YOUNG PEOPLE'S LITERACIES IN THE DIGITAL AGE

What do young people really do with digital media? *Young People's Literacies in the Digital Age* aims to debunk the common myths and assumptions that are associated with young people's relationship with digital media. In contrast to widespread notions of the empowered and enabled 'digital native', the book presents a more complex picture of young people's digital lives.

Focusing on the notion of 'critical digital literacies' this book tackles a number of pressing questions that are often ignored in media hype and political panics over young people's digital media use, including:

- In what ways can digital media enhance, shape or constrain identity representation and communication?
- How do digital experiences map onto young people's everyday lives?
- What are young people's critical understandings of digital media and how did they develop these?
- What are the dominant understandings young people have of digital media and in whose interests do they work?

These questions are addressed through the findings of a year of fieldwork with groups of young people aged 14 to 19 years. Over the course of eight chapters, the experiences and views of these young people are explored with reference to various academic literatures, such as digital literacies, media and communication studies, critical theory and youth studies. Starting with their early socialisation into the digital context, the book traces the continuities, contradictions and conflicts they encounter as part of their practices. Written in a detailed but accessible manner, this book develops a unique perspective on young people's digital lives.

Luci Pangrazio is a Research Fellow at the Centre for Research for Educational Impact (REDI), in the Faculty of Arts and Education, Deakin University, Australia. Her research focuses on critical digital literacies and the changing nature of digital texts. Luci is currently researching young people's practices and understandings of personal data.

YOUNG PEOPLE'S LITERACIES IN THE DIGITAL AGE

Continuities, Conflicts and Contradictions

Luci Pangrazio

Routledge
Taylor & Francis Group

LONDON AND NEW YORK

First published 2019
by Routledge
2 Park Square, Milton Park, Abingdon, Oxon OX14 4RN

and by Routledge
52 Vanderbilt Avenue, New York, NY 10017

Routledge is an imprint of the Taylor & Francis Group, an informa business

British Library Cataloguing in Publication Data
A catalogue record for this book is available from the British Library

Library of Congress Cataloging-in-Publication Data
Names: Pangrazio, Luci, author.
Title: Young people's literacies in the digital age : continuities, conflicts and contradictions / Luci Pangrazio.
Description: Abingdon, Oxon ; New York, NY : Routledge, 2018. | Includes bibliographical references.
Identifiers: LCCN 2018036536| ISBN 9781138305564 (hardback) | ISBN 9781138305557 (pbk.) | ISBN 9780203728918 (ebook)
Subjects: LCSH: Internet and children. | Computers and children. | Digital media--Social aspects. | Information society. | Computer literacy. | Internet literacy.
Classification: LCC HQ784.I58 P34 2018 | DDC 004.67/8083--dc23
LC record available at https://lccn.loc.gov/2018036536

ISBN: 978-1-138-30556-4 (hbk)
ISBN: 978-1-138-30555-7 (pbk)
ISBN: 978-0-203-72891-8 (ebk)

Typeset in Bembo
by Taylor & Francis Books

Printed and bound in Great Britain by
TJ International Ltd, Padstow, Cornwall

For Henry and his friends.

CONTENTS

FIGURES

ACKNOWLEDGEMENTS

This book could not have been written without the involvement of the 13 young people who participated in the fieldwork. I am extremely grateful for their enthusiasm and willingness to become involved in the research. The openness and honesty with which they shared their stories enabled a rich and detailed view of their digital worlds.

I am also grateful to the two schools and the community arts centre where the fieldwork took place. The assistance and support of the staff and students at these three locations, particularly the school principals, teachers and educators, was much appreciated.

I would also like to thank colleagues who took the time to read parts of the book and provide me with valuable feedback – Neil Selwyn, Ilana Snyder, Julian Sefton-Green, Cameron Bishop and Sophie Rudolph.

On a practical note, I am grateful for the editorial work that goes into the process of book publishing. I would like to thank Lucinda Knight, Vilija Stevens and Matt Bickerton and all of the editorial team at Routledge.

Finally, I would like to thank my family Cam and Henry for their love and support.

BEGINNINGS

When I first met Mitch in 2014, he was a savvy 16 year old at an outer-suburban high school in Melbourne. He lived in one of the city's 'growth corridors', where farming land was rapidly being turned into residential housing to make way for the expanding population. Like most of the residents in the area, Mitch was white and middle class. Most days, Mitch could be found in a classroom, at the library or walking to and from school. Mitch could also be found online in spaces such as Facebook, where he communicated with friends and classmates; Steam, where he 'met up' with friends and played games; and YouTube, where he subscribed to various channels, browsed for entertainment or looked for a tutorial to help him with his mathematics homework.

Mitch described himself as a 'gamer' and spoke in an animated way about the various games he played. On Steam, Mitch had created an avatar called 'Maestro'. He had constructed this digital identity carefully to reflect his interest in music and performance. The name of his avatar also revealed something about Mitch's capability and confidence in digital spaces. Part of his confidence came from having a 'tech specialist' uncle, who had given Mitch some tips and short cuts on using digital media. As a result, Mitch's digital practices were niche to his needs and interests. On Steam, for example, Mitch and his friends used an application called 'Mumble', which enabled them to chat and give each other tips while playing.

During our meetings, Mitch talked a lot about his future and explained that he wanted to be a film director when he 'grew up'. The videos he had seen on YouTube by amateur filmmakers had inspired him to start making his own movies. He had created several short films, which he had uploaded to the platform to share with friends, family and his YouTube community. To Mitch, YouTube was an important starting point on his journey to becoming a filmmaker. While Mitch's skills and practices were relatively complex and sophisticated, much of what he had learnt over the last ten years had come from informal experiences with friends and family.

Mitch's experiences were typical of many young people across the world today. His story highlights the way his experiences spread across online and offline contexts to support his interests, educational needs and social relationships. Reflecting on the digital platforms Mitch uses, we might consider the many and varied ways he can develop his gaming skills and the opportunities he has to express his identity and connect with others. Digital media, in the form of online forums and videos, also helped Mitch develop his filmmaking skills—from videoing and editing to production and dissemination. At first glance, there is much to be celebrated in this account of how digital media helped Mitch to imagine and develop his interests, social relationships and career.

However, Mitch's use of these platforms was not only shaped by his interests, but also by the structural and discursive connections that exist between digital platforms. Steam, for example, has a YouTube channel, which includes videos from the ten most popular games, based on how many users were recommending these games to friends. Similarly, Google has a video tab that links directly to YouTube with a list of videos that match that particular search.

Participation on digital platforms can therefore be seen as both an active *and* impelled choice. In addition, most of these platforms have publicly displayed metrics and comments, which are intended to provide feedback on the social 'value' of a user's posts. This can create mixed emotions for individual users, as this feedback is immediate and sometimes unforgiving. While this presents challenges for all users, for young people like Mitch, who are just starting to experiment with professional or social identities, negative feedback—or worse still no feedback at all—can be dispiriting.

Many questions emerge about Mitch's narrative, including how he uses digital media to learn and the role that his school played in helping him to act on his career goals. However, the questions I'm interested in, and which I explore in later chapters, include: In what ways have digital media enhanced, shaped or constrained Mitch's identity representation and communication strategies? How are digital experiences incorporated into Mitch's everyday life? How was Mitch socialised into the digital context? What are his critical understandings of digital media, and how and where did he develop these understandings? I am also interested in the dominant understandings Mitch and other young people have of digital media and in whose interests they work. Such questions are about theory and focus. They are also about methodological questions over how to research young people's relationship with digital media in ways that are generative for researchers and educators, as well as the young people themselves.

What this book is about

This book is about how a group of young Australians use digital media in their everyday lives. Throughout the 2014 academic year, I met with three different groups of young people aged 14 to 19 to understand how they thought about and used digital media in their everyday life. A focal point for the meetings was a series of creative workshops, in which the young people visualised, modelled and reflected upon their experiences with and understandings of the digital. We engaged in group conversations about their creations and the process of making. I was interested in how they used the materiality of the media (i.e. paint colour, texture) to represent their digital experiences and what the act of making revealed to them about their own digital practices and understandings. These conversations were clarified through one-on-one interviews and online observations.

The research documented: the young people's digital practices; their dispositions toward digital media; the critical understandings that these young people brought to their digital practices; and how and where these understandings were developed. In particular, the project focused on how digital media use played a part in their capacity to form and represent their identities, communicate with others and participate in society. This book is the culmination of the research.

This focus of this book is both local, through its examination of the everyday socialities of young people, and global, as multinational technology companies now mediate these socialities through ubiquitous digital platforms. It explores the ways in which these young people appropriate digital platforms, such as Facebook and Instagram, to suit their needs and interests. The tension between the local and the global can be exciting and confusing for these young people, as they strive to forge identities, social relationships and career paths. In various ways and to varying degrees, the digital mediates their experiences, interactions and future prospects. This topic is fraught with assumptions and anxieties. Many people, parents in particular, have concerns about what their children are doing online and want to know what they can do to support their practices and help them to be 'safe'. They are particularly sensitive to the popular press's claims about the 'unhealthy' relationship young people have with digital media—that they are 'addicted' to their devices, that they do not know how to communicate face to face, and that they cannot spell or write.

An article in *The Atlantic* by Jean Twenge (2017), with the provocative title 'Have smartphones destroyed a generation?' attracted significant interest on publication. Twenge argued that mobile phones are the reason why mental health issues and suicide rates among young people have escalated significantly in recent years. While this argument was subsequently criticised by researchers (see Rideout, 2017; Cavanagh, 2017), the article has attracted significant interest in the mainstream media, including local and national radio and print press. Twenge tapped neatly into adult fears about the effects of mobile media on young people's health and well-being. However, the reporting of Twenge's assertions overlooked her conflation of correlation with causation. Mental health issues in young people *have* unfortunately increased in recent years (see Beyond Blue, 2017), but there is no evidence to suggest that this is *caused by* mobile phones. Teenagers who are suffering from depression and anxiety might be more inclined to communicate via their mobile phones, but this does not necessarily lead to feelings of negativity, and could in fact be a positive support for young people who are feeling socially isolated.

Twenge's article is typical of a media panic (Drotner, 1992) in which there is an exaggerated emphasis on the harm that media might cause young people. Similar to moral panics, media panics are based around the idea that media are causing some kind of corruption or demise of social order. The ensuing debate is often emotional, heated and polarising. Adults are often positioned as 'protectors' within this discourse, discouraging children from some media, while encouraging others (Buckingham & Jensen, 2012). Once these binary ways of thinking about social phenomena have been invoked, they can be difficult to move beyond. For example, the argument that video games increase violence among young people still circulates even though there is no rigorous evidence to prove this is the case (see DeCamp & Ferguson, 2017; Kühn et al., 2018). Despite this, media panics tend to set the agenda for research, distracting researchers, educators and adults from addressing the more complex and hidden issues at play.

When it comes to understanding young people and their relationship with digital media, stereotypes abound. Labels like the 'digital native', 'net generation' and 'iGen' are regularly used in both academic and popular discourse to describe young people in contemporary society. These labels are based on the assumption that young people have a natural affinity with digital technologies because they have grown up surrounded by them. Despite this rather simplistic logic, the view of the empowered 'digital native' has certainly taken hold in the popular imagination (see Chapter 2). These labels simplify the complex social and cultural issues that underpin digital media use and homogenise the variety of young people's digital experiences and capabilities. While many notable empirical studies have found labels such as 'digital native' to be inaccurate, they are clearly influential in characterising a generation.

This book contributes to a growing counter-commentary that seeks to explore the *diverse* and *divergent* experiences young people have with digital media. I adopt a sociocultural approach to understanding young people's digital literacies *in context*, and do not assume that there is a fundamental problem with how young people are using digital media. At the same time, I recognise that technology is not a neutral tool or conduit for social practices. I explore the technical and social factors that constrain and limit young people's digital experiences. In particular, I focus on the influence of the coded architectures of the digital platforms, together with the social and cultural factors in which digital practices are embedded, to map out the complex ways that young people experience 'digital' contexts.

An apt example of the complex interplay between the technical and the social can be seen in the rising trend of Fake Instagram (aka 'Finstagram') accounts. Finstagram is a secondary Instagram account where users are free to share unedited depictions of themselves to a more intimate group of followers. 'Finstas', as they are commonly referred to, are typically teenage girls looking for some freedom from the pressure to perfect their Instagram image. However, the media have widely reported the tendency for these accounts to become more explicit, including images involving nudity and drugs (Sun, 2017; Patterson, 2016). Not surprisingly, the response from adult commentators has been one of alarm and dismay.

While there may be 'Finstas' who deliberately use inappropriate images, young people's desire to present a more 'honest' digital identity highlights the pressures associated with mainstream social media platforms, as well as their adept methods of working around these. From a different perspective Finstagram might be seen more positively. Psychologist Sandy Rae contends that the freedom afforded through a Finstagram account potentially synchronises private and public personas, which is healthy for identity formation (Brown, 2015). Nevertheless it is ironic that young people feel more 'authentic' or true to themselves on Instagram accounts that are labelled as 'fake'.

The issues raised by the Finstagram trend highlight the complex nature of identity representation and social relationships in the digital age. Not only are there pressures from technology companies for users to present one 'authentic' digital identity, but also the visual nature of posts and feedback from followers and friends encourage particular forms of communication. Young people must also find a way of negotiating parental and educational reactions to the media panic that ensues when journalists focus on the most extreme examples of social media use. While digital media offer young people an array of possibilities for representation and communication, individual dispositions and capabilities determine the extent to which these potentialities may be realised.

Who this book is for

This book is written for educators and researchers who work with young people. I was first drawn to this area of research during my time as a high school English teacher when I noticed how important digital media were in the lives of the young people I taught. In particular, issues on social media would frequently spill over into the classroom, occupying the minds of my students and creating antagonisms between them that could not be ignored. These were not issues that could be solved through extra cybersafety classes or a ban on social media in school, and often involved a mix of social and technical challenges that spanned online and offline worlds. Despite the prevalence of these issues among students, through discussions with colleagues I noticed there were few resources and limited understandings about how to help support young people in negotiating these complex, multilayered problems.

From an academic perspective, the last two decades have seen the emergence of a large body of work exploring young people's relationships with digital media. However, much of the empirical research is based on descriptive data. There have been many ethnographic studies on how young people use digital media in their daily life. While these are useful accounts to have, I was interested in investigating the dynamics of this relationship and its implications for young people's literacies, including the way they view themselves and others. I started this research with questions that could not be answered through an ethnographic study—I needed to talk *with* young people so we could identify these issues together. To do this effectively I needed to research appropriate strategies that might facilitate an open dialogue. I also needed an understanding of the platforms the young people used, as well as what was already known about how young people were using them.

In considering the contributions of this book to the field of digital literacies, one might ask to what extent the findings and insights can be generalised. Specifically, how might this book be useful to researchers and educators working in different contexts and with different cohorts of young people? While this book focuses on the *particularities* of these young people's digital experiences, it seeks to develop insights into the conditions and processes that shape these experiences. I seek to reveal how the motivations of platform operators play out in the young people's social experiences and how these culminate in paradigms of practice (Postigo, 2016). This shifts the focus from media texts onto what people actually *do* with media texts (Couldry, 2012). And what people *do* with media texts is shaped by the social, economic, cultural, historical and political factors and discourses that are particular to their time and place. The insights gathered from this picture will help educators and researchers develop a more nuanced picture of young people's literacies, so that programmes and the curriculum might be more responsive to their needs.

Outline of the book

Chapter 1 outlines the main themes, issues and debates that underpin the book. Young people's lives are perceived as intertwined with digital media, meaning they have significant bearing on the formation and representation of their personal and social identities. Drawing on critical theories of digital media, I argue that these are not neutral tools for representation and communication. Digital media (and social media in particular) broker sociality in particular ways and for particular purposes. I argue that understanding these converged and complex assemblages of the social and technical require critical digital literacies. From this perspective, the chapter asks how and where young people might encounter the resources and skills that would enable them to develop a critical digital disposition. The chapter concludes by introducing the young people and the methods and approach that were used in the research project that is integral to the book.

In Chapter 2, I present a picture of young people's digital practices across time. I argue that early interactions and experiences with digital technologies and the internet are important in establishing patterns and practices, and that these play out in various ways across young people's digital lives. I begin by outlining the dominant discourses associated with young people's use of digital media: the 'digital native' discourse and the protectionist discourse. Throughout the research, a digital narrative was developed for each of the 13 participants. Here, I focus on one of these narratives in detail, using 15-year-old participant Rachel as a case study. I analyse her early digital experiences, identifying the institutions, discourses, resources and significant others that shaped her values, beliefs and expectations of digital media, and compare and contrast these against the other young people in the group. In doing so, I examine the connections in Rachel's digital narrative between the past and the present; the digital and non-digital; the technical and the social. I focus on her initiation into digital contexts, examining the moments of change in particular aspects of her life and the factors that contributed to this.

Chapter 3 focuses on the young people's current *dispositions* toward digital technologies, and how these shape their ways of making meaning in, and of, digital media. Drawing on the research data, the chapter shows how these young people often held clear, well-established understandings that guided their digital practices. Dispositions are constructed through a complex interplay of discourses, social norms, personal experience, and formal and informal education. I use Foucault's (1980) notion of dispositif to explore the heterogeneous ensemble of elements that influence the young people's disposition toward the digital. Using the research literature and the research data, I analyse the digital dispositif experienced by these young people. This provides a critical framework for the study, highlighting that the young people's agency is distributed across a range of digital and non-digital elements drawn together through the dispositif.

Chapter 4 explores how young people use digital media to represent their *identities*. It outlines theories and approaches to identity relevant to this research area. Expanding upon Chapter 3, I use Deleuze and Guattari's (1980/2013) notion of 'becoming' to think through the opportunities the young people have to explore and experiment with different identities within the digital dispositif. The chapter then looks at how young people negotiate these opportunities. It examines the way they use different components to represent aspects of their identity and how these are influenced by the social milieu in which they are embedded, as well as the architecture of digital platforms. Despite the opportunities that emerge, these young people's formation of online identities remained closely 'tethered' to their offline corporeal identities—constraining the fluidity and flexibility of practice popularly associated with the internet.

In Chapter 5, I examine how young people negotiate the materialities of digital platforms to *communicate and connect with others*. I present a detailed exploration of the specific qualities that digital platforms introduce into these young people's communication practices and the effect they have on patterns of sociality and behaviour. I start by reviewing the literature on platform participation. I then provide a detailed examination of the five main ways the young people used digital media to connect with others. Communicative strategies ranged from one-way projections of information to more involved interactions with others. Drawing on literature from media and communication and critical internet studies, I make the argument that the ideologies of technology companies shaped the communication practices of young people more strongly than first thought. Despite this, these young people developed ways to work around and resist the practices and subjectivities promoted by digital platforms.

In Chapter 6, I take stock of what has emerged over the last five chapters and examine the kinds of critical understandings these young people have of digital media. I critically examine the tensions between the immediate, local concerns associated with identity representation and communication and the universalistic structures of digital platforms that these young people must negotiate as part of their digital media use. In doing so, I highlight the limited tools and resources these young people were able to draw on in order to understand the more complex and interconnected practices they experienced through their use of digital media. I conclude the chapter by considering the problematic gaps that exist between these young people's experiences of digital media, academic theorisations of this relationship, and common educational approaches to digital literacies.

In the final chapter, I argue for the need to focus more strongly on building skills and understandings about the technological and social processes involved in digital media use. Drawing on the findings of the research, I put forward a model to develop critical digital literacies called 'Critical Digital Design'. I then focus on how the various groups who have a stake in young people's digital practices might work to improve the current situation. These groups include: academic researchers; schools and education officials; parents and families; technology companies; and of course young people themselves. The notion of critical digital literacies holds different meanings for each of these groups. An overarching conclusion is that cultivating critical and agentic digital practices involves a more consistent approach that draws on a wider range of people and resources. In this sense, how to support young people's literacies in the digital age exemplifies how we, as a society, perceive the transformations brought about by digital media.

References

Beyond Blue (2017). Stats and facts. Retrieved from: www.youthbeyondblue.com/footer/stats-and-facts

Brown, V. (2015). How teens are hiding their real lives with 'fake' Instagram accounts. *News.com*. Retrieved from www.news.com.au/lifestyle/relationships/family-friends/how-teens-are-hiding-their-real-lives-with-fake-instagram-accounts/news-story/bc52a4959c6c05430b713ff5eb7119d9

Buckingham, D., & Jensen, H. (2012). Beyond 'media panics': Reconceptualising public debates about children and media. *Journal of Children and Media*, 6(4), 413–429.

Cavanagh, S. R. (2017). No, smartphones are not destroying a generation: The kids are gonna be all right. *Psychology Today*. Retrieved from www.psychologytoday.com/blog/once-more-feeling/201708/no-smartphones-are-not-destroying-generation

Couldry, N. (2012). *Media, Society, World: Social Theory and Digital Media Practice*. Cambridge, UK: Polity.

DeCamp, W., & Ferguson, C. J. (2017). The impact of degree of exposure to violent video games, family background and other factors on youth violence. *Journal of Youth and Adolescence*, 46(2), 388–400.

Deleuze, G., & Guattari, F. (1980/2013). *A Thousand Plateaus*. London and New York: Bloomsbury Academic.

Drotner, K. (1992). Modernity and media panics. In K. Schroder & M. Skovmand (Eds.), *Media Culture: Reappraising Transnational Media* (pp.42–62). London: Routledge.

Foucault, M. (1980). *Power/Knowledge: Selected Interviews & Other Writings*. New York: Pantheon Books.

Kühn, S., Kugler, D. T., Schmalen, K., Weichenberger, M., Witt, C., & Gallinat, J. (2018). Does playing violent video games cause aggression? A longitudinal intervention study. *Molecular Psychiatry*. doi:10.1038/s41380-018-0031-7

Patterson, D. (2016). What the Finsta?! The darker world of teenagers and Instagram. *The Huffington Post*, 28 September. Retrieved from www.huffingtonpost.com/entry/what-the-finsta-the-darker-world-of-teenagers-and_us_57eb9e03e4b07f20daa0fefb

Postigo, H. (2016). The socio-technical architecture of digital labor: Converting play into YouTube money. *New Media & Society*, 18(2), 332–349.

Rideout, V. (2017). Some thoughts on the Atlantic's 'Have smartphones destroyed a generation?'. *Parenting for a Digital Future*. Retrieved from http://blogs.lse.ac.uk/parenting4digitalfuture/2017/08/11/some-thoughts-on-the-atlantic/

Sun, D. (2017). Teens live digital double lives on 'Finsta', or fake Instagram. *Wichita News*, 3 May. Retrieved from www.kwch.com/content/news/Teens-live-a-digital-double-life-on-Finsta-421243444.html

Twenge, J. M. (2017). Have smartphones destroyed a generation? *The Atlantic*, September. Retrieved from www.theatlantic.com/magazine/archive/2017/09/has-the-smartphone-destroyed-a-generation/534198/

1

YOUNG PEOPLE'S DIGITAL LIVES

An introduction

Young people's relationship with digital media is widely discussed, yet there is something significant about this relationship that merits sustained attention. During the teenage years, young people start to develop a sense of themselves as independent of family, with peers and social networks taking on far greater importance. The digital is very much bound up with these changes. It has become an important part of how identities are experimented with and represented and how socialities are enacted. It is also how careers are imagined and realised. But digital technologies are not just neutral tools in any of these actions—they broker processes and interactions in particular ways. Social media platforms, for example, do not just enable socialities, but influence the audience and purpose of communicative acts. As with many changes, there are advantages and disadvantages. Such changes can occur incrementally and often go unnoticed. Yet how young people negotiate and understand these changes, and the tensions and issues that accompany them, is increasingly connected to their future prospects as socially engaged and informed citizens.

Young people

Adolescence is a stage in life marked by biological, cognitive and social change. In the teenage years, young people begin to contemplate what their future might look like, as they try and test different identities and career pathways. These fledgling identities and dispositions have a certain fragility.

This fragility is not particular to young people—any stage in life that involves change is challenging. However, young people have not usually had the repertoire of experiences that enable them to see these moments of change as a normal part of life. While the demands of their social lives are grounded in the now, young people are routinely encouraged to be mindful of the future and how the decisions and choices they make might affect their prospects. They are required to consider the subjects, courses and programmes they need to take in order to get on the right 'track' to a particular career or vocational path.

At the same time, it is becoming increasingly difficult for young people to reach the traditional milestones of adulthood, such as full-time employment, independent living and home ownership. We now see young people living at home for longer periods of time, sometimes well into their adult years, in order to have financial and material support (Muir et al., 2009). Amidst these challenges, precarities and tensions, there are competing academic perspectives on children and young people, each with a different theoretical focus and ontological viewpoint.

Attempts to delineate and define 'young people' as a distinct social group brings to light many of the theoretical tensions that underpin 'youth studies'. I have already used several different terms in the opening pages of this book—'young people', 'teenagers' and 'adolescents'—yet each term has slightly different uses and connotations. The term 'teenager', for example, is used to refer to someone in the age range of 13–19 years, and came into popular use in the 1950s as a marketing category (Buckingham, 2008). It therefore has problematic associations with advertising and consumption. Although there is some variation in definition, a 'young person', is generally considered to be someone between the ages of 12–25 years (McGorry et al., 2006). Psychologists adopt the term 'adolescence' to refer to the time between childhood and adulthood. Sociologists, on the other hand, tend to use the term 'youth', which, in a similar way to psychology, is defined as the stage between childhood and adulthood. Andy Furlong (2013) argues, however, that 'youth is a broader category than adolescence' as it is *not* linked to 'specific age ranges nor can it be linked to specific activities, such as paid work or having sexual relations' (p.19).

Throughout this book I use the term 'young people' to refer to the participants in the research. This avoids the associations that the label 'adolescence' has to psychological theories, which tend to position young people as somehow incomplete or simply in transition to adulthood. I approach young people as 'complete', even if they are looking to build future careers and lifestyles. As Kehily (2007) explains, the transitional period of young personhood is 'between being dependent and becoming independent' (p.3), rather than any form of arrested adulthood. In a similar way, I have made a conscious decision to avoid labelling the young people as 'youth'. While there is a diverse body of work on the sociology of youth, the term has become associated with normative or correctional processes, which inadvertently position young people as needing education, regulation or help; i.e. 'youth at risk' (Capuzzi & Gross, 2014).

In exploring the digital lives of these young people, I start from the premise that their experiences are unique, meaning they should not be treated as a homogenous group. As Helsper and Eynon (2010) point out, young people vary greatly in their skills, resources and motivations when using digital media, meaning their dispositions towards it vary markedly. In the context of this book, 'disposition' is taken to mean the attitudes and beliefs young people have toward digital media, which predisposes them to particular digital practices. In Chapter 3 I trace the origin of these dispositions using Foucault's (1980) concept of the 'dispositif'. As such, my use of the term 'disposition' differs from Bourdieu's, who sees it as a set of pre- or unconscious inclinations that lead to a particular 'way of being' or 'habitual state' (Bourdieu, 1977/2011, p.214). By contrast, I analyse the array of discursive and non-discursive factors that shape young people's beliefs about the digital, as well as their sense of agency in this context.

The digital age

Digital technologies have changed the arrangements and patterns of contemporary life. Much of this is to do with the explosive growth of the internet and its capacity to connect people, open markets, redefine boundaries and carve out new spaces for cultural engagement. Social media have opened up new avenues for participation. While crowdsourcing, citizen journalism and online activism often fall short of their promise, such developments have undoubtedly changed the ways in which civic and social life are enacted (Hinton & Hjorth, 2013). At the same time, the increasing commingling of bodies with technologies, principally in the form of wearables, such as fitness trackers, ear buds, smart watches and virtual reality headsets, is imbued with both excitement and trepidation with regard to what the technological future might hold. Key here is the fact that these technologies are built on and operated by code, which is invisible and pervasive, making it very difficult to identify and understand the potentialities and pitfalls that might unfold.

Bearing this in mind, Arthur and Marilouise Kroker (2008) suggest three implications for what it means to live in the digital age. First, they argue digital culture 'literally remaps, rewires, and recodes life itself using complex algorithms' (Kroker & Kroker, 2008, p.3). Through algorithms and machine learning, the processes that drive the functioning of everyday digital culture are increasingly automated, meaning that many of the decisions that shape the spaces and processes of sociality happen without our knowing. Due to algorithmic profiling, we are often not aware of the myriad identities that are created on our behalf. As Cheney-Lippold (2017, p.6) notes, 'online you are not who you think you are' due to how various digital traces are generated and processed by unknown actors in the digital economy. There is a pressing need for us to understand how socialities are reshaped through algorithmic processing, and the implications this has for embodied experience.

Second, they contend digital code blurs boundaries between 'flesh, machine and images' (Kroker & Kroker, 2008, p.3), where clear distinctions once existed. In doing so, the motivations instantiated by machines are seamlessly intertwined with those of the individual, raising questions of agency and autonomy. Finally, while much is made of the potential for digital transmission to take place almost instantaneously, it inevitably slows when it interacts with 'putatively solid objects of society—bodies, politics, economy, gender, sexuality' (p.3). It is easy to see how ideas of borderless, ubiquitous digital communication quickly translate into utopian promises for liberation, freedom and democracy. Yet, despite its boundless potential, when digitality is inflected with the very real and material qualities of the world, it is 'all the more physical, concrete, stubborn, as regressive politically as it is progressive' (Kroker & Kroker, 2008, p.3). O'Neil (2016) argues that digital processing has actually *increased* inequalities, particularly with regard to the datafication of everyday life.

As with many sociotechnical phenomena, the digital is neither wholly utopian nor dystopian—its determination lies in the interplay between human practices and values and the capabilities of digital technologies. However, many of these issues have their antecedents in the principles of digital encoding. While 'the digital' is made manifest through digital devices and systems, a more granular understanding of digital encoding provides an important lens through which to view the themes and concerns of this book.

At the most basic level, the digital can be described as a binary code in which there are only two possible states: off and on, symbolised by 0 and 1. The flow of information that is 'captured' by binary code is discrete and discontinuous, so that each tenth of a second on a clock may be captured, for example, but not each point in between. By comparison, analogue processing continuously translates information via electric pulses of varying amplitude. The aim of code, then, is to ensure that the output is always greater than the input. These changes can be traced back to the invention of the Turing machine in 1936, which Kittler (2008, p.45) argues, 'banished the infinity of numbers' involved in coding to just 0s and 1s. With technology, code has been put into 'the practice of realities' (Kittler, 2008, p.44). However, with it came an inevitable reduction that enabled the exactitude of computer science.

Encoding information digitally has advantages. By using binary code, large amounts of information can be compressed so that transmission and storage of data is far more efficient. Further, being composed of only two signals, data are more easily decoded. In short, digital data are easier to store, manipulate and replicate, affording the user greater control and precision of information. Analogue, by comparison, has infinite values of data so the process of decoding is more time consuming and prone to errors. While the vast amount of information involved in analogue transmission is its greatest shortcoming, analogue is able to represent changing values and continuously variable qualities, which is more akin to the way humans experience the world. It is easy to see why many commentators have lauded this as an era of change and transformation. While these changes are being driven by financial and governmental factors, digital technologies are also implicated in many of these developments. However, it would be short-sighted to focus on digital technologies as the sole catalysts of change.

The mutual shaping theory of technology sees technology and society as mutually influencing and shaping each other. I draw on the work of Williams (1974) and Buckingham (2008, p.12), which explains that technology is 'socially shaped and socially shaping'. Seen in this way, what people *do* with technologies is determined by the 'inherent constraints and possibilities which limit the ways in which it can be used', which are, in turn, 'largely shaped by the social interests of those who control its production, circulation, and distribution' (Buckingham, 2008, p.12). This book pays close attention to the relationship between the technical and the social, as well as the economic and political systems in which they are embedded. With the recent proliferation of digital technologies, this relationship has been thrown into sharp relief, as individuals increasingly rely on technology to carry out their everyday lives.

Young people in the digital age

In May 2017, *The Australian* newspaper leaked a document that Facebook, the largest social media platform in the world, has the capacity to share details about the psychological state of teenage users with its advertising partners. According to the document, Facebook can identify when teenagers are feeling 'insecure', 'anxious', 'depressed', 'silly', 'useless' and 'a failure', which can help advertisers pinpoint when these young people might be interested in 'working out and losing weight' or 'needing a confidence boost' (Levin, 2017). Over 6.4 million young people use Facebook in the Australian and New Zealand region. According to the report, Facebook have detailed information about these young people's communicative practices on the platform, such as the days in the week when they are likely to be 'broadcasting achievements' or 'building confidence'. Facebook issued an apology for their 'oversight' (which has not led to any changes in policy)—it was the first time they had tacitly admitted that they collect and exploit young people's social media data.

This is not the first time Facebook has been found taking advantage of their users. In 2014, Facebook manipulated the News Feed of almost 700,000 users to investigate the influence of emotional contagion (see Kramer et al., 2014). In early 2018, it was revealed that Cambridge Analytica, a British political consulting firm, paid US$1 million to harvest tens of millions of Facebook user profiles to target individuals with messaging that aimed to change their opinion on issues. These large-scale intrusions into privacy and the capacity to affectively manipulate users' opinions are indicative of the power held by such companies. For many individuals, the desire to connect with others overrides concerns over security and privacy, meaning that individuals unwittingly become a party to the agenda of large multinational companies. On social media, users share detailed and emotional information with their friends and followers, making these platforms rich sources of personal data for the platform operators.

These issues relate to people of all ages who use social media, not just young people. It is perhaps not surprising that the age requirement on Facebook, Instagram and Snapchat of 13 years coincides with the age at which the Children's Online Privacy Protection Act (COPPA) in the US allows companies to collect personal data *without* parental consent. Despite corporate surveillance and the commodification of personal data, many parents and adults still believe their children are safer on social media than in 'real-life' public spaces. This has made young people particularly reliant on digital media as a space to develop an identity separate from the family. As a result, young people are turning to digital media to engage in practices that traditionally would take place in public spaces—to 'hang out, jockey for social status, work through how to present themselves, and take risks that will help them to assess the boundaries of the social world' (boyd, 2007, p.21).

These digital practices blur distinctions between public and private, which has raised concerns over how young people maintain control over their digital content and online relationships. Berriman and Thomson (2015) counter this concern by arguing that young people have more nuanced understandings of privacy and control over digital media than first thought. They put forth the idea of 'spectacles of intimacy' to explain the graduated levels of visibility and risk young people negotiate when using digital media. As they explain, 'Young people are constantly experimenting and realising the affordances of social media, combining these creatively with face-to-face socialities, and trading off visibility and participation' (pp.595–596). Young people's social media practices are therefore shaped by societal trends, peer expectations and the specific qualities of these digital platforms. The intentions and motivations of platform operators are another important part of this discussion, as they are a powerful but often unseen modulator of young people's social experiences.

Digital identities

It is now commonly accepted that digital media offer many opportunities for identity expression and experimentation. For example, informal digital writing involves play and communication but, as Merchant (2005) points out, complex identity performances are simultaneously taking place. Such practices inevitably spread into offline contexts, influencing interactions at school, home and in the community. While many commentators have criticised the relevance of making distinctions between the online and the offline, like McMillan Cottom (2017), I use this dualism for analytical purposes in order to explore the interplay between online 'space' and offline 'place'. Similarly, how individuals negotiate their peer networks both online and offline is indicative not only of how they perceive themselves, but also how others perceive them. Recognition by others, whether face to face or via online communication, emerges as an important aspect of identity formation and representation in the contemporary era.

Several researchers (Potter & Banaji, 2011; Sunden, 2003) argue that what digital media afford young people is not a new process of identity formation, but the opportunity to make these processes visible. For example, boyd (2007) writes that digital profiles are a type of *digital body* where the individuals must write themselves into being. While the audience might know the offline identity of the individual, the online identity that is presented through a digital profile works in an aspirational way. boyd contends that in a digital context, individuals are 'inclined to present the side of themselves that they believe will be well received by these peers' (p.13). Similarly, Sherry Turkle (2011) writes that an online profile is an avatar of sorts or 'a statement not only about who you are, but also who you want to be' (p.180).

Other researchers have argued that digital media create places where roles and identities can be worked through. Dean and Laidler (2013) write that for their female participants, Facebook afforded them a space that sat outside the dichotomous representations of femininity presented in popular culture. On Facebook they could circumvent 'some of the disadvantages of binding feminine identity with consumerism', enabling them to 'dress, look and feel more naturally' (p.7). According to Dean and Laidler 'The Facebook Girl' is able to transgress these binaries as new means of self-expression are afforded through social media. In a similar way, Selwyn (2009) details how the Facebook page was a place where the university students in his study could become familiar with the 'identity politics' of being a student. It became a space where the issues that arise from university staff, academic conventions and expectations could be reported and reflected upon.

Mendelson and Papacharissi (2011) examined the role of Facebook photo galleries in introducing the self and performing identity. For the new college students in their study, the repetition of photos of the individual or the individual with friends served to introduce and assert an identity independent of family. Further, the 'collectively performed narcissism' (p.269) was thought to be a step toward self-reflection and self-actualisation, rather than self-absorption. This positive reading of the role narcissism plays in the process of identity formation appears to counter many of the mainstream concerns that designate narcissism as inherently problematic. Perspective is important, as how a particular behaviour or instance is interpreted is dependent on the background of the viewer. The idea that identity is socially constructed, fluid and multiple underpins the theorising of identity in this book.

What these studies highlight is that significant changes are at work when considering how identity and digital media intersect and these need close examination. If narcissism does serve a purpose, as Mendelson and Papacharissi (2011) contend, the flip side must also be considered. For example, if the emphasis is on appearance and social groupings, rather than other features of identity, then what sort of anxieties does this create in the user? For each assumption, another question emerges, suggesting that perceived benefits often bring with them new socialities that also need consideration.

Local identities in a global context

While I focus on the particularities of these young people's digital experiences, changes occurring at a global level are shaping the context for their socialities. Facebook, Google, YouTube and Amazon are now worldwide, meaning similar methods of search, self-representation and interaction occur in diverse places across the world. In his research Danny Miller (2016) reveals how people adapt these platforms to their own individual needs and purposes. Yet the digital 'substrate' upon which these practices take place is essentially similar, if not the same. Digital platforms facilitate particular practices, but they also encourage similar dispositions toward fundamental concepts, such as privacy and trust. In this way, digital platforms not only facilitate meaning-making practices, but also *condition* them.

The concept that there is a distinction between public and private life (Fuchs, 2014; Turkle, 2011) has shifted through digital platforms. Through digital technologies, we can connect to almost any social network to engage and interact with others. boyd (2010) calls social media 'networked publics', referring both to the space where individuals engage online and the imagined community that emerges from the intersection of people, technology and practice. However, socialising or connecting in a 'networked public' often takes place *in private* and involves sharing *personal* information—all of which blurs the boundaries between public and private spheres. Indeed, the very purpose of mediation is often to share and connect, which fundamentally depends on a public, rather than a private, sense of self. Further to this, platform operators are able to commodify these social interactions, as they take place in a liminal space that is neither public nor private.

Much has been written about the double standard that emerges when the profits of commodifying the personal information and interactions of users remain within private companies (Srnicek, 2017; Fuchs, 2014). However, incursions into the social sphere have been taking place for some time and extend well beyond the internet. Neoliberalism has encouraged the spread of the market into private life and by doing so has significantly changed notions of privacy. The New London Group (1996) argue this has eroded the autonomy and intimacy necessary for personal growth and freedom. However, other scholars (Palen & Dourish, 2003; Marwick & boyd, 2014) have argued that privacy has always been negotiated in context, meaning that it should be seen as networked and dialectical.

Digital platforms have also played an important role in shifting notions of trust. If you were to give a stranger the keys to your house ten years ago, people might have thought you were irresponsible or just plain foolish. Similarly, giving away your bank account details online might have appeared extremely naïve. Yet through digital platforms like Airbnb and eBay, these are now everyday practices. Trust expert Rachel Botsman (2017) argues that digital platforms have fundamentally changed who and what we trust. Instead of a hierarchical model of trust, where we are conditioned to trust those in positions of authority or power, we have moved to a 'distributed' model of trust, where we are more likely to trust strangers over government officials and authorities. Trust in the government and media is at an all-time low (see Ries et al., 2018). Implicit to a distributed model of trust is users' faith in the mechanisms of the platform and the motivation of platform operators to generate and deliver services. Blind trust in digital platforms, however, clearly has implications for other aspects of digital media use, including information and news sourcing.

Throughout the study, I sought to understand how digital platforms *conditioned* young people's digital practices not only through their architecture, but also through the discursive shifts in key concepts such as privacy, commodification and trust. I was interested in whether the young people were critically aware of these changes, and if not, how they might be supported to become so.

Digital literacies

Throughout this book, I adopt a literacies perspective to theorise young people's digital practices. Before explaining this perspective, preceding questions might be: Why literacies? Why not competencies, capabilities, or skills? In particular, what does 'literacy' bring to an understanding of young people's digital practices? As stated earlier, my interest in writing this book lies in furthering understandings of how researchers and educators might support young people to develop critical and reflective digital practices. Alongside a focus on the sociocultural context, a literacies perspective helps to understand the process of meaning-making for different social and cultural groups, including a consideration of the conventions, norms, values and beliefs on their practices.

I adopt a social approach to literacies, and therefore use the plural 'literacies' to acknowledge the multiple and varied practices young people draw on to make meaning of the world. While this research is grounded in the social literacies tradition and adopts descriptive methods to capture the young people's digital practices, I am also interested in how this intersects with young people's educational experiences. There are several reasons for this. First, school is a prominent place in young people's lives. In Australia, a typical teenager is expected to attend school for 1,500 hours a year. In taking a holistic account of young people's digital lives, it is necessary to understand not only how they use digital media *in* school, but to what extent their digital media use *outside* school is informed or acknowledged by the school curriculum.

Second, critical understandings of media are rarely developed *ad hoc*, so I am interested in the extent to which the school, as a place of both formal and informal learning, might provide young people with these understandings. This approach fits with Street's (1994) reframing of literacy as a critical social practice in that it seeks to 'take account of the historical as well as cross-cultural perspectives' and maintains that a goal should be 'to help students locate their literacy practices' (p.119) as they take place across contexts, media and modes.

Yet how young people navigate digital platforms and their architecture has been largely overlooked by literacies research. While there is a strong body of work on the digital lives of young people, particularly in sociology (Robards & Bennett, 2011; Dyer, 2015), health (Byron et al., 2013; Hendry, 2017), and citizenship and globalisation (Harris, 2008; McCosker et al., 2016), there has been a lack of empirically grounded, theoretically rich accounts of what young people's everyday digital experiences mean for literacies and literacies education. In particular, it is unclear how young people develop a critical awareness of the language in and around their digital media use. With this in mind, I seek to explore the practices, languages and dispositions that young people have cultivated in relation to digital platforms and the networked socialities that now characterise contemporary life, with a particular focus on the implications these practices have for literacies education.

What are digital literacies?

Defining 'digital literacy' has proven complicated, as the spaces, texts and tools which contextualise such practices are continually changing. Perhaps for this reason, some commentators adopt deliberately broad definitions of digital literacies. Thorne (2013), for instance, defines digital literacies as 'semiotic activity mediated by electronic media' (p.192). While accurate, this definition avoids outlining the more specific skills and practices required. Other definitions of digital literacy have tended to fall into the categories of either mastery and operational proficiency, or evaluation and critique (Lankshear & Knobel, 2011). Jones and Hafner (2012) define digital literacy along proficiency-related lines, which involves operating digital tools and 'the ability to adapt the affordances and constraints of these tools to particular circumstances' (p.13). Gilster (in Pool, 1997, p.9) argues digital literacy is about 'knowledge assembly' and 'how to assimilate the information, evaluate it, and reintegrate it'. While these definitions have all been successfully operationalised in various settings, there is a growing sense that none of these can account for the diverse and dispersed range of digital practices and processes of everyday life.

The increased complexity of contemporary digital contexts has prompted several researchers to call for new frameworks and approaches to study and develop these new and dynamic literacies (Potter & MacDougall, 2017; Avila & Pandya, 2013; Coiro et al., 2008). Further tensions arise when faced with the task of defining what it means to engage *critically* with digital media. It could be considered a set of 'skills and practices' (Avila & Pandya, 2013, p.2), a form of curatorship (Potter, 2012) or empowering consumers to shape content (Jenkins, 2008). The variety of approaches to developing *critical* digital literacies reflects the array of academic disciplines involved with this area of research and their different theoretical underpinnings and goals. There is clearly a need to challenge and test what is meant by 'critical digital literacies' in the complex, contemporary digital landscape.

Approaches to digital literacies

Generally speaking, three main approaches to literacies can be applied to digital texts and contexts. While these approaches clearly overlap, each has different points of emphasis. The first of these follows in the critical literacies tradition. Beginning in the late 1980s, a variety of models built on sociocultural perspectives of literacy and sought to contextualise digital practice within history, culture and power. Within these models, criticality is framed so that it can be translated across contexts and media. Green's (1988) three-dimensional model of literacy involves operational, cultural and critical dimensions, thereby scaffolding the individual into transforming and producing meaning through their literacy practices. At the time, this represented an expanded notion of literacy, with the operational concerned with effective language use, the cultural concerned with meaning-making and the critical with understanding manifestations of power (Green, 2002, p.27).

Complementing these ideas, Janks (2000) identifies an ability to 'understand and manage the relationship between language and power' (p.175) as the key concern of critical literacy. She argues that issues of domination, access, diversity and design should be seen as enterprises that are 'crucially interdependent' (p.178), and that 'deconstruction without reconstruction or design reduces human agency' (p.178). Similarly, Luke's (2000) definition of critical literacy involves three components. The first is 'metaknowledge' of 'meaning systems and the sociocultural contexts in which they are produced and embedded', the second involves the technical skills to negotiate these systems, and the final 'involves the capacity to understand how these systems and skills operate in the interests of power' (p.72).

In response to this more objective approach to critique, another strand of critical digital literacy has emerged which seeks to highlight the personal experiences of individuals. In this approach, the ideological is downgraded, while the 'politics of pleasure' (Alvermann, 2004) is foregrounded. UK media theorists like Buckingham (2003) and Sefton-Green (1998) have drawn attention to young people's everyday use of digital texts in which a 'correct' ideological reading of these texts is less important than how they connect with learners' lives. The problem with contemporary forms of critical literacy, Buckingham (2003) asserts, is that they tend to be based around one commonly perceived reading of political correctness that educators impart to their students. In this model, students are seen as 'victims of media manipulation' (p.118), while educators act as gatekeepers over the knowledge and skills that will liberate them from the repressive ideologies expressed through popular media. Like Buckingham and Sefton-Green, Potter (2012) adopts a more personal approach to critique, describing the production and representation of identity through digital media as a type of 'self-curatorship'.

Other approaches in this vein have also focused on the individual in developing critical practices in specific digital contexts. Burnett and Merchant's (2011) 'Tripartite Model' of critical practice specifically targets social media. Building on Greenhow and Robelia's (2009) idea of 'advantageous online community practices' (p.136), Burnett and Merchant advance a conceptual model that highlights the inter-relationships between identity, practice and networks that take place around, through and outside social media. This shifts the focus of the model from the media to be critiqued to how the individual engages with these media, integrating identity with critical practice. They write:

> Critical practice in this context may be less about digital technology as an abstract force (one that considers how it might structure our thoughts and actions) and more about an interrogation and evaluation of what we and others are actually doing on and off-line.
>
> *(Burnett & Merchant, 2011, p.51)*

This model marks a shift in the locus of practice that may be more suitable for networked, fluid texts like social media. They argue that using social media is usually a pleasurable pursuit, so any critical practice needs to balance young people's interest with more serious pedagogical aims (Burnett & Merchant, 2011). Their approach treats young people's personal responses to digital forms as a type of 'resource' from which to explore the formation of their beliefs, values and responses. In this approach, critical literacy is thus linked to the process of shaping social identities.

Sitting alongside the corpus of work on critical engagement with digital media is a more recent perspective on how key issues of digital literacy can be addressed. The 'design turn' in literacy studies refers to the idea that unpacking and examining the processes of digital design in an educational setting leads young people towards a critical and practical knowledge of digital text production—a critical digital literacy. The New London Group (1996) introduced 'design' as a key component of literacy education in their work on multiliteracies to acknowledge, among other things, the changes in communication brought about by new technologies. In its original instantiation, design was seen as a key tool that young people might draw upon to devise their 'social futures' (p.4). However, in recent years the idea of design has focused more specifically on the digital context and is becoming an increasingly popular method of digital literacy education.

Variations on the design theme have arisen in the work of Sheridan and Rowsell (2010), Jenkins (2006), and Gauntlett (2011). Unlike the two approaches described earlier that originate from non-digital contexts, digital design literacies respond more specifically to the digital context and therefore represent a potential way forward for critical digital literacy. This approach is focused on the outcomes of making, creating and producing, providing an avenue for young people to express their ideas, values and beliefs and therefore mobilise personal or affective responses to digital texts.

While some of these models acknowledge elements of all three orientations—the critical, the personal, and digital design—each orientation has a particular emphasis. In the digital context, it therefore becomes difficult for any one of these models to account completely for the increasing complexity and diversity of digital practices. As Burnett and Merchant (2013) point out, 'the very process of locating literacy can imply a certain boundedness or fixity which is at odds with the more fluid, hybrid landscapes and timescapes of the digital age' (p.37). As a result, it appears difficult for any of the approaches outlined to explore affective and creative responses to digital forms *and* critique broader concerns to do with discourse, ideology and power in a way that takes into account the complexity of the digital era.

Critical digital literacies

In focusing on and looking for evidence of critical practices, this book explores what young people *do with* digital media, rather than assessing a set of rarefied skills or capabilities. However, what young people *do with* digital media is shaped by the materialities of the media they are using. By materialities, I refer not only to the 'physicality of hardware, software, digital objects and processes', but also the material conditions of production, including 'social relations, political context, and aesthetic experiences' (Munster, 2014, p.328). While materialities refer to the overarching systems in which digital literacies are embedded, digital texts or media are where practices typically take place.

An increasingly important way for digital texts to be organised and experienced is via digital 'platforms', such as Google, Facebook and YouTube. While some scholars foreground the technical definitions of the term (see Bogost & Montfort, 2009), the 'platform' has become a dominant way for digital media companies to position themselves in the market. The term 'platform' is both discursive, in that it shapes how users, developers and technology companies come to think about its function (Gillespie, 2010), *and* technical, as it refers to an architecture structured by software (Helmond, 2015). I use 'architecture' to refer to the 'system's overall structure and function', including the interface specifications, as well as the algorithms and processes that 'govern relationships among components and allow them to interoperate' (Baldwin & Woodard, 2008, p.7). To develop insight into the materialities of the everyday digital media young people were using, I draw on fields of research dedicated to understanding the politics of digital platforms (Srnicek, 2017; Beer, 2016; Bratton, 2015) and the architecture of social media (see van Dijck, 2013; Hands 2013; Rieder, 2012; Bucher, 2012).

Software is rapidly evolving, and identifying the challenges presented by networked digital media can be difficult. The most recent moment of 'fake news' highlighted some of these concerns, as researchers and educators struggled to agree on what young people need to know about these emergent and evolving digital texts (boyd, 2017; Wardle, 2017). Some of these challenges are familiar, but some are new. Like older forms of media, social media platforms seek to make a profit through users' interactions and representations; however, the business models adopted by large multinational technology companies such as Facebook and Google are clearly different (Buckingham, 2017). Indeed, the ways in which information, interactions and relationships are commodified through digital platforms have implications for the kinds of social practices that take place in and around these sites. Bearing this in mind, we could expect that young people have tacit understandings of the materialities of digital texts and have already developed critical social practices that account for these changes.

To advance the academic debate about critical digital literacy, I take stock of the needs and practices of young people. In everyday life, individuals move fluidly between the ethical and the personal; the objective and the subjective; the creative and the critical. Practices spread across digital contexts and include social, cultural and political elements. Rather than contextually bound notions of skills and practices, this book understands and explores criticality from the perspective of the individual, through the notion of 'disposition', or more specifically, a 'critical disposition'. One of the goals of this book is to support the young people in this study to develop a critical digital disposition.

A critical digital disposition can be thought of as encompassing a form of curatorship, as well as a degree of scepticism or even 'radical scepticism' (Green, 1991), in their digital practices. In this way, the culture that created such tools and practices might also be critically evaluated (Honn, 2013). From this perspective, practices and devices no longer appear as a series of 'natural', inevitable processes that become uncritically inscribed into daily life. It can be difficult to cultivate a dispassionate, critical perspective in a context that invests deeply in the personal and affective. I seek to identify how, when and why young people move between critical, personal and technical mindsets, and how these articulate with and manifest through their everyday digital practices. For this reason, I look for the resources that young people draw on to develop critical literacies, as well as the significant others they turn to when in need of clarification and help.

Fieldwork

To explore the themes and concerns arising over the course of these two chapters, I conducted a year of fieldwork with young people. Over the course of the 2014 school year, I met with three groups of young people located in different areas across metropolitan Melbourne. Given the significance of school in young people's lives, two of the groups that I worked with were based in a school. The third group was at a youth arts centre in the outer east of Melbourne. I met with the groups at the school or centre at various times throughout the year to talk about their digital experiences and build, make, draw and model particular themes and ideas that related to their thoughts and reflections. The young people were also interviewed three times throughout the year and observed online, primarily on the most commonly used platforms including Facebook, Instagram, YouTube and Steam.

Provocation as a means of generating data

While a range of studies have described how young people use digital technology (Ito et al., 2010; Davies & Eynon, 2013; boyd, 2008, 2014), this research aimed to provoke young people to think differently and critically about their use of digital media. In doing this, the fieldwork sought to understand why young people use digital media in the ways they do. The Italian collective Ippolita (2013) argues that to critically examine our immersion in this technological world we need to be distanced from our digital objects: 'If we start from collective findings, we can derive individual conclusions, in a process of estrangement that starts from the inside out' (p.16). In this context, a provocation is a way of 'estranging' or 'defamiliarising' digital concepts and tools that are so familiar they have become 'invisible'. These concepts are then re-presented afresh, encouraging new insights and ideas.

The idea of defamiliarisation can be traced back to the work of Russian formalist Viktor Shklovsky (1917/1965), who wrote that art is a technique of thinking with images. A key goal of art, Shklovsky contends, should be to present familiar concepts in a new way. This is achieved by making forms difficult to recognise so that the process of perception[1] is prolonged. In this way, perception becomes an 'aesthetic end in itself', so that the object itself is less important than the *experiencing* of the 'artfulness of the object' (Shklovsky, 1917/1965, p.18). Shklovsky writes that humans are inclined to adopt an 'algebraic' method of thought in which perception becomes 'over-automatised' or reliant on recognition, as opposed to seeing things in their entirety. This argument seems prescient today, as algorithms do, in some ways, direct digital practices and identities. By decontextualising or defamiliarising an object, as is common practice in art, the viewer might perceive things as they are, rather than as they are known or thought to be. This process attempts to resist an 'over-automatisation' of perception.

The fieldwork aimed to defamiliarise and make strange digital practices—to prolong perception, to disrupt common processes of recognition, to provoke alternative methods of thought—so that digital materials and technologies and human practices in and around them may be seen for what they are, and not for how they are commonly recognised or popularly known. In particular, I used creative and visual methods to provoke the young people to critically reflect on both their *own* digital experiences, as well as the attributions, ideologies and discourses that shaped their understandings of digital media. This encouraged the young people to reflect upon issues relating to their use of digital platforms that would have been overlooked or remained hidden through more conventional research approaches. Representing their digital histories and practices through such creative techniques encouraged them to critically consider their engagement with digital platforms and the understandings and strategies they generated as a result.

The fieldwork was based on a series of creative 'provocations' (Pangrazio, 2017) that supported the young people in model-making, painting, mapping and digital design. Working with a visual artist, the creative activities were based around four different provocations, designed to encourage young people to think critically about their current digital practices. These four provocations were: *mapping digital and non-digital experiences; visualising the internet; timelining digital practices*; and *re-articulating the icons of the internet*. For a more detailed description of these provocations, see Appendix 1. The approach taken in this fieldwork marks a critical break with typical sociocultural literacies research, which tends to adopt methods based around descriptive, ethnographic accounts of practices. My goal was to work with young people in generative ways to open up new perspectives and insights on the digital context and share these with researchers and educators who are also interested in developing these practices in young people.

The fieldwork generated a significant amount of data and required careful analysis. The aim in analysing the data was twofold. First, it sought to build a digital narrative of each young person involved in the fieldwork. In particular, it focused on the role digital media played in their identity representation and formation; their communication and relationships with others; and their participation in society. Second, it sought to explore the critical social practices (Street, 1994) of the young people as they used digital media, including: their disposition toward digital technologies; their critical capabilities and where these were acquired; the language used; and the type of approach they considered effective in building these capabilities. Particular attention was directed toward the context in which digital practices took place, to understand how these related to their wider digital networks. To capture the complexity of each case and to enable comparisons to be drawn across cases, two techniques were employed to analyse the data: narrative analysis and thematic analysis.

Conclusions

In terms of the theoretical propositions outlined in the first two chapters, in the chapters that follow I explore the following questions:

- How are digital media used in young people's day-to-day lives, and how has this changed across time?
- How are young people shaping and shaped by the digital systems and devices they use?
- What are their understandings of the digital platforms and the coded architecture that influence their experiences?
- What literacies do they draw on and demonstrate as part of their practices?

I develop answers through the four themed empirical chapters that follow. Returning to the central questions of how these insights can be generative for literacy researchers and educators, the final two chapters draw together the critical understandings and practices that the young people demonstrated and suggest ways in which they might be better supported to cultivate their digital literacies. Let us begin by developing a temporal picture of young people's digital practices, so we might better understand their socialisation into the digital context.

Note

1 In this context, the definition of perception is a sensory one, in which the physical characteristics of the object—its colour, shape and size, for example—are sensed by the eye.

References

Alvermann, D. (2004). Media, information communication technologies, and youth literacies. *The American Behavioural Scientist*, 48(1), 78–83.

Avila, J., & Pandya, J. (2013). *Critical digital literacies as social praxis*. New York: Peter Lang Publishing Inc.

Baldwin, C. Y., & Woodard, C. J. (2008). *The architecture of platforms: A unified view*. Harvard Business School Working Paper. Retrieved from www.hbs.edu/faculty/Publication%20Files/09-034_149607b7-2b95-4316-b4b6-1df66dd34e83.pdf

Beer, D. (2016). *Metric Power*. London: Palgrave Macmillan.

Berriman, L., & Thomson, R. (2015). Spectacles of intimacy? Mapping the moral landscape of teenage social media. *Journal of Youth Studies*, 18(5), 583–597.

Bogost, I., & Montfort, N. (2009). *Platform studies: Frequently asked questions.* Paper presented at the Digital Art and Culture Conference, University of California, Irvine.

Botsman, R. (2017). *Who Can You Trust? How Technology Brought Us Together and Why it Could Drive Us Apart.* London: Penguin.

Bourdieu, P. (1977/2011). *An Outline of a Theory of Practice.* Cambridge, UK: Cambridge University Press.

boyd, d. (2007). Why youth (heart) social networking sites: The role of networked publics in teenage social life. In D. Buckingham (Ed.), *MacArthur Foundation Series on Digital Learning—Youth, Identity and Digital Media* (pp.119–142). Cambridge, MA: The MIT Press.

boyd, d. (2008). *Taken Out of Context: American Teen Sociality in Networked Publics.* (PhD), University of California, Berkeley, CA. Retrieved from: www.danah.org/papers/Ta kenOutOfContext.pdf

boyd, d. (2010). Social network sites as networked publics: Affordances, dynamics, and implications. In Z. Papacharissi (Ed.), *Networked Self: Identity, Community, and Culture on Social Network Sites.* New York and London: Routledge.

boyd, d. (2014). *It's Complicated: The Social Lives of Networked Teens.* New Haven and London: Yale University Press.

boyd, d. (2017). Did media literacy backfire? *Data & Society: Points.* Retrieved from https://p oints.datasociety.net/did-media-literacy-backfire-7418c084d88d

Bratton, B. (2015). *The Stack: On Software and Sovereignty.* Cambridge, MA: The MIT Press.

Bucher, T. (2012). Want to be on the top? Algorithmic power and the threat of invisibility of Facebook. *New Media & Society*, 14(7), 1164–1180.

Buckingham, D. (2003). *Media Education: Literacy, Learning, and Contemporary Culture.* Cambridge, UK & Malden, MA: Polity Press.

Buckingham, D. (2008). Introducing Identity. In D. Buckingham (Ed.), *Youth, Identity and Digital Media.* Cambridge, MA: The MIT Press.

Buckingham, D. (2017). Teaching social media: A critical media education approach. *Media Education Blog.* Retrieved from https://davidbuckingham.net/2017/11/02/teaching-socia l-media-a-media-education-approach/

Burnett, C., & Merchant, G. (2011). Is there a space for critical literacy in the context of social media? *English Teaching: Practice and Critique*, 10(1), 41–57.

Burnett, C., & Merchant, G. (2013). Points of view: Reconceptualising literacies through an exploration of adult and child interactions in a virtual world. *Journal of Research in Reading*, 37(1), 36–50.

Byron, P., Albury, K., & Evers, C. (2013). 'It would be weird to have that on Facebook': Young people's use of social media and the risk of sexual health sharing. *Reproductive Health Matters*, 21(41), 35–44.

Capuzzi, D., & Gross, D. R. (2014). *Youth at Risk: A Prevention Resource for Counselors, Teachers and Parents* (6th ed.). Hoboken, NJ: John Wiley & Sons.

Cheney-Lippold, J. (2017). *We Are Data: Algorithms and the Making of Our Digital Selves.* New York, NY: New York University Press.

Coiro, J., Knobel, M., Lankshear, C., & Leu, D.T. (2008). Central issues in new literacies ad new literacies research. In J. Coiro, M. Knobel, C. Lankshear, & D.T. Leu (Eds.), *Handbook of Research on New Literacies* (pp.1–21). New York: Lawrence Erlbaum Associates, Inc.

Couldry, N. (2012). *Media, Society, World: Social Theory and Digital Media Practice.* Cambridge, UK: Polity.

Davies, C., & Eynon, R. (2013). *Teenagers and Technology.* London and New York: Routledge.

Dean, J. (2005). Communicative capitalism: Circulation and the foreclosure of politics. *Cultural Politics*, 1(1), 51–74.

Dean, M., & Laidler, K. (2013). A new girl in town: Exploring girlhood identities through Facebook. *First Monday* [online], 18(2–4).

Deleuze, G., & Guattari, F. (1980/2013). *A Thousand Plateaus*. London and New York: Bloomsbury Academic.

Dyer, H. (2015). All the web's a stage: The effects of design and modality on youth performances of identity. In S. L. Blair, P. N. Claster, & S. M. Claster (Eds.), *Technology and Youth: Growing Up in a Digital World*. Bingley, UK: Emerald Group Publishing Limited.

Foucault, M. (1980). *Power/Knowledge: Selected Interviews & Other Writings*. New York: Pantheon Books.

Fuchs, C. (2014). *Social Media: A Critical Introduction*. London: Sage

Furlong, A. (2013). *Youth Studies: An Introduction*. London and New York: Routledge.

Gauntlett, D. (2011). *Making is Connecting*. Cambridge, UK: Polity Press.

Gillespie, T. (2010). The politics of 'platforms'. *New Media & Society*, 12(3), 347–364.

Goffman, E. (1959). *The Presentation of Self in Everyday Life*. New York: Doubleday Publishing Group.

Green, B. (1988). Subject specific literacy and school learning. *Australian Journal of Education*, 32(2), 156–179.

Green, B. (1991). Reading 'readingS': Towards a postmodernist reading. In C. D. Baker & A. Luke (Eds.), *Toward a Critical Sociology of Reading Pedagogy: Papers of the XII World Congress on Reading*. Philadelphia, PA: John Benjamins Publishing Company.

Green, B. (2002). A literacy project of our own? *English in Australia*, 44(3), 25–32.

Greenhow, C., & Robelia, B. (2009). Informal learning and identity formation in online social networks. *Learning, Media and Technology*, 34(2), 119–140.

Hands, J. (2013). Introduction: Politics, power and 'platformativity'. *Culture Machine*, 14, 1–9.

Harris, A. (2008). Young women, late modern politics, and the participatory possibilities of online cultures. *Journal of Youth Studies*, 11(5), 481–495.

Helmond, A. (2015). The platformatization of the web: Making web data platform ready. *Social Media + Society*, July–December, 1–11.

Helsper, E.J., & Eynon, R. (2010). Digital Natives: Where is the evidence? *British Educational Research Journal*, 36(3), 503–520.

Hendry, N. A. (2017). Social media bodies: Revealing the entanglement of sexual well-being, mental health and social media in education. In L. Allen & M. L. Rasmussen (Eds.), *The Palgrave Handbook of Sexuality Education*. London: Palgrave Macmillan.

Hinton, S., & Hjorth, L. (2013). *Understanding Social Media*. London: Sage.

Honn, J. (2013). Never neutral: Critical approaches to digital tools and culture in the humanities (Blog post). *The Centre for Digital Humanities @ Princeton*. Retrieved from: https://digitalhumanities.princeton.edu/2013/10/21/never-neutral-critical-approaches-to-digital-tools-culture-in-the-humanities/

Ippolita. (2013). *The Dark Side of Google*. Amsterdam: Institute of Network Cultures.

Ito, M., Horst, H., Antin, J., Finn, M., Law, A., Manion, A., Mitnick, S., Schlossberg, D., & Yardi, S. (2010). *Hanging Out, Messing Around and Geeking Out: Kids Living and Learning with New Media*. Cambridge, MA: The MIT Press.

Janks, H. (2000). Domination, access, diversity and design. *Educational Review*, 52(2), 176–186.

Janks, H. (2010). *Literacy and Power*. New York: Routledge.

Jenkins, H. (2006). *Confronting the challenges of participatory culture: Media education for the 21st century*. Macarthur Foundation White Paper.

Jenkins, H. (2008). *Convergence culture*. New York: New York University Press.

Jones, R. H., & Hafner, C. A. (2012). *Understanding Digital Literacies: A Practical Introduction*. London and New York: Routledge.

Kehily, M. J. (2007). Introduction. In M. J. Kehily (Ed.), *Understanding Youth: Perspectives, Identities and Practices*. London: Sage Publications.

Kittler, F. (2008). Code. In M. Fuller (Ed.), *Software Studies: A Lexicon*. Cambridge, MA: MIT Press.

Kramer, A. D. I., Guillory, J. E., & Hancock, J. T. (2014). Experimental evidence of massive-scale emotional contagion through social networks. *Proceedings of the National Academy of Sciences*, 111, 8788–8790.

Kroker, A., & Kroker, M. (2008). *Critical Digital Studies: A Reader*. Toronto, Canada: University of Toronto Press.

Lankshear, C., & Knobel, M. (2011). *New Literacies: Everyday Practices and Social Learning* (3rd ed.). Buckingham, UK: Open University Press.

Levin, S. (2017). Facebook told advertisers it can identify teens feeling 'insecure' and 'worthless'. *The Guardian Australian*. Retrieved from www.theguardian.com/technology/2017/may/01/facebook-advertising-data-insecure-teens

Luke, A. (2000). Critical literacy in Australia. *Journal of Adolescent & Adult Literacy*, 43(5), 448–461.

Marwick, A., & boyd, d. (2014). Networked privacy: How teenagers negotiate context in social media. *New Media & Society*, 16(7), 1051–1067.

McCosker, A., Vivienne, S., & Johns, A. (2016). *Negotiating Digital Citizenship: Control, Contest and Culture*. London: Rowman & Littlefield International.

McGorry, P., Parker, A., & Purcell, R. (2006). Youth mental health services. *In Psych*. Retrieved from www.psychology.org.au/publications/inpsych/youth_mental_health/

McMillan Cottom, T. (2017). Black cyberfeminism: Ways forward for intersectionality and digital sociology. In J. Daniels, K. Gregory, & T. McMillan Cottom (Eds.), *Digital Sociologies* (pp.211–231). Bristol, UK: Policy Press.

Mendelson, A. L., & Papacharissi, Z. (2011). Look at us: Collective narcissism in college student Facebook photo galleries. In Z. Papacharissi (Ed.), *A Networked Self: Identity, Community, and Culture on Social Network Sites*. New York: Routledge.

Merchant, G. (2005). Electric involvement: Identity performance in children's informal digital writing. *Discourse: Studies in the Cultural Politics of Education*, 26(3), 301–314.

Miller, D. et al. (2016). *How the World Changed Social Media*. London: UCL Press.

Muir, K., Mullan, K., Powell, A., Flaxman, S., Thompson, D., & Griffiths, M. (2009). *State of Australia's young people: A report on the social, economic, health and family lives of young people*. Social Policy Research Centre.

Munster, A. (2014). Materiality. In M. L. Ryan, Emerson, L., Robertson, B.J. (Ed.), *The Johns Hopkins Guide to Digital Media*. Baltimore, MD: Johns Hopkins University Press.

The New London Group (1996). A pedagogy of multiliteracies: Designing social futures. *Harvard Educational Review*, 66(1), 60–92.

O'Neil, C. (2016). *Weapons of Math Destruction: How Big Data Increases Inequality and Threatens Democracy*. UK: Penguin Random House.

Palen, L., & Dourish, P. (2003). *Unpacking 'privacy' for a networked world*. Paper presented at the SIGCHI Conference on Human Factors in Computing Systems, Ft. Lauderdale, FL.

Pangrazio, L. (2017). Exploring provocation as a research method in the social sciences. *International Journal of Social Research Methodology*, 1–12. doi:10.1080/13645579.2016.1161346

Pool, C.R. (1997). A new digital literacy. *Educational Leadership*, 55(3), 6–11.

Potter, J. (2012). *Digital Media and Learner Identity*. New York: Palgrave Macmillan.

Potter, J., & Banaji, S. (2011). Social media and self-curatorship. *Comunicar*, 38, 83–91.

Potter, J., & MacDougall, J. (2017). *Digital Media, Culture and Education: Theorising Third Space Literacies*. London: Palgrave Macmillan.

Pratt, M. B. (1984/1988). Identity: Skin, blood, heart. In E. Bulkin, M. B. Pratt & B. Smith (Eds.), *Yours in struggle: Three Feminist Perspectives on Anti-semitism and Racism*. Ithaca, NY: Firebrand books.

Rieder, B. (2012). What is in PageRank? A historical and conceptual investigation of a recursive status index. *Computational Culture: A Journal of Software Studies*. Retrieved from http://computationalculture.net/2012/08/29/what_is_in_pagerank/

Ries, T. E., Bersoff, D.M., Adkins, S., Armstrong, C., & Bruening, J. (2018). *2018 Edelman Trust Barometer—Global Report*. Retrieved from http://cms.edelman.com/sites/default/files/2018-02/2018_Edelman_Trust_Barometer_Global_Report_FEB.pdf

Robards, B., & Bennett, A. (2011). My tribe: Post-subcultural manifestations of belonging on social network sites. *Sociology*, 45(2), 303–317.

Sefton-Green, J. (1998). *Digital diversions: Youth culture in the age of multimedia*. London: UCL Press.

Selwyn, N. (2009). Faceworking: Exploring students' education-related use of a Facebook. *Learning, Media and Technology*, 34(2), 157–174.

Sheridan, M.P., & Rowsell, J. (2010). *Design Literacies: Learning and Innovation in the Digital Age*. London: Routledge.

Shklovsky, V. (1917/1965). Art as technique. In L. T. Lemon & M. J. Reiss (Eds.), *Russian Formalist Criticism: Four Essays* (pp.17–23). Lincoln, NE: University of Nebraska.

Srnicek, N. (2017). *Platform Capitalism*. Malden, MA: Polity Press.

Stagoll, C. (2010). Becoming. In A. Parr (Ed.), *The Deleuze Dictionary*. Edinburgh, UK: Edinburgh University Press.

Street, B. (1994). The New Literacy Studies: Implications for education and pedagogy. *Changing English*, 1(1), 113–126.

Thorne, S. L. (2013). Digital literacies. In M.R. Hawkins (Ed.), *Framing Languages and Literacies* (pp.192–218). New York: Routledge.

Turkle, S. (2011). The tethered self: Technology reinvents intimacy and solitude. *Continuing Higher Education Review*, 75.

van Dijck, J. (2013). *The Culture of Connectivity: A Critical History of Social Media*. New York: Oxford University Press.

Wardle, C. (2017). Fake news. It's complicated. *First Draft News*. Retrieved from https://medium.com/1st-draft/fake-news-its-complicated-d0f773766c79

Williams, R. (1974). *Television: Technology and Cultural Form*. Glasgow: Fontana.

Zielinski, S. (2006). *Deep Time of the Media. Toward an Archaeology of Hearing and Seeing by Technical Means*. Amsterdam: Amsterdam University Press.

2

DIGITAL NARRATIVES

A case study

Ben Pasternak is a young Australian entrepreneur who some believe might be the 'next Mark Zuckerberg' (Francis, 2014). In 2014 he was a year 9 student at a private school in inner Sydney. Bored in science class, he began developing an iPhone game. The result was Impossible Rush—a game designed to test your 'brain's reflexes'.[1] Impossible Rush quickly became a worldwide hit in the App Store, peaking at number seven in Sweden, number 16 in the US and 18 in Australia. At age 15 Ben was the youngest person to receive venture capital funding for his next mobile app, Flogg (Rivero, 2016), which enables young social media users to buy and sell things in safe and secure ways. At 16 Ben was the CEO of Flogg and managing a team of developers and designers—all of whom were several years his senior. Ben now lives in New York and is the co-founder of an American technology and social media company, Monkey.

While Ben is clearly talented, his digital narrative highlights just how important the early years were in creating and establishing digital opportunities. His passion for technology started at age eight when he became 'obsessed' with the social gaming site Club Penguin (Francis, 2014). By 11 he had his own YouTube channel, where he would review the latest devices on the market. At 13 he was making his own digital games and designs. It helped that his parents were able to financially support his ventures. As well as purchasing devices for him, his mum explains they poured 'thousands of dollars' (Francis, 2014) into funding Impossible Rush. Ben's narrative highlights the importance of personal background and life circumstance to digital opportunities and success.

With this need for personal contextualisation in mind, this chapter focuses on the importance of digital histories on current practices. Using the case study of 15-year-old participant Rachel, I focus on how her historical patterns of engagement manifest in current practices. Research tells us that early experiences with digital media are important as they can directly impact how young people are positioned to climb the 'ladder of opportunities' offered by digital technologies (Livingstone et al., 2011). How digital media are encountered across different contexts, namely home and school, illustrates the digital connections and disconnections in Rachel's life. I examine her initiation into digital contexts and the moments of change, as well as the factors that contributed to these. However, Rachel was only one of 13 participants. For a brief introduction to each of the young people involved in the study, please see Appendix 2.

Narrative analysis

Over the course of fieldwork, I used narrative analysis (Elliot, 2005) to build a picture of the young people's digital practices across time. A narrative approach was generative for the young people, as it encouraged analysis and self-reflection on digital practices, as well as the identification of significant moments in their digital past. The young people were asked and provoked to tell a story about their relationship to digital media—how they had shaped it and how it had shaped them. This helped to shift the focus of the discussions from what happened, to how they made sense of these moments and experiences. As the storyteller of their digital experiences, the young people were encouraged to 'interpret the past rather than reproduce it as it was' (Riessman, 2004, p.9). This aligns with the approach taken toward theorising identity outlined in Chapter 1, which recognises the self as fluid and reflexive. At the same time it enables the young people to trace the aspects of their personal identity that have remained stable across time (Ricoeur, 1991).

Discourses of young people's digital media use

Developing a narrative of each of the young people's digital lives encouraged identification of the institutions, resources and significant others that were influential in their early years online and how these experiences and interactions manifest in their current digital practices. In contrast to much digital research, which tends to focus on current practices and media texts, exploring digital narratives helps us to see digital practices as part of a broader life trajectory. While there might be similarities and patterns to the way young people in a given culture are socialised to the digital, this chapter is *not* based on the assumption that there are particular norms and customs to be attained. Yet there are dominant discourses associated with their use that have bearing on their narratives.

If aspects of identity are socially constructed, it follows that discourse (in addition to a range of other elements) has an important role to play in shaping these young people's digital experiences. Specifically, mainstream views and perceptions can have a significant influence upon young people's attitudes toward and engagement with digital media. Smith, Hewitt and Skrbis (2015) contend that young people's perceptions of digital media and the internet can actually *reproduce* social inequalities, meaning that their socialisation to the digital is inherently connected to their digital futures. They identify three related processes that are influential in this regard:

(1) young people internalize status-specific values about what constitutes beneficial and capital-enhancing use from influential others (e.g. parents, siblings, teachers, and peers); (2) these values are reinforced by mechanisms (e.g. norms, rules, and expectations) that reward certain uses and marginalize others; and (3) this further differentiates them in their access to the economic, social, cultural, and technological resources needed to comply with the internet uses expected of them.

(Smith et al., 2015, p.1024)

In this chapter I use Foucault's (1969/2002) notion of discourse, or discursive formations, to analyse how these young people's digital practices reflected socially accepted principles and understandings of digital media use. To Foucault, discourse is a way of producing knowledge systems or 'epistemes' that engender dominant ways of thinking about concepts and which become associated with particular historical periods or eras (Foucault, 1969/2002). An important aspect of discourse is that it is neither existent nor permanent, but instead an emergent 'space' in which 'various objects emerge and are continuously transformed' (Foucault, 1969/2002, p.36). In this way, discourse creates and transforms social practices, objects and ways of thinking.

A discourse or discursive formation can be approximated to a discipline (like political science, literature or medicine), or 'divisions or groupings with which we have become so familiar' (Foucault, 2002, p.24). Using medical science as an example, Foucault explains that from the 19th century practitioners began to 'presuppose the same way of looking at things' and that medicine was organised by a 'certain style' and 'series of descriptive statements' (p.37). O'Farrell (2005) explains discursive formations are 'a bit like the grammar of a language [and] allow certain statements to be made' (p.79). In this way discursive formations provide a 'space in which various objects emerge and are continuously transformed' (Foucault, 2002, p.36). A key point is that discursive formations create systems of knowledge that affect the world we live in.

Discourses emerge at the intersection of power and knowledge. Based upon 'expert knowledge', discourses create commonly accepted truths and are often used to establish and maintain power (Foucault, 1975/1991). Discourses of young people's use of digital media are typically focused on instilling practices of 'correct use'. What constitutes 'correct use' is determined by adults, typically researchers or law makers working in the area. The goal of these narratives is to guide and discipline young people through the transitional period of adolescence in order to create responsible and productive adults. As such, these narratives overlap with the principles of neoliberalism (Owen, 2014). One goal of this research was to identify the ways in which discourses around young people's use of digital media were constructed, and critically evaluate the effect they have on their digital experiences. As such, the research is concerned with questions of power, knowledge and subjectivity.

There are two significant discourses in regard to young people's use of digital media that are worth outlining—the 'digital native' discourse and the protectionist discourse. As we shall see, these discourses are not only oppositional in the claims they make and their recommendations for practice and policy, but are also dependent upon each other as a way of validating the claims and counterclaims that are made. These discourses are also relevant in the next chapter, where I use dispositif (Foucault, 1980) to analyse both the discursive *and* non-discursive elements that underpin young people's dispositions towards the digital.

The 'digital native' discourse

One of the most influential discourses in shaping both popular and academic conceptions of young people and digital media is that of the 'digital native' (Prensky, 2001a, p.2). Prensky coined the term 'digital native' to make the argument that young people (typically those born after 1980) are highly skilled users of technology, whom 'digital immigrants' (those born before 1980) struggle to teach. In his original conception of the 'digital native', Prensky (2001b, n.p.) even argued that 'teenagers brains are almost certainly physiologically different' from those of adults due to their time in front of computers.

While Prensky (2009) later distanced himself from his original argument, it is still a popularly referenced and researched concept (see Ebner & Schiefner, 2010; Palfrey & Gasser, 2008). The discourse of the 'digital native' has been debunked by several notable empirical studies (Helsper & Eynon, 2010; Hargittai & Hinnart, 2008; Kennedy et al., 2007), which demonstrate that *not* all young people are equally transformed by technology or as adept as the discourse suggests. Yet it still continues 'to have an influence on policy and practice', particularly in education (Jones & Czerniewicz, 2010, p.318).

The protectionist discourse

As explained in the opening chapter, popular media have played a significant role in raising adult fears around the relationship that young people have with digital media, turning it into what Drotner (1992) calls a 'media panic'. This panic appears to have taken hold in Australia, with reports that parents fear their children using social media and technology more than anything else, including drugs, alcohol and smoking (Griffiths, 2018). The protectionist discourse attempts to find normative solutions and strategies to such problems, which has led to the proliferation of cybersafety programmes in schools, as well as restrictions and monitoring of children's and young people's use of digital media.

Cybersafety programmes tend to focus on developing people's skills to manage and control their 'digital footprint', or the data trails and traces they leave behind when using digital media (Roddel, 2006). It is also concerned with issues of cyberbullying and 'stranger danger' in the online context. Cybersafety is most often directed at children and young people and their parents, and uses a didactic approach that seeks to enhance privacy and security practices. However, Hope (2013) argues that in adopting a protectionist discourse, cybersafety positions young people in constraining ways. Indeed, binary language structures the discourse where young people are positioned as 'innocent victims' or 'dangerous perpetrators'; 'naïve technology users' or 'rational "digital natives"' (pp.87–92). The competing claims of these two discourses lead to a complex set of propositions for young people to navigate.

So how are these dominant discourses constructed and communicated to young people? And how do they navigate the subjective positions they create? Using Rachel as a case study, I explore the emergence and effect of these discourses across the history of her digital experiences. As we shall see, there are other influences that shape her practices, but discourse is clearly a way that adults and other authorities in her life are able to establish hierarchies of knowledge and power in the digital context.

Rachel's story

Rachel's first experiences with digital media were in grade 3 when she was allowed to play maths and English games on the desktop computers in the classroom. In maths, online games were used as a reward if students finished their work early. Also in grade 3, Rachel and her classmates started using the internet to research information for school projects. Rachel found Wikipedia to be a particularly useful website. Not only did it expand her learning and knowledge-seeking practices, but with Wikipedia Rachel felt she had the ability to find out or learn about anything *independent* of others.

However, she soon found that the more official uses of digital media in primary school were repetitive and revolved around drill-based English and maths games. After a couple of years such games lost their appeal, especially when compared with the more exciting things she was doing online *outside* school. Her attitude toward Wikipedia also changed. As she explained, in upper primary school students were warned not to use Wikipedia because it was thought to lack credibility. Rachel no longer uses Wikipedia because, as she says, 'I don't trust it!' She now knows 'the best sites to go on, not just like Wikipedia and stuff', and attempts to validate the information she finds on the internet through other sources. However, she acknowledges that this is not always possible due to time constraints.

Early on Rachel's digital practices were guided by her interest in gaming and play, as well as a growing sense of individual creativity. Rachel enjoyed 'dress up game' websites, where users choose a character and dress them in clothes and accessories. Even as a teenager she regularly revisited this website, but as she explains this was more for nostalgic reasons, and had become a source of embarrassment: 'It's really silly, it's like a guilty pleasure. I just do it when I'm bored.' While she might have downplayed the significance of these websites in group discussion, it was clearly significant to her. Indeed, two other young people in the study, Trent and Mitch, also returned to the websites they had used in the past. As

Trent explained, he regularly returned to Club Penguin, 'to get those pretty good memories back'. Whether out of curiosity or for pleasure, returning to these sites helped to invoke memories of the past, which appeared to be a source of comfort for each of these young people.

Gaming was another important part of Rachel's digital practices. When she turned eight Rachel opened an account on Club Penguin. Club Penguin is a massive multiplayer online game, containing a range of games and activities, and with some social networking capabilities. While Rachel enjoyed playing the games, she recognised the importance of Club Penguin in shaping her interest and confidence in social networking, particularly with regard to establishing what constituted 'appropriate' online communication. Not long after opening an account she quickly found that she was visiting Club Penguin to communicate with friends rather than to play games. At this time, she also started using MSN Messenger. However, she stopped using it because it 'just got out of fashion!' She went on to explain that she only used MSN Messenger because she 'didn't have Facebook', indicating how significant Facebook had become to her online communication.

Over time Rachel began to use school email more regularly, and at the time of the fieldwork saw it as an important support to her learning. Email was the method she used to communicate with teachers and more official figures in her life. The main thing Rachel had learnt at school in regard to her use of digital media was cybersafety. Cybersafety lessons at Rachel's school were often in response to a specific incident and were occasionally delivered by the police. While some students at the same school found these classes and workshops to be useful, Rachel described them as negative and repetitive. Indeed, she felt her formal school experiences had provided her with few opportunities to expand and develop her digital skills.

While many of her friends started using Facebook in grade 5, Rachel was not allowed to open an account until year 7. When she was allowed to open an account, her best friend provided her with help on how to use the social networking site: 'I think it was in grade 5 everyone was on Facebook, but I wasn't allowed to have it till grade 7, so I got it then and my best friend showed me it and started from there.' At the same time, Rachel was required to open a school email account, but among friends she finds Facebook to be more effective as it is 'quicker than emails because people check it more often'. This was particularly the case when she needed to contact people in her class to find out about homework or school information. When she started on Facebook, she explained 'mum was like kind of supervising'. In the beginning, this was not a problem; however, as she grew older, having her mum as a 'friend' became a source of anxiety for Rachel. To deal with this, Rachel organised her Facebook conversations into 'groups' to have some privacy from her mother.

The bulk of Rachel's digital practices during the research period took place on social media sites, namely Facebook, Instagram and Snapchat. Rachel mentioned several times that she saw the internet and social media as the main way to communicate with people when not at school. This was because her mother did not allow her to go out in public much, so the internet was key to socialising and communicating with her boyfriend and friends. Another benefit to social media was that it was free. Rachel often ran out of credit on her phone so Facebook was a more dependable form of communication than text messaging.

While opening a Facebook account was noted as a significant moment in the development of her social identity, there was some ambivalence about her use, particularly in regard to the pressures of having 'friends' and accruing 'likes'. In 2012 and 2013, Rachel described being 'very into' having 'all these friends and stuff'. However, two years later, Rachel appeared to be more reflective and responsive about how particular websites and experiences made her feel. Two years prior she had closed her Tumblr account because she was following too many 'depressing blogs'. Rachel described the situation as getting 'out of hand' to the point where she would 'feel upset' and 'influenced by it'. For Rachel, the easiest solution was to simply shut down her account.

Facebook was integral to Rachel's friendships and relationships and she described her experiences on the platform in more positive terms. In particular, photos were an important way to build social relationships and intimacy. Rachel was particularly focused on this and changed her profile photo regularly to reflect the evolving nature of her relationship with boyfriend Chris (see Figure 2.1).

Displaying the various facets of the relationship in this way not only strengthened the couple's bond, but also encouraged friends and family to acknowledge their partnership. The feedback they received on their posts and photos provided a kind of public validation for their relationship and reaffirmed Rachel's choice in him as a partner. With each new photo came a stream of likes from friends and family and, most notably, words of affection from her boyfriend. This commentary occasionally became extreme, with one Facebook exchange between the couple ending with another participant in the study posting: 'Alright guys, we get it!'

Rachel's boyfriend Chris reciprocated these practices, including her in his profile photos and posts. However, leaving the other out of posts or photos could culminate in a sense of guilt, as she explained:

> His friend took a photo of him and it doesn't have me in it and he made it his profile picture and Chris's is all like panicking it doesn't have you in it and I'm freaking out. And I'm like it's ok. So I kind of have all my photos of him because he is an important person to me as well.

Rachel developed her friendships and extended her social networks through photos and cover photos, as well as sharing links to YouTube clips and online articles. As such, an important part of developing friendship and intimacy was having connections in both online and offline contexts.

Aside from building social relationships, Facebook enabled Rachel to explore different aspects of her identity and represent these publicly. Sometimes she might

FIGURE 2.1 Rachel's Facebook profile photos, June–December 2014

share a piece of artwork she had completed at school or post about an experience (see Figure 2.2).

Rachel's Facebook posts marked her independence from family and signalled an increasing engagement with the wider world. Rachel also used Facebook to express her opinions. These more opinionated posts would range from a brief review of a film she had recently watched or a commentary on school life. While these were occasionally her own original posts, they were often made up of embedded tweets, reposts or articles. For Rachel, the extended networks offered through Facebook introduced her to new social issues that she could quickly respond to and comment on, giving her confidence to form and present an opinion. This was assisted by the architecture of the platform, which helped her to present her opinion in the form of comments and reposts, and was soon an important part of her identity.

While Rachel did not use Instagram and Snapchat as much as Facebook, she did use each platform for a specific purpose. Instagram was used as a kind of real-time 'diary' of what she was doing, whereas Facebook was used to represent her identity in more detailed and deliberate ways:

Today I went to Ikea for the first time in my life
They sell good meatballs and have my dream bathroom
and it was fun — 🙂 feeling ikea with

Like · Comment · Share

👍 13 people like this.

FIGURE 2.2 Rachel's Facebook post, March 2014

> Yeah well for Instagram I don't really like post a lot of photos or selfies or anything, I just post stuff that I'm doing. So if I'm watching a movie I'll go 'I'm going to the movies'. But if I'm on Facebook I'll probably write a status or I'll take a photo of it and stuff.

At the time of the fieldwork, Rachel had only been using Snapchat for six months and during some of this time her phone was not working, so in many respects she was developing her practices on the platform. While Rachel's social media use continued to grow, her gaming practices declined. Several Facebook posts around the lack of female characters suggested she felt marginalised by the overwhelming masculinity of some of the more popular games today.

Despite her commitment to social networking, there was some uncertainty about her practices. For example, once Rachel started using Facebook she quickly found that there were expectations about platform participation that were not immediately obvious. What made for appropriate content or a 'successful' post was learnt through trial and error and took some time to master. Other young people in the study were under the watchful eye of an older brother [Maddy] or uncle [Mitch], who would provide feedback on their social media practices. Maddy, for example, said she used to post a lot of comments, but when her brother, who was four years her senior, told her 'you post too much on Facebook', she started to be more careful and selective with what she posted. With time Rachel became accustomed to the social expectations associated with Facebook use. Nevertheless, there was some embarrassment associated with the younger version of self presented on social media, as one post revealed (Figure 2.3).

Although it is difficult to determine whether this post was covering up a more serious anxiety, it enabled Rachel to show she had moved on from the 'embarrassments' of the past. The high number of reposts suggests that it struck a chord in her network, which comprised largely teenage girls. It surfaces the idea that a younger self was more naïve and embarrassing—a notion that perhaps many young people would not consider without prompting. It also encourages a more performative and purposeful representation of identity online. A unique feature of social media platforms is that they allow one to scroll back through time, allowing for a reflexive understanding of the self across time.

Some of Rachel's most significant digital experiences involved writing websites, most notably Wattpad. She found out about Wattpad through a friend:

> I had a friend on Tumblr and he liked to write and he's like, 'Do you write online?' Because I had sent him a message and he's like, 'But do you write online?' And I'm like, 'No I don't'. He's like, 'Well try out Wattpad and see'.

FIGURE 2.3 Rachel's Facebook post, October 2014

Rachel would upload her writing on Wattpad and receive feedback and ideas from other users. These exchanges were important to Rachel and, at particular times in her life, dominated her online communication. As a budding writer, Rachel did not have many opportunities offline to explore this aspect of her identity and better her skills. Internet sites like Wattpad and Quotev provided her with that space: 'I wasn't overly open about what I wrote, I always kept it a secret, but then if I'd never found Wattpad I'd still be really secretive about my writing and stuff'. While her visits to the site had declined, she clearly viewed these interactions as a large and valuable part of her digital practices.

Digital media, particularly social media, appeared central to Rachel's life and identity. As she explained in interview, it not only expanded the people she could communicate with and the topics she was interested in, but also enabled her to explore different aspects of her personality. She explained:

> I don't know on social media I'm kind of like very ummm I feel like I'm different … I don't know how to explain it, like I'm very honest and open on social media and kind of am in person as well but … I don't know I never get real opportunities to be honest and open in real life as I am on social media.

How Rachel represented herself online influenced how she came to see herself more broadly. For example, she would like to see herself as a writer, with connections to the wider world and digital media had helped her achieve that. For Rachel the internet provided opportunities for her to develop new social and creative identities, but these were opportunities that she had sought out of her own accord and were not replicated or extended in a formal school context.

Themes and trends in Rachel's story

In examining Rachel's story, a number of recurring influences and issues emerge that merit more detailed analyses. Rachel's digital narrative involved socialisation into three broad areas of practice: information and content seeking; communication and relationships; and presentation of self. These areas of practice intersected and overlapped in the variety of digital contexts that Rachel experienced. They were often rehearsed and developed alongside other digital practices, such as gaming or writing and sharing stories on Wattpad. Rachel's digital narrative demonstrated the lasting influence of early practices in establishing future patterns of engagement. Like other participants, her early internet practices bore some resemblance to what she was currently doing online, as she explains: 'I feel like what I was doing on the internet five or six years ago I'm doing now. Like I've recently got into playing online games on the internet and maybe dress up games laid down a foundation for those that were to come.' For Rachel the first websites used were like an initial stepping stone on a 'path' of websites that involved similar digital practices (i.e. Club Penguin to MSN Messenger to Facebook).

Place and space

Rachel's narrative took place across a variety of places and spaces. For analytical purposes, 'place' can be thought of as a physical destination in the *offline* world, whereas 'space' could be thought of as the *online* sites individuals visit (McMillan Cottom, 2017). Traditionally, place has been thought of as a unique or self-contained location. However, Hopkins (2010) explains that 'place' is increasingly recognised 'as having open and permeable boundaries, shaped by complex webs of local, national and global influences' (p.11). A school's learning management system, for example, means that the school is both a space *and* place for young people. As such, there is an increasingly complex interplay between place and space, which young people must navigate as part of their digital practices.

Complicating things further is the fact that the specificity of the place or space is integral to identification and the development of identity (Hopkins, 2010, p.11). These shifts are evident in Rachel's biography as her sense of self is developed across home and school, and shaped by friends, family and teachers. Indeed, Rachel has cultivated a range of digital identities that enable her to participate across a variety of contexts from gaming platforms to social networking sites, often enacting these at the same time. While technology has enabled global connections, Rachel's biography highlights that the recognition of her identities tends to take place at the local level, often with people whom she knows intimately and cares about.

Common to the digital narratives of the participants was the importance of place and physicality in the recognition and authentication of their identities. However, working out the tacit rules that underpinned these expectations and assumptions was far from straightforward. For example, Rachel recounted her participation on Facebook with some consternation, as she felt compelled toward behaviours she was not entirely comfortable with. Rachel's narrative highlights the complex intersections of place and space, as well as play, education, work, mobility and immobility in the construction of her socialities (Farrugia, 2015). Her understandings and dispositions toward digital media were formulated in response to school-based programmes, family and friends, to name but a few. I critically analyse the heterogenous elements involved in shaping digital dispositions in Chapter 3.

Specifically, school was significant in introducing Rachel to several digital practices. For example, she reported that classroom teachers had used computer games as a reward for finishing school work. Despite her initial interest, the games did not change across her primary school years and quickly became repetitive and boring. What was missing from Rachel's experience was what young people identify as constituting a good game—'opportunities for engagement, socialising, challenge and accumulation' (Beavis et al., 2015, p.39). Instead, what Rachel experienced was more akin to busy work or repetitive exercises albeit in digital form. Educational uses of digital media, no matter how prosaic, were often viewed positively as they were thought to lead to opportunities and empowerment. Like many young people from schools in low socioeconomic areas, Rachel had not encountered any of the more innovative technologies currently being used in schools, such as 3D printers or programmable robots. Instead her experiences involved repetitive, drill-based activities that were deemed pedagogically acceptable through their digital mediation.

School was also significant for the unofficial digital learning that took place. Rachel describes her friends introducing her to games and social media at school and wanting to use the same platforms and websites. The school did not officially endorse students using some of these websites and platforms (i.e. Facebook, You-Tube), suggesting that the social conventions of the spaces and places involved in her digital practices were often in tension. However, school was also where many of the young people were introduced to the practice of information and content seeking. In her early years, Wikipedia was an important site for Rachel to find out about the world; however, by secondary school it was discouraged or simply used as a starting point for finding more credible sources.

Rachel's introduction to the digital also took place at home, most typically when a significant other introduced it or, in the case of parents, allowed her to use a new social networking site. With restrictions and protocols on language use and behaviour, Rachel's parents possibly felt that Club Penguin was a safe site for her to use unsupervised. Rachel's experiences are indicative of the restrictions many young people feel in regard to their personal freedom due to parental fears for their safety in public places. In many respects, the space of the game occupies the place of the public park or recreation centre. Once habituated these early digital practices shaped Rachel's patterns of digital engagement.

Many websites were common across the group, suggesting that there were similarities in the ways these young people were socialised into the digital context. In particular, these were often inscribed along gender lines, with four of the six boys beginning online communication via gaming platforms, in particular Miniclip, Nickelodeon and Pokémon. On the other hand, the girls often learnt about online communication through sites like Club Penguin, Farmville and Moshi Monsters. For Rachel social networking quickly superseded any gaming practices that might have taken place on these sites. Nevertheless, these early sites played a significant role in these young people's digital narratives, which explains why three of them regularly returned to visit the websites of their childhood, highlighting the importance of these spaces for the young people in their teenage years.

Digital cultures

Rachel's digital biography also highlights the significance of different digital cultures on her emerging sense of self. As many researchers have shown, cultural practices provide opportunities for young people to rehearse and represent their identities and their relationships with others (see Robards & Bennett, 2011; Morgan & Warren, 2011). Of significance is the fact that youth cultural practices are not 'imposed' upon young people, but instead are 'reflexively constructed by active and effectively empowered social subjects' (Bennett, 2015, p.776).

Rachel's use of Wattpad was a good example of her developing identity as a writer, with the opportunities to communicate with other writers and provide feedback on their work key to this process. Holland, Lachiotte, Skinner and Cain (2001) use the concept of 'figured worlds' to account for how young people engage with virtual worlds, and the worlds of popular culture and fantasy, to *create* identities for themselves. When participating in figured worlds, 'People tell others who they are, but even more importantly, they tell themselves and they try to act as though they are who they say they are' (Holland et al., 2001, p.3). Each one of these figured worlds is underpinned by social conventions, which guide the development of practices.

The internet has also made youth cultures more accessible, opening up available subject positions for young people like Rachel. As Bennett (2004) explains, youth cultures are 'cultures of "shared ideas", whose interactions take place not in physical spaces such as the street, club or festival field, but in the virtual spaces facilitated by the internet' (p.163). Gee (2004) contends that many cultural practices—whether they take place in the online or offline world—involve more than just participation in a culture or community, and include a type of informal learning. Gee puts forward the notion of 'affinity spaces' to describe 'a place or set of places where people affiliate with others based primarily on shared activities, interests, and goals, not shared race, class, culture, ethnicity, or gender' (p.67).

On the internet affinity spaces potentially enable young people to transcend physical and geographical limitations to engage and learn with others about their own personal interests and hobbies. Rachel found affinity spaces on Facebook, Tumblr and Wattpad, to name but a few, and she describes learning from these experiences in different ways. As she puts it, she can be someone different in each of these communities. These were not always positive involvements, as she explained with Tumblr and occasionally Facebook; however, these were experiences she was able to learn from.

Significant others

Unlike other young people in the study, Rachel did not mention any 'significant others' in her biography to guide or help in the development of her digital practices. Teachers were largely absent from her discussions and parents tended to play a more supervisory role ensuring Rachel was 'safe' online. Rachel's experience contrasts with other participants who had older siblings [Maddy], cousins [Penny, Grace and Simon], and parents [Chantelle] to provide suggestions, ideas and tips on their digital practices. For example, Grace's cousin introduced her to Club Penguin and then to Facebook, encouraging and guiding her into these new social spaces. Simon's cousin introduced him to the gaming platform Steam. On Steam they could meet up virtually to play games and 'chat'. These instances and interactions expanded these young people's digital practices and helped foster a sense of confidence and purpose in the digital context.

While some participants mentioned a significant other had encouraged them to expand their practices or develop a sense of appropriateness, none except Mitch mentioned a more knowledgeable mentor to help develop critical or advanced digital practices. Digital technology might have enabled young people to learn more autonomously, but there is still a need for a mentor or teacher to expand and develop digital skills and critical thinking. It might seem paradoxical, but Warschauer (2007, p.45) points out that 'people only develop the ability to work autonomously, whether in online or offline realms, only through processes of being instructed or mentored by others'. Apart from learning to work autonomously, mentors also help young people to make critical connections through their digital practices, such as 'making ties to content knowledge and the world, problem solving, and innovative thinking' (Gee, 2012, p.419). Analysis of Rachel's biography reveals an absence in this regard.

Analysing Rachel's narrative through discourse

It is now possible to see how the trends and themes in Rachel's narrative reflect the dominant discourses associated with young people's digital media use. Throughout Rachel's narrative there were moments in which particular values about digital media were internalised and rewarded, while other practices were described in more negative ways. For example, educational uses of technology, no matter how banal, were valued and rewarded by teachers and adults, whereas social networking was to be approached with caution due to its supposed risk.

On the one hand analysis of Rachel's narrative suggests that the adults in her life conceive of her as a 'digital native', as there appear to be few attempts to support or develop her digital skills. On the other hand, however, the school-based cybersafety lessons and her mum's close monitoring of her Facebook account position her as vulnerable and naïve, and in need of adult protection. This culminates in a complicated and sometimes contradictory set of messages for Rachel to interpret. Nonetheless a result of these discourses is that each stakeholder (including young people themselves) has a set of descriptive statements they can draw on to explain and validate their actions. In the next chapter, I focus on how the participants themselves use dominant discourses to explain their beliefs and attitudes toward digital media.

A notable absence in Rachel's narrative was that of a more knowledgeable mentor or teacher to develop and extend her understandings and practices with digital media. While it is beyond the scope of this research to provide a conclusive explanation as to why this was the case, it could be that Rachel's teachers and the school community view their students as 'digital natives', who need little help from adults to build their digital competence. If adults assume that young people are 'highly skilled' users of technology then it is easy to see why teachers and parents would believe they have little role to play in young people's digital lives. Instead, the approach taken by the adults in Rachel's life might be explained through the protectionist discourse. Rather than inspiring Rachel to use digital media in innovative and creative ways, the role of teachers, the school and her parents tended to be one of protector, curtailing her digital practices, rather than encouraging exploration and development.

In particular, Rachel reported secondary school programmes as doing little to expand or further develop her practices and instead focused on developing protective skills and strategies. Cybersafety education was the main form of digital media education that took place in these years. As the most frequently used sites were banned at school (i.e. Facebook and YouTube), Rachel had come to see the school site as digitally disconnected or at least different from other sites encountered in her everyday life. Such paternalism does little to empower young people to ask questions of digital media and how it shapes their view of the world. In short, it does little to develop critical use of digital media.

Each of the discourses creates a 'space' in which practices, objects and ways of thinking about digital media use are theorised and transformed, culminating in a set of practices that appear eclectic and often contradictory. Clearly, each of these discourses does play an important role; however, problems arise when the discourse begins to 'presuppose' (Foucault, 1969/2002) ways of thinking about and understanding young people's use of digital media. This can hamper reasoned debate as arguments tend toward the extreme, creating what Drotner (2005) calls 'discursive dichotomies', in which children and young people are positioned as either 'empowered' or 'at risk'. Despite the need to understand the influence of dominant discourses, as well as the various contexts and stakeholders on young people's digital practices, there is a lack of studies that are focused on such details (Vandewater, 2013).

Conclusions

This chapter has developed a temporal picture of digital experiences through a detailed exploration of Rachel's narrative. In doing so we have explored the connections and disconnections across her various contexts of use, building rich and detailed insights into what has motivated and influenced her practice. Rachel's experiences contrast with those of Ben, whose story opened this chapter. Unlike Ben, who appeared to have few structural or financial barriers to his digital practices, Rachel's digital experiences were hamstrung in several ways. Not only did she experience financial difficulties, such as running out of credit on her mobile phone, but she also noted feeling limited by the expectations others had of her use. Having few opportunities to cultivate her digital skills at school was another significant factor.

But how do digital narratives manifest in the young people's *current* attitudes toward the digital? I now investigate the young people's digital dispositions. Using Foucault's dispositif I unpack the matrix of discursive *and* non-discursive elements that underpin young people's attitudes. As we shall see, the non-discursive elements are not only more influential than the discursive elements, but can also be more difficult for the young people to identify. The temporal picture of digital practices built in this chapter provides an important foundation for this discussion, as we trace where these understandings and practices come from.

Note

1 See: https://itunes.apple.com/au/app/impossible-rush-official-version/id910248027?mt=8

References

Beavis, C., Muspratt, S., & Thompson, R. (2015). 'Computer games can get your brain working': Student experience and perceptions of games in the classroom. *Learning, Media and Technology*, 40(1), 21–42.

Bennett, A. (2004). Virtual subculture? Youth identity and the internet. In A. Bennett & K. Kahn-Harris (Eds.), *After Subculture: Critical Studies in Contemporary Youth Culture*. Basingstoke, UK: Palgrave.

Bennett, A. (2015). Youth and play: Identity, politics and lifestyle. In J. Wyn & H. Cahill (Eds.), *Handbook of Children and Youth Studies*. Singapore: Springer Science + Business Media.

Buckingham, D., & Jensen, H. (2012). Beyond 'media panics': Reconceptualising public debates about children and media. *Journal of Children and Media*, 6(4), 413–429.

Drotner, K. (1992). Modernity and media panics. In K. Schroder & M. Skovmand (Eds.), *Media Culture: Reappraising Transnational Media* (pp.42–62). London: Routledge.

Drotner, K. (2005). Mediatized childhood: Discourses, dilemmas and directions. In J. Qvortrup (Ed.), *Studies in Modern Childhood*. Basingstoke, UK: Palgrave Macmillan.

Drotner, K. (2013). The Co-construction of media and childhood. In D. Lemish (Ed.), *The Routledge International Handbook of Children, Adolescents and Media* (pp.15–21). London and New York: Routledge.

Ebner, M., & Schiefner, M. (2010). *Looking Toward the Future of Technology-Enhanced Education: Ubiquitous Learning and the Digital Native*. Hershey, PA: IGI Global.

Elliot, J. (2005). *Using Narrative in Social Research*. Thousand Oaks, CA: Sage Publications.

Farrugia, D. (2015). Space and place in studies of childhood and youth. In J. Wyn & H. Cahill (Eds.), *Handbook of Children and Youth Studies*. Singapore: Springer Science + Business Media.

Foucault, M. (1969/2002). *Archaeology of Knowledge*. Abingdon, Oxon, UK: Routledge.

Foucault, M. (1975/1991). *Discipline and Punish: The Birth of the Prison*. London: Penguin Books Ltd.

Foucault, M. (1980). *Power/Knowledge: Selected Interviews & Other Writings*. New York: Pantheon Books.

Francis, H. (2014). Is this 15-year-old Australian the next Mark Zuckerberg? *The Sydney Morning Herald*. Retrieved from www.smh.com.au/technology/is-this-15yearold-australian-the-next-mark-zuckerberg-20141008-10rrzm.html

Gee, J. P. (2004). *Situated Language and Learning: A Critique of Traditional Schooling*. New York: Routledge.

Gee, J. P. (2012). The old and the new in the new digital literacies. *The Educational Forum*, 76, 418–420.

Griffiths, M. (2018). Parents fear social media and technology more than drugs, alcohol or smoking. *The Age*. Retrieved from www.abc.net.au/news/2018-03-11/parents-fear-social-media-tech-more-than-drugs-alcohol-smoking/9535712

Hargittai, E. & Hinnart, A. (2008). Digital inequality: Differences in young adults' use of the Internet. *Communication Research*, 35(5), 602–621.

Helsper, E. J. & Eynon, R. (2010). Digital Natives: Where is the evidence? *British Educational Research Journal*, 36(3), 503–520.

Holland, D., Lachiotte, W. J., Skinner, D., & Cain, C. (2001). *Identity and Agency in Cultural Worlds*. Cambridge, MA: Harvard University Press.

Hope, A. (2013). The politics of online risk and the discursive construction of e-safety. In K. Facer & N. Selwyn (Eds.), *The Politics of Education and Technology: Conflicts, controversies and connections* (pp.83–98). London: Palgrave Macmillan.

Hopkins, P. E. (2010). *Young People, Place and Identity*. London and New York: Routledge.

Jones, C., & Czerniewicz, L. (2010). Describing or debunking? The net generation and digital natives. *Journal of Computer Assisted Learning*, 26, 317–320.

Jones, R. H., & Hafner, C. A. (2012). *Understanding Digital Literacies: A Practical Introduction*. London and New York: Routledge.

Kennedy, G., Dalgarno, B., Gray, K., Judd, T., Waycott, J., Bennett, S., Maton, K., Krause, K., Bishop, A., Chang, R., & Churchward, A. (2007). The net generation are not big users of Web 2.0 technologies: Preliminary findings from a large cross-sectional study. In R. Atkinson, C. McBeath, A. Soong, & C. Cheers (Eds.), *Providing choices for learners and learning: Proceedings of the 24th annual conference of the Australasian Society for Computers in Learning in Tertiary Education* (pp.517–525). Singapore: ASCILITE.

Lankshear, C., & Knobel, M. (2011). *New Literacies: Everyday Practices and Social Learning* (3rd ed.). Buckingham, UK: Open University Press.

Livingstone, S., Haddon, L., Görzig, A., & Ólafsson, K. (2011). *EU Kids Online: Final Report*. London: EU Kids Online, London School of Economics & Political Science.

Mavoa, J., Gibbs, M., & Carter, M. (2017). Constructing the young child media user in Australia: A discourse analysis of Facebook comments. *Journal of Children and Media*, 11(3), 330–346.

McMillan Cottom, T. (2017). Black cyberfeminism: Ways forward for intersectionality and digital sociology. In J. Daniels, K. Gregory, & T. McMillan Cottom (Eds.), *Digital Sociologies* (pp. 211–231). Bristol, UK: Policy Press.

Meyers, E. M., Erickson, I., & Small, R. V. (2013). Digital literacy and informal learning. *Learning, Media and Technology*, 38(4), 355–367.

Morgan, G., & Warren, A. (2011). Aboriginal youth, hip hop and the politics of identification. *Ethnic and Racial Studies*, 34(6), 925–947.

O'Farrell, C. (2005). *Michel Foucault: Key Concepts*. London: Sage.

Owen, S. (2014). Framing narratives of social media, risk and youth transitions: Government of 'not yet' citizens of technologically advanced nations. *Global Studies of Childhood*, 4(3), 235–246.

Palfrey, J., & Gasser, U. (2008). *Born Digital: Understanding the First Generation of the Digital Natives*. New York: Basic Books.

Pool, C. R. (1997). A new digital literacy. *Educational Leadership*, 55(3), 6–11.

Prensky, M. (2001a). Digital natives, digital immigrants, part 1. *On the Horizon*, 9(5), 1–6.

Prensky, M. (2001b). Digital natives, digital immigrants, part 2: Do they really think differently? *On the Horizon*, 9(6), 1–6.

Prensky, M. (2009). H sapiens digital: From digital immigrants and digital natives to digital wisdom. *Innovate: Journal of Online Education*, 5. Retrieved from www.wisdompage.com/Prensky01.html

Ricoeur, P. (1991). Life in quest of narrative. In D. Wood (Ed.), *On Paul Ricoeur*. London and New York: Routledge.

Riessman, C. K. (2004). Narrative analysis. In M. S. Lewis-Beck, A. Bryman, & T. F. Liao (Eds.), *The Sage Encyclopedia of Social Science Research Methods*. Thousand Oaks, CA: Sage Publications.

Rivero, T. (2016). Meet the 16-year-old CEO of mobile app 'Flogg'. *Wall Street Journal*. Retrieved from www.wsj.com/video/meet-the-16-year-old-ceo-of-mobile-app-flogg/A4795880-8A1C-4E39-BE08-6F02960CA03A.html

Robards, B., & Bennett, A. (2011). My tribe: Postsubcultural manifestations of belonging on social network sites. *Sociology*, 45(2), 303–317.

Roddel, V. (2006). *Internet Safety Parents' Guide*. Morrisville, NC: LuLu Press.

Selwyn, N. (2015). The discursive construction of education in the digital age. In R. H. Jones, A. Chik, & C. A. Hafner (Eds.), *Discourse and Digital Practices: Doing Digital Analysis in the Digital Age*. London and New York: Routledge.

Smith, J., Hewitt, B., & Skrbis, Z. (2015). Digital socialization: Young people's changing value orientations towards internet use between adolescence and early adulthood. *Information, Communication & Society*, 18(9), 1022–1038.

Thorne, S. L. (2013). Digital literacies. In M.R. Hawkins (Ed.), *Framing Languages and Literacies* (pp.192–218). New York: Routledge.

Vandewater, E. A. (2013). Ecological approaches to media and children. In D. Lemish (Ed.), *The Routledge International Handbook of Children, Adolescents and Media* (pp.46–54). London and New York: Routledge.

Warschauer, M. (2007). The paradoxical future of digital learning. *Learn Inq*, 1, 41–49.

3

DIGITAL DISPOSITIONS

There is an entirely different attitude to privacy among young people than there was perhaps a generation ago.

(George Brandis, Australian Attorney General, 2017)

There is much speculation and public debate about young people's attitudes and beliefs toward digital media. Research findings are similarly divided, particularly with regard to attitudes toward online privacy. Research from the University of Sydney, for example, shows that young Australians are more likely to *disagree* with the idea there is no privacy online than older Australians (Goggin et al., 2017). This contrasts with research from the Annenberg Center for the Digital Future in the US, which concluded that young people *are more willing* to allow access to their personal data or web behaviour than their older counterparts (Cole et al., 2013). Given the socially and culturally situated nature of young people's digital practices, such variation in findings is not surprising. Young people's dispositions toward digital media are not universal. Rather what we find are dispositions that are responsive to the local context, but can be understood as part of the global paradigm of networked digital culture.

Having developed a temporal picture of the young people's digital practices in Chapter 2, the aim of this chapter is to identify and explore what young people know and believe about digital media, and how and why they arrived at these *digital dispositions*. In the previous chapter, I outlined two dominant discourses that shape young people's digital understandings and practices—the 'digital native' discourse and the protectionist discourse. However, Rachel's narrative demonstrated that her use of digital media was not shaped by discourse alone. Indeed, the 'digital native' discourse appeared a rather simplistic way of theorising the complex issues Rachel was negotiating as part of her digital experiences. Discourse is only one aspect in a milieu of elements, including institutions and materialities, which shape these young people's dispositions toward digital media.

In this chapter, I analyse the young people's knowledge and understandings about digital media through Foucault's (1980) theory of dispositif. Dispositif (or *apparatus*—see Bussolini, 2010) is literally anything that has the capacity to shape, constrain, determine or intercede in the behaviours, beliefs and opinions of human beings. By analysing what the young people told me about digital media throughout the study, I construct a digital dispositif. While dispositif shares etymological similarities with the word disposition, there are some differences. Disposition refers to an individual's natural or mental outlook or an inherent quality or characteristic. Like dispositif, it also refers to the particular arrangement or placement of objects and subjects, and the influence this has on the formation of attitudes and beliefs. However, dispositif draws attention to the material and ontological composition of these attitudes.

While the young people's digital dispositions can be identified and read at a fairly superficial level, the theoretical lens of the dispositif enables a deeper level of analysis. Through the digital dispositif we can map the influence of discursive, material and affective notions of the digital on the young people's beliefs and practices. Throughout this chapter, I use the word 'disposition' to refer to the young people's beliefs and attitudes toward the digital, while 'dispositif' helps me to trace the *ontologies* of these beliefs and attitudes. Specifically, ontology is concerned with how the young people were positioned as both individuals *and* as subjects through various elements of the digital dispositif.

What is a dispositif?

Dispositif emerged in Foucault's later writings and interviews after he acknowledged the methodological impasse of an exclusively discursive focus. Discourse alone could not account for the recursive and relational ways power was nuanced across various elements of society. With dispositif, Foucault was aiming for something more general than the episteme. In this way, the dispositif is

> a thoroughly heterogeneous ensemble consisting of discourses, institutions, architectural forms, regulatory decisions, laws, administrative measures, scientific statements, philosophical, moral and philanthropic propositions—in short, *the said as much as the unsaid.*
>
> *(Foucault, 1980, p.194, emphasis added)*

Discursive formations are focused on an analysis of language and discourse; however, the dispositif takes into account the non-linguistic, particularly visual and spatial arrangements (Lambert, 2016). Given the importance of the visual and the affective in the digital context, the dispositif is a particularly useful analytical frame for this study. Drawing on Foucault and those who followed him, in this chapter I articulate the various elements of the digital dispositif.

Due to differences and difficulties in translation, dispositif has become a notoriously illusive Foucaultian concept (see Peltonen, 2004). However, applied to the young people's digital dispositions, it becomes more tangible. I analyse how the different elements of the dispositif conditioned the young people to experiencing and understanding digital media. This has implications for their practices (see Chapters 4 and 5). In particular, I focus on how they accept, resist or work around these understandings and subject positions. This involves negotiations of power and knowledge. Indeed, the digital dispositif is 'always inscribed in a play of power' (Foucault, 1980, p.196).

Foucault used dispositif to analyse how power was enacted across a range of non-discursive and discursive elements and the outcomes that resulted from these arrangements. This is not to suggest that the outcomes of any given dispositif were necessarily planned or preordained—dispositifs change and shift across time and context. Instead the dispositif was a way of answering the question: 'why were very different things in the world gathered together, characterised, analysed and treated' (Foucault, 2001, pp.171–172). Specifically, it can be thought of as 'the network that is established *between* these different elements' (Agamben, 2009, p.5, emphasis added). It focuses on how normative positions are formulated according to specific contextual arrangements, rather than generalised, universal ideals (Rohle, 2005). Through the dispositif I analyse how power and knowledge are connected and condensed across the heterogenous elements associated with digital media use to produce subject positions for these young people. Rather than arriving at a totalising or technologically determinist theory, through analysis of the dispositif the realities of these young people's digital experiences and the factors that conditioned them can be critically analysed.

The materialities of digital media play an important role in the dispositif. Specifically, the architecture of digital platforms as well as the social practices these instantiate. This influences how affect is mobilised across digital networks, encouraging acts and behaviours in ways that are experienced and felt rather than consciously articulated. While affect has been applied in a number of contexts, throughout this book I draw on social scientific applications of affect (Massumi, 2002, 2015; Gregg & Seigworth, 2010; Hillis et al., 2015). Every behaviour, practice or language event comes about through conscious dimensions of experience *as well as* through subconscious, embodied reactions. Affective reactions might complement, contrast or contradict the more official discourses and representations of the digital that drive its implementation in society.

Nevertheless, like most dispositifs, the digital dispositif is created as a way of improving society or providing a solution to a pre-existent problem (Foucault, 1980). Popular depictions of digital media promise connection, creation and prosocial forms of community participation. Indeed, 'the capture and subjectification of this desire in a separate sphere constitutes the specific power of the apparatus' (Agamben, 2009, p.17). Dispositifs are created to be functional and effective; however, they can have unforeseen outcomes. Revealing the latent desires and motivations implicit to the digital dispositif provides opportunities for critique, as well as revealing opportunities for alternative behaviours and subject positions. This corresponds with one of the key goals of this study, which was to find ways to support the development of critical and agentic digital practices.

Much research into young people's relationship with digital media rightfully focuses on their practices. However, as we shall see in Chapters 4 and 5, digital practices are socially, affectively, discursively and materially constructed. In developing a digital dispositif, I map how power and knowledge move across online and offline contexts to reveal the ways in which collective and individual subject positions are circumscribed for these young people (Rohle, 2005). By locating these young people within the digital dispositif, the particular challenges they face become all the more evident. So too do the ways in which they might be supported to address these. As Franco Berardi (in Cote, 2011) explains, if we are to develop digital practices for the better, 'we have to recombine those elements that are disseminated in the social milieus' (p.383).

The digital dispositif

Extending on the discussion of discourse in Chapter 2, I construct here a dispositif of digital media based on these young people's attitudes, understandings and experiences of the digital. I use dispositif to reveal the various elements that shape these young people's dispositions toward the digital, and to identify how they accepted, resisted or worked around these elements. I organise the analysis into two parts, which correspond to different aspects of the dispositif including: the influence of *discursive elements* such as the protectionist and 'digital native' discourse; and the *non-discursive elements*, including the influence of affect and embodiment; and the materialities of digital media.

Discursive

In explaining their digital practices or how they arrived at particular understandings, many of the young people would draw on the discourse of the 'digital native' (Prensky, 2001a, 2001b), outlined in the previous chapter. This discourse positioned the young people as adept and skilful users of digital media. They appeared to accept this positioning, and used it to justify their behaviours and beliefs. Sean explained: 'Most young people are very much adept at computers from a very young age, because they were raised around them.' To Mitch, young people were simply 'born into it'. Not only were they 'born' into using digital technologies, but they were also born into the dispositif, as their life experiences were oriented by the digital in many different ways.

Several young people also believed their 'generation' was more inclined to experiment and adapt to digital technologies due to greater confidence. As Trent said, 'It's our generation too—we adapt', while in Grace's view, young people's disposition towards digital technology means they are more willing to try things out:

I think the problem with older people, who don't know how to use it, is they don't want to try things, because they think they're going to break it. Whereas we would just click things and work it out ourselves.

Echoing Prensky's (2001a, 2001b) argument more directly, Mark explained that the issue is visible in education, where teachers are just not as accomplished at using technology as young people:

I think if they actually got—no offence to schoolteachers—but if they actually got some people that do spend a considerable amount of time on the internet and know how to navigate around it like young people do, it would be a lot easier to teach younger audiences.

While it was not evident that these young people exhibited different digital practices from adults, it appears they have accepted their discursive positioning as 'digital natives'. They identified as highly skilled users of digital media, leading to a certain confidence and willingness to experiment.

At the same time six of the young people described the relationship that humans have with digital technology in sceptical, sometimes quite negative ways. This led to tensions and complications in the way they felt about and described their *own* digital practices. On the one hand they appeared to have adopted the idea that they were 'digital natives'. Yet on the other hand they idealised non-digital or face-to-face communication, believing it to be more meaningful or real. This privileging of non-digital communication was sometimes justified in surprisingly conservative ways. This was particularly evident in some of the rather dystopian futures predicted by several young people.

In some instances, technology and nature were represented in a binary relationship, where technology was often seen replacing or encroaching on face-to-face experiences. This was exemplified in Sean's map of digital and non-digital experiences—a type of family tree—that replaced the tree, roots and branches with cables and wires (Figure 3.1).

Sean saw digital media as 'an artificial way of connecting people'. He went on to say that 'the digital side is a bit less … it's a bit faded, so it's not as strong but it's still there'. Chantelle's position was the most extreme. She depicted technology as a 'dark … enveloping cloud that is sort of sweeping over humanity'. In the middle of her map she wrote 'family', 'safe', 'life' and 'friends'. As she explained, her map depicted 'family units' as 'cheerful and bright', but then there was this 'cloud sort of internet connection' that was 'destroying that' (Figure 3.2).

In both images the young people represent the digital as kind of abstracted strata, connecting and permeating different aspects of their lives. At the same time, the artworks could be co-opted as representations of how the young people experience the digital dispositif. Seen from this perspective the digital is an example *par excellence* of the dispositif.

FIGURE 3.1 Sean's 'map' of digital and non-digital experiences

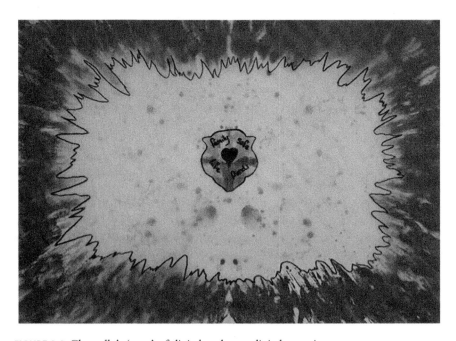

FIGURE 3.2 Chantelle's 'map' of digital and non-digital experiences

Two other young people predicted a dystopian technological future for society. Stacey believed that 'people, teenagers and parents are spending too much time on new advanced technology' and that this will lead to an existence like that proposed in the movie *Wall-E*:

> If we keep going I believe that's how we are going to be. We are not going to see the beauty of what we actually have. We're just going to be stuck to our screens 24/7. There'll be no break because like we sleep, wake up straight on.

In a similar way, Trent drew on the *Terminator* movies to explain that 'eventually we'll lose control of it [digital technology]—it will become such an intelligence that we won't have *any* control over it … like a "Skynet" reality'.

These opinions appeared to stem not only from the protectionist discourse, which emphasised the more negative possibilities of digital media use, but also from dominant tropes in popular culture. As discussed in Chapter 2, the protectionist discourse emphasises the more dangerous and risky aspects of digital media use in an attempt to keep young people safe online. While the protectionist discourse, and the cybersafety programmes and practices that result, seek to be useful, it is not surprising that young people might have some negative feelings toward digital technologies as a consequence.

This idea is reinforced by popular culture, where representations of digital technologies tend to accentuate their negative capabilities. The dynamics of the relationship that humans have with digital technology, and the latent fears and concerns it evokes, have provided rich material for many creative projects over the years. For example, film directors have tended to see the relationship humans have with technology in dystopian terms, predicting an apocalyptic domination by machines. While these young people identify as 'native' to the digital, there is a sense of trepidation as they describe and depict technologies as encroaching, entwining, dominating or overshadowing human experience. Implicit to these discussions was that humans had little control over technological systems. This contradicted the confidence with which they identified as 'digital natives'.

There was a more general sense among the young people that being on the internet was a 'waste' of time. As Dylan explained: 'I don't want to waste a whole Saturday that I could have gone outside and found something very exciting or I could have made time with my friends to build a social connection.' Mitch thought that people should limit the time spent on digital media, suggesting one could never be quite as productive online as offline: 'I think you need to understand that you know, you can turn it off, there are other things to do besides waste … or well spend your time on the internet.' Such remarks complicate the popular image of young people as addicted to their devices.

While the young people accepted and identified with the label of digital native, this contrasted with the beliefs they held. Given the widespread use of terms like 'net generation', 'digital native' and 'cyberkids' in various formal and informal discourses, the young people were left little choice but to identify with these labels.

Yet the digital dispositif was also constructed through popular culture and the protectionist discourse, which both highlight the negative potentialities of digital technology. Analysed through the dispositif we can see the multilayered negotiations that the young people were making through the range of digital experiences and discourse they were exposed to and entangled in.

When it came to issues of risk and safety, the protectionist discourse, most commonly experienced as 'cybersafety', was clearly influential in shaping the young people's understandings of digital media. It guided their practices in regard to privacy and security, the use of anonymity and the circulation of content. Cybersafety worked to both contain and limit the young people's digital practices in order to 'keep them safe' online. It also worked rhetorically, shifting their opinion and initiating a particular set of values for digital media use.

Most of the participants addressed questions of privacy and security in terms of social media. Of the young people on Facebook, only Dylan had what might be considered low privacy settings, where anyone on the social media platform could see his profile, posts and status updates. This might be explained by his rather extroverted social media identity: Dylan had cultivated a distinct social media persona that, unlike others in the group, purposefully aspired to gaining the attention of others. I discuss Dylan's identity practices in further detail in Chapter 4. Keeping privacy settings low no doubt helped him to attract and 'friend' ever increasing numbers of people.

All of the other young people had strict privacy settings, meaning that only the people they were 'friends' with on social media could see their profile. This discussion was not driven by concerns over privacy, but rather the ability to control where their content and information went and what others might do with it. As Stacey said, 'I only want my information to go out to certain people'. Maddy also considered what might be done with that information: 'Well I make sure everything's on private and then like no one can access it.' But for Rachel, privacy also meant keeping certain posts private from particular 'friends' and family. 'Friending' her mother on Facebook was a case in point:

> I've got my mum on Facebook and stuff but I kind of, this is going to sound kind of bad, but I don't block her, but I make sure she doesn't see some of my posts. Not that they're that bad but I don't know.

Evident here is one of the most significant tensions within the digital dispositif—between the demands of the protectionist discourse and those of the peer-based social network. The young people referred to this tension time and again throughout the study.

Another issue with regard to risk and safety was deciding when to become 'friends' with someone online. For Penny, who had over 1,200 friends on Facebook, the number of mutual friends she had with another user was a deciding factor: 'If I have enough mutuals I just add them.' Algorithms created by platform operators also suggest 'friends' according to the user's history of platform participation. Here the architecture of the social media platform plays an important role in guiding Penny in the 'friending' process and providing her with a sense of security through the measure of mutual friends.

Penny also recounted a 'rule' about 'friending' that had come from a policeman who visited her school, which provided a counter to the prompts and suggestions of the platform:

> He was talking about as long as you know they're a real person, and they're either friends or friends with people you know … He's like it doesn't matter how many friends you have as long as you've met them at least once before so you know they're a real person.

While all the girls at City College followed this rule, it was not a failsafe technique. As Penny explained, sometimes Facebook 'friends' become 'creepy': 'You block them if they're like creeping you out and you don't want to talk to them.' However, when it came to forming an online relationship, knowing someone face to face first was considered to be the socially responsible course of action, even if it meant using a long chain of 'mutuals' to do so. This time the protectionist discourse was in tension with the architecture of the platform.

While Dylan was less concerned with his privacy settings on social media, like Simon, he related the issue of privacy to banking and other formal transactional practices. Both boys saw themselves as 'safe' because they did not yet have a bank account and were not disclosing that information in the digital context. In this way, Simon and Dylan equated safety with being robbed or losing money, as Simon explained:

> I don't think it's an issue [privacy] because I think I'm relatively safe in that regard. Like I don't think I'm at risk of having my details stolen, because I don't go onto Facebook and post all like location and bank account details and I don't do online banking or online shopping.

Interestingly, Dylan's and Simon's privacy practices were framed in financial terms. Given there has been a good deal of media focus on online financial fraud, this is not surprising.

Both Sean and Chantelle saw privacy in more technical terms, demonstrating an awareness of the complex ways information can be accessed and used. Sean explained that he was 'fairly careful' online and had a 'virus protection program' to ensure he would not 'get key logged or anything like that'. Chantelle considered the issue of privacy in terms of 'data mining and all that'; however, her father 'puts a lot of anti-hacking' software onto the family's computers. Both Sean and Chantelle found solutions to privacy issues in the platform settings and felt relatively protected and safe online. This solution was imparted to them from a more tech-savvy other. For example, Sean relied on his friends, while Chantelle's father, a website designer, was clearly influential.

When asked about the most important information they had received in regard to the internet, three in the group answered that it was around privacy and security. For Mark this information was learned at school: 'I just guess all the safety assemblies we've had, how to like use the privacy and not to put too much information on there about yourself.' For Heidi the most important information she had learned was in regard to 'being able to control' where information went and only 'allowing access to certain people'. In more general terms, Trent reported that being told to 'always read the terms and conditions' was most important to him. The other young people could not think of *any* information they had learned or picked up over the years that was valuable when using the internet. Presumably, their attitudes were shaped most strongly by the digital platform and the social practices of their peers.

Outside of what took place on Facebook, it is not within the scope of this research to confirm whether the young people actually practised what they reported. However, the young people described a rather proactive disposition when it came to privacy and security and, despite the muddiness of broader laws and conventions on these issues, they deemed this to be the sole responsibility of the individual user. As Heidi explained, individuals were responsible for what they put online, so others could not be held accountable when things went wrong. When asked whether she would be concerned if an advertising company used her unsolicited photos in a campaign, Heidi reasoned: 'I did put it up there so … if you send someone something and then you think, "Oh I wish they didn't have it now because *you* did it, so …"'

The positioning of the young people as individually responsible for their privacy and security was the result of the protectionist discourse. The role of parents and guardians contributed to this, as did the cybersafety programmes at school, which emphasised individual safety and security practices. Rather than trusting and supporting the young people to make the right decisions online, the role of the adult was to oversee and check on the young people's behaviours. While some participants did have meaningful discussions with their parents and guardians over some digital matters, this was not the norm for this group of young people.

Several participants relied on the architecture of social media platforms to protect their privacy and security; however, two young people in the group were keenly aware that privacy settings could only ever give you a false sense of security. Mark likened privacy to a fake security camera: 'I guess I see Facebook privacy as one of those fake cameras you put up that don't actually work, but it makes people think you've got a camera on your house.' Rachel saw her privacy online as completely permeable and potentially under threat: 'I kind of feel … well someone's probably reading all my messages right now, not that they would be but that's what I think.' Evident here is a burgeoning critical disposition toward the security processes of digital platforms.

Several males in the group expressed the idea that being 'anonymous' online offered more safety and protection. Again this practice came from the school-based cybersafety programmes. For example, when I asked Simon whether he drew on any skills or knowledge learnt at school, he replied:

Yes … that would be like being anonymous, as you've progressed into high school that's when they expect kids to have Facebook and Twitter and Tumblr and all that stuff, so don't give out *all* your information. And that's why … the only information that is displayed for me is my username, which usually *isn't* Simon Cooper.

On the gaming platform Steam he used an avatar, 'Agent North'; however, this identity was still known to his friends. Mark saw anonymity as more of a default position to the way he represented his identity online: 'I was just like I don't really want to have my face on the internet because it isn't necessary, so I'll just have this anonymous person on there.' Despite the boys' descriptions these were, at best, 'anonymous-like practices', as Mark's closer friends and family could easily identify his online identities. These explanations uncovered the underlying belief that being anonymous led to greater safety and security online, and once again highlighted the power of the cybersafety discourse in shaping practices.

The young people also used anonymity in a more nuanced way to reflect and reinforce levels of social intimacy as well as develop skills more covertly. Simon's and Trent's close friends were aware of their identities on Steam, but other game players, with whom they may well have been friends on Facebook, did not. In a similar way, Rachel disclosed her 'true' identity to the friend who introduced her to the writing website Wattpad, but apart from that was anonymous on the site. In this sense, anonymity imparted a sense of freedom to experiment and develop different versions of self, free from the gaze of more critical others. I discuss this tendency to interpret people's identities in relation to an embodied, 'authentic' form and the limitations this imposes on practices in Chapter 4. However, this instance highlights that elements of the dispositif could also coalesce in unforeseen ways to instigate behaviours and subjectivities that were liberating for these young people.

Also arising from the cybersafety discourse were practices concerning the circulation of content. This was an extension of the individualised responsibility discussed earlier, in that individual 'control' over personal content only exists *before* it goes online; after that it was thought of as available and, in a sense, free, for anyone to use. Five of the young people expressed this idea at various points across the study. As Maddy said, 'I don't really put anything up that's not, I wouldn't care if they used it, it wouldn't be a big deal'. While Sean explained, 'I don't really put anything up that I wouldn't want to happen', meaning that a prerequisite for deciding what to put online was whether he would be happy for *anything* to happen to that content (i.e. be spread widely or manipulated). Grace simply said: 'Don't post things that you don't want *everyone* to see.'

Evident in these sentiments is an acknowledgement of the automated nature of the architecture of the digital platform, and how it can be manipulated to achieve particular social ends. Indeed, stories of embarrassing images 'going viral' were frequently recounted throughout the study. It is not surprising that this translated into conservative practices in which some of the young people, like Grace, claimed they didn't 'post much stuff on the internet'. At the same time, when asked about their digital footprint (the trail or traces people leave behind them when online), three of the young people at one school reported that they didn't think about it, because they posted very little online.

Given that the young people had been subject to cybersafety programmes from upper primary school, it was not surprising that, like Rachel in the previous chapter, the protectionist discourse shaped their disposition toward digital media more than any other. Heidi explained that the cybersafety message was 'drilled' into students there 'since we were maybe 10'. Mark also used the term 'drilled' to describe the school-based cybersafety programmes he had encountered: 'I've just had all this internet stuff drilled into my head before I've even had it [the internet], so it's just not really something that I talk about.'

At City College and Bankview College cybersafety 'lessons' occurred a 'few' times each year. Rather than a designated programme, these were often presented in response to a specific incident. Trent explained that at Bankview College the content had become 'a bit more frightening the older we get'. It seemed there was a tendency for cybersafety programmes to be framed in juridical terms, particularly with regard to issues of cyberbullying. Several well-publicised teen suicides in Melbourne and around the state of Victoria had increased the intensity with which this discourse was presented to the young people. While there were benefits to what was learnt through these programmes, the repetition of a message that sought to constrain and limit could be counteractive to encouraging critical and agentic digital practices.

Materialities

Acquiring information was an important part of why these young people used the internet. As they saw it, information was infinite online—it was simply up to the individual to find it. Mark saw little impediment to accessing particular sites or completing tasks online. As he explained, it just 'depends on where you want to go on the internet'. Chantelle believed that there was an 'infinite amount of information' available on the internet, involving 'journeys of discovery or research'. She described a circuitous pattern to seeking information: 'each road you go on takes you to a different road, takes you to another, takes you to another one and then eventually you wind up back at the thing you were originally looking at.' All the young people believed that in the digital context information is in abundance.

At the same time, the young people had a strong sense of the structure of the internet and the implications this had on accessing and acquiring knowledge. In discussing the structure of the internet, Mark and Simon described some websites as essential. YouTube and Google, they explained, were 'core internet features', meaning the majority of their practices took place on these platforms. To Mark, YouTube was one of the two 'powerhouses of the internet'. Not only do they consider these 'core' to their experiences, but they believe they are 'core' to all other users as well. According to Mark and Simon, secondary to YouTube and Google were other websites, including Facebook, gaming platforms, 'sharing' and online shopping sites. Mark explained that 'the centre is the more popular areas and then as we branch out we go into vaster areas where there are less people'. This is not only a description of their own practices, but also what they believed others did online.

While the bulk of his regular practices might have taken place on these 'core' sites, Mark acknowledged that the less frequently visited areas could yield more unique and valuable digital 'resources': 'Like me and my friend have a running joke where if we find a weird video on YouTube we say we've gone to the outside of YouTube, like the border.' This is an almost geographical or topographical account of the way YouTube is structured, where the most popular videos are at the centre and the less viewed ones are on the outer edges. Once again the young people imagine the digital as kind of strata, overlaying experiences. Mark and Simon were confident about what they could do online. This disposition led them to create a YouTube channel: 'We originally had an idea, me and Mark and a few other friends, we had an idea that we'd start this YouTube page and that's what we've done.' The sense of possibility enabled through both the discursive and technical features of the platform, combined with their confidence as 'digital natives', led Mark and Simon to feel productive and agentic within the digital context.

Like Mark and Simon, Sean identified three platforms as 'key' to the internet. At the centre of Sean's timeline of digital practices were three intertwined branches coloured green, blue and red to depict the websites Google, Facebook and YouTube, respectively (Figure 3.3). Sean described these sites as having 'been very core' to his digital practices from the very beginning. He went on to explain that 'most people'

FIGURE 3.3 Sean working on his timeline of digital practices

would consider them 'core things' as well. According to Sean, Google was the 'lionshead of internet search history'. He described Facebook and YouTube as 'similar sorts of platforms' in that they 'interconnect in … what they do'.

In fact, all but three young people in the study depicted Google, Facebook and YouTube as key to their use of the internet. When asked why this was the case, Rachel answered 'because they're of their own kind … there are like other websites … but not as good'. Penny argued 'because that's where everyone is', demonstrating the power of network effects in directing partici- pation. On the other hand, Mark believed it was a matter of originality: 'For instance with Google and YouTube, they're completely original … they were there basically since the beginning so they've had all this time to build up a reputation.' For these young people, Google, YouTube and Facebook have been there from the 'beginning' of their internet use. However, clearly the way that these platforms are marketed and the structural connections they have to other digital platforms, mean they have acquired an important status in the young people's minds, and this in turn shaped their dispositions toward the digital significantly.

While the young people were well aware of the fact that few companies monopolise the internet, only Sean saw this as a problem. Not only did he describe it as the 'commercialisation of the internet', but he believed it would be difficult to establish any alternatives to these core websites:

> I was wondering if as these things become more established, is there any room for different things to overtake them? Like Google's ingrained in our culture, it's what we use, like everyone uses Google, even if they don't use the same explorer.

To Sean the internet was actually becoming smaller as the search engines and platforms that help organise the vast amounts of information, actually mean users encounter less information. As he explained, information 'will all rein into large companies'. Sean's descriptions were both detailed and critical. He was able to reveal and explore some of these issues through the research provocations and the discussions that followed. With this knowledge in mind, Sean was poised to con- sider alternative platforms and practices.

However, the rest of the young people did not perceive the monopolisation of the internet by one or two tech companies to be a problem. As Stacey argued, more variety would be 'creating conflict' among users. Mitch elaborated further: 'Somebody would have this website and be like, "Hey, check this out!" And then somebody else would go, "Oh nah I like this website better".' To Mitch and Stacey this situation could only lead to conflict. On the other hand, Heidi descri- bed the future in terms of technological convergence, where different digital plat- forms would evolve to perform or enable similar tasks and actions: 'I think things like SoundCloud, YouTube and Snapchat will all become one … It's like these were once separate things.'

That the notions of convergence and monopolisation underpinned the thinking of the majority of the young people suggested that these concepts were perceived as simply part of the digital. While the provocations and discussions did help to create awareness of the issues, whether they were significant enough for the young people to act on is another matter. These platforms bring together a series of practices and behaviours fundamental to the digital dispositif. When asked whether they had tried an alternative search engine to Google, Chantelle replied that she had tried Dogpile, and several had also used Bing, but they found them to be inferior services. Heidi best summed up the discussion when she said that 'the most common thing searched on Bing is Google'.

Analysis of the research data suggested that the platform interface was integral to how these young people understood power and agency in the digital context. Notions of popularity and status, in the form of publicly displayed likes, shares and comments, were commonly referenced. It not only shaped the young people's use of digital media, but also how they perceived and interpreted others' practices. As Stacey explains: 'People are trying to get to the top and control everything … and try and control others so they know that they're the top dog.' In this case 'getting to the top' meant having a lot of followers or friends on social media, which led to more likes and shares of their posts and photos.

Popularity on the internet was also thought to give individuals greater agency and control in the digital context and beyond. The YouTube platform was a key exemplar for this as the notoriety of the YouTube 'star' figured prominently in discussions. Comedian and web-based producer PewDiePie and his girlfriend CuteyPie, both YouTube celebrities, were touchstones of popular culture for several young people in the study. As such, they were regularly referenced as a way of making sense of how knowledge and power are channelled on the internet, specifically YouTube, as Mark explains:

> So again with PewDiePie whenever he plays a new game that's come out, every one of his fans like buys that game and the game becomes popular. And that's why there's advertising and all that …

To Mark, popularity was a kind of 'currency' online: 'I see popularity online as a currency. It's just something that you use to become more popular and have more power over things.' In this way, social media were seen to be an important tool in becoming famous. Simon contended that a lot of famous people would not be famous if it were not for YouTube: 'Like a lot of people that are famous on YouTube, if there wasn't a place that's really as famous as YouTube they wouldn't be recognised, we wouldn't know about them.' In this sense the architecture of the digital platform exerts a kind of force capturing and orienting the behaviours and gestures of individuals.

How young people come to adopt these interpretations of others' behaviours is a complex confluence of the social and the technological. It might be explained by the fact that on social media platforms the social has collapsed into the technological, as these markers of 'value' strongly influence how they read and interpret others' digital practices. While these young people had a well-developed sense of what metrics were important to pay attention to, these were interpreted in an almost intuitive or subconscious way. Metrics are important in gauging size, engagement and affect; however, Baym (2013) notes they 'can distort what they are seen to measure' (n.p.). Indeed, the network effects of the platform mean additional likes, shares or friends lead to increased value of the object or individual it is attached to, but exactly what that value is referring to can be difficult to discern.

Affect and embodiment

As mentioned earlier, the young people would often draw on binary descriptions to contrast the experiences of online and offline contexts. This was also used when discussing the affective qualities of digital experiences. In contrast to face-to-face relationships, which the young people described as implicitly expressive and emotive, online interactions were thought to be lacking in emotion. For example, Mark said 'people stop showing emotions online because they don't have to. It's just text on a screen'. Trent felt that his relationships online were 'fading' and 'less intense … because there's no emotion online'. Others believed people become less responsive to and respectful of others' emotions when using digital media, which led them to assume that digital networks were devoid of emotion.

To these young people, emotions were associated with the corporeal; without seeing an embodied reaction, emotions did not consciously 'register' with others. For this reason it was often difficult for the young people to discuss their reasoning for particular behaviours and practices, as the majority of these were motivated by emotions and affect. Even though affective responses were not deemed significant to digital media use, Trent's description of being online suggested it was important: 'It feels like chaos half the time … it's like popups everywhere, it feels like your heart is beating at a million miles an hour and the world is in slow motion or something.' Such a description points to the kinetic and emergent nature of digital networks. It suggests that bodily reactions to digital media, while only occasionally rising to consciousness, are key to using digital media. Platforms, like YouTube, 'mediate desires' and create a series of 'travelling affects' (Kofoed & Ringrose, 2012, p.16), or emotional responses that circulate through people and digital media. The notions of movement and dynamism are key to affect, as in its most simple form, it is the 'capacities to act and be acted upon' (Seigworth & Gregg, 2010, p.3). In digital networks, affect emerges, condenses and dissipates across human and non-human components in a multitude of ways across the dispositif.

For example, Rachel uploaded an arresting cover photo depicting her visiting her grandmother when she was sick in hospital. The act of uploading the photo was most likely the culmination of affects: the love and care she has for her grandmother; the sadness she felt over her sickness; the pressures from Facebook to document important events in life; and the expectations friends have of Rachel as a person and Facebook friend. Presenting the event on Facebook increased the significance of this moment for both Rachel and her friends. In this way, Rachel's actions were also about the affective relationships she had with people *other* than her grandmother. Interestingly, it was difficult for Rachel to articulate why she posted the photo to Facebook. This is not to suggest that each digital practice should be accounted for, or that there is a correct interpretation of these. However, this does highlight the power of the non-linguistic elements in inculcating gestures and practices. The affective qualities of the experience and pressures of the platform sat just beneath the surface of consciousness and were difficult for Rachel to articulate. These sensations did not always come together in seamless ways. For example, that this cover photo was quickly changed suggested that there might have been some discomfort in revealing such an intimate moment on Facebook.

Throughout the study, the young people described moving seamlessly between online and offline space, and indeed, many of them were continuously connected to the internet through their mobile phones. However, it was clear that once digitally mediated, social experiences and relationships were expressed and experienced differently. The young people articulated a different set of rules around acceptability and appropriateness, suggesting that the online space, particularly social media platforms, was based around a different set of social conventions. In this way, their disposition toward themselves and others was different in the digital context.

A common refrain was that people were 'different' online. As Simon explained, 'In my personal opinion and some experience I reckon people can change online'. In a similar way, Rachel said, 'Like there's a person I know … yeah like they're all positive but then when you see them offline they're all like the opposite'. Trent noted that the different context could be both good and bad, 'because you can like really get to know people because they will say more things online than face to face'.

The digital space allowed for different types of relationships and identities to emerge, and these young people imagined and approached it in this way. Penny had 'some really good friends' on Facebook, but when she saw them at school they 'barely talk'. These comments highlight the proliferation of subject positions via the dispositif. Through digital media young people can explore different aspects of their identities and connect with different people. But each of these identities and relationships were circumscribed by a different set of social and technical conventions, which the young people were simultaneously drawn to and confused by.

Developing an understanding of these conventions and processes took place in a rather *ad hoc* way, often through trial and error or observing friends online. Two of the young people reported that they spoke to their parents about some of the things that happen on social media, but this was only in response to particular situations. As Mitch observed, 'If somebody were to talk to me negatively on Facebook or something, I'd go up to my parents and be like "Oh yeah, this is a problem that I'm having" and then they'd try and help me'. Whether or not one could or should ever be cognisant of the role that affect plays in shaping their digital experiences could be debated. However, there would be benefit to drawing young people's attention to the ways in which affect can motivate digital practices.

Digital subjectivities—implications for knowledge, power and agency

In revealing the heterogenous elements of the digital dispositif and the connections between these, several issues emerge. The majority of the young people's practices took place on digital 'platforms', as opposed to websites, webpages or other digital media. While other elements played a role, it is significant that the young people described these platforms as 'core' to their digital practices. They did not approach the internet as a series of interconnected 'texts', but rather as a 'core' of digital platforms. While other elements were significant, including the dominant discourses and social practices of peers, it was the architecture of platforms that was an overriding organisational feature. This influenced the young people's subjectivities, as well as how they understood knowledge, power and agency in the digital context.

Discursively the young people were positioned in three main ways: as skilful and adept 'digital natives'; as vulnerable digital victims; and as self-responsible cybersafe users. Each subject position was distinct from the other, encouraging different behaviours and practices. Not all the young people assumed these subjective positions. Some, like Dylan, simply ignored the warnings of the protectionist discourse. Others acknowledged and referenced these discourses, yet in practice were just as likely to ignore them.

However, discourse is only *one* element that influences the young people's digital dispositions. As we have seen, practices, materialities, institutions and affectivities are also influential (Rohle, 2005). An example of this was how the social pressures of peers contrasted with the principles of the protectionist discourse. While the young people spoke of working around these tensions, these negotiations could lead to anxiety. For example, Rachel had organised her Facebook 'friends' into 'groups' to keep her mum separate from her peer network. However, there was a sense of guilt about this as she felt obliged to be an honest and dutiful daughter. Part of the problem is cybersafety's narrow focus on the individual and their safety and security practices. Thompson (2016) suggests extending cybersafety programmes to include 'relationship building practices, friendship expectations, and impression management strategies' (p.13). This could work to ameliorate the tensions between the protectionist discourse and the social pressures these young people described.

Binary terms were used to describe aspects of digital technology and digital media use. At least four participants described the technological future in dystopian terms, while another two saw online communication as inferior or 'a waste of time'. This aligns with several US studies that have highlighted just how fearful people are of technology (Think Artificial, 2007; Ledbetter, 2015), demonstrating how cultural representations become powerful frameworks for thinking about digital technologies. It also highlights the impact of overlooking more nuanced interpretations of digital technologies in the quest to entertain (Pangrazio & Bishop, 2017). Fear and trepidation are not conducive to agentic digital practices, and as several studies have shown, can lead to a sense of powerlessness, particularly with regard to privacy and personal data (see Andrejevic, 2014; Lupton & Michael, 2017).

These findings complicate young people's identification and labelling as 'digital natives'. More importantly this becomes a tension with which young people must contend as they negotiate the different elements of the digital dispositif. While many academics have argued that the term 'digital native' can do more harm than good (see Buckingham, 2008; Herring, 2008), it resonates strongly with the general public and is regularly reinforced by mainstream media through stories of the digital 'wunderkind', like Ben Pasternak, whose story opened Chapter 2. It is not surprising that the young people in this study identify as 'digital natives'. When digital experiences do not live up to expectations this subjective positioning can become confusing *and* limiting. What's more, as 'digital natives' they are not inclined to seek help. Several young people held competing ideas with regard to the digital context: the digital context is essentially where they should feel most comfortable; *but* that it is a separate and inferior world to the non-digital.

The young people and those they encountered online had tacit understandings that were specific to the digital context. Many of the young people did not see the online as continuous or embedded in the offline, but instead viewed it as a separate, almost autonomous space. This contrasts with other studies in which young people did not distinguish between online and offline contexts (see Salaway & Caruso, 2008; Carrington, 2015). Some of these young people spoke of how online behaviours 'spilt over' into the offline; however, most saw digital identities as different and somehow removed from other offline identities. Further, if the young people had greater 'barriers' to getting online (i.e. they could not move 'seamlessly' between the two), then the difference between the online and the offline was greater. In the case of at least two young people, whose access to the internet had been limited either in the past or present, the digital context was seen and described as a distinct 'space'.

Many of the young people believed they were solely responsible for their online behaviours, as well as how others interpreted and acted upon them. This represents a further elaboration on the concept of responsibilisation (see Wakefield & Fleming, 2009). Not only was online safety the responsibility of the individual user, but so too was what would happen to this content once it was uploaded. As a result, the overriding rule was that one should be prepared for any of their online content to be spread publicly by others. This idea comes from protectionist discourse, most commonly experienced in the form of cybersafety programmes, and it does work to make young people mindful of what they share online. However, narratives of correct use of social media are also about the government and regulation of young people (Owen, 2014). So while these initiatives might be done with good intentions, they can diminish notions of digital agency and resilience. This discourse ignores the growing body of literature that highlights the potential for social media to build social ties (Ellison et al., 2007; Valenzuela et al., 2009), as well as develop more complex understandings of subjectivity (Pearson, 2009).

Rather than seeing the architecture as something they could master and reimagine, the young people approached it as having a power of its own. A new materialist reading of this situation might be that young people saw their agency as distributed across the human and non-human parts of the digital dispositif (Cote, 2014). Yet implicit to these statements is that the balance of power *does not* lie with the individual user. The participants noted others can exploit the automated nature of the platform architecture to disseminate unflattering images or posts of their peers. The fear of an embarrassing image 'going viral' was a point of concern for many of these young people. Given the various pressures on young people to both promote *and* protect themselves on digital platforms it is perhaps not surprising that three of the young people described sitting on the digital 'sidelines', too anxious to post something in case it led to social recriminations. Such a disposition can lead to conservative and staid digital practices (see Pitcan et al., 2018), despite the capacity for the digital dispositif to be much more.

The young people held clear understandings of how knowledge and information were structured in the digital dispositif, with the platform being an overriding organisational feature. Indeed, what the young people described and depicted throughout the study was nothing like the 'map' that dominates more common ways of imagining the internet. According to Galloway (2011), the internet is commonly understood as having a 'hub-and-spoke cloud aesthetic' with 'minuscule branching structures' that cluster together to form 'intricate three-dimensional spaces' (p.90). He argues that this kind of depiction can obscure the ideologies that underpin information flow. By contrast, the young people's descriptions and responses to the research provocations focused upon exploring how the architecture of platforms shaped socialities and participation. This involved identification of critical issues underpinning the dispositif, such as convergence and monopolisation. A critical point here was that the young people did not see these as socio-economic constructs, but rather as somehow inherent to the structure of the internet.

Most described internet practices taking place on only two to three platforms, which are owned by even fewer corporations. For example, the 'core' of the internet described by Mark, Simon and Sean is actually owned by one company, since Google bought YouTube in 2006 for US$1.65 billion.[1]Lovink (2011) explains that this core is the result of 'power patterns', which are well known patterns of practices that encourage people toward particular sites: 'ordinary users do not want to look uncool and cannot afford to be left out in this informal reputation economy; this is why they feel forced to follow the herd' (p.15). Mark also used the herd metaphor to describe people's online behaviour describing them as 'a flock of sheep … and they all flock to whatever's the new thing'. Following this logic, digital practices become linked to an in-group, out-group mentality in which feelings of belonging, status and self-esteem become entangled with particular websites and platforms, highlighting the ways in which the outwardly disparate digital elements are connected through the dispositif.

With the heterogenous elements being channelled into digital platforms, the dispositif is becoming increasingly *homogenous*—convergent, merging and expanding. Dispositifs change across time. This analysis allows us to 'account for the difference between historical time periods while also accounting for a substantial overlap of objects, means, and discourses' (Bussolini, 2010, p.88). Indeed, some aspects of the dispositif have remained constant, such as parental fears over their children's use of social media. However, other things have clearly changed. For example, these young people's digital experiences contrast sharply with how the potentialities of the internet were once imagined. Prominent media and literacies scholars of the 1990s were optimistic about how digital media might operationalise post-structural theories of texts (Landow, 1992; Bolter, 1991; Snyder, 1996). They saw the potential for the digital to decentre and disrupt the linear nature of texts, thereby overturning traditional distinctions between author/text/reader.

What these young people describe, however, is a situation in which knowledge and power are funnelled through two or three dominant platforms. The young people imagined the internet as something which is hierarchically organised, most notably by popularity and status. These concepts were used to justify and explain the digital practices of themselves and others. In this way, the young people understood that power was 'symbolic and material, as relational, as microphysical' and circulating in networked formations (Cote, 2014, p.124). These were detailed, critical and complex understandings that had been acquired and cultivated within the digital dispositif.

With little formal and technical knowledge to draw on, the young people appeared to focus more strongly on the social processes that it facilitated, rather than considering how the architecture of platforms encouraged and constrained particular practices. A corollary of this is that vernacular social practices were shaped by more affective and material elements of the dispositif. When the young people were asked about the structure of the internet or more critical aspects of digital media use, their knowledge was often derived from popular media or learnt through the internet itself. The structure of the internet and the architecture of platforms appeared to be more intuitively or affectively 'felt' than cognitively understood. Closer attention to affect, and the way it intersects with the material and discursive, helps us to understand the far-reaching influences of the digital dispositif on these young people's everyday lives.

Conclusion

In this chapter I have analysed the dispositif that shaped these young people's digital dispositions. In doing so, we have opened up the 'analytical "blackbox"' that underpins young people's attitudes and beliefs toward the digital to arrive at deep understandings of why they think and act in the way they do. As individual differences and life circumstance also have bearing on the formation of these digital dispositions, this can never be an entirely comprehensive account. Instead, what I have presented in this chapter are the trends and issues that emerged across this particular group of young people.

As we have learned, the dispositif comprises discursive and non-discursive elements, each of which connects, contradicts or contrasts with other elements. This leads to a proliferation of subjectivities. The tensions and inconsistencies these young people navigate as a result of this are an important, but largely unspoken part of using digital media. Having established the foundations of young people's knowledge and dispositions in this chapter and the last, it is now time to turn to how the young people operationalise these in their digital practices. In the next two chapters I focus on the young people's digital practices, including how they reconcile the various discourses, conventions and institutions through their experiences.

Note

1 See: www.nbcnews.com/id/15196982/ns/business-us_business/t/google-buys-youtube-billion/#.VV5FStqqqko

References

Agamben, G. (2009). *What is an apparatus? And other essays*. Stanford, CA: Stanford University Press.

Andrejevic, M. (2014). The big data divide. *International Journal of Communication, 8*, 1673–1689.

Arvidsson, A. (2011). General sentiment: How value and affect converge in the information economy. *The Sociological Review, 52*(2), 39–59. doi:10.1111/j.1467-954X.2012.02052.x

Baym, N. (2013). Data not seen: The uses and shortcomings of social media. *First Monday, 18*(10).

Bolter, J. D. (1991). *Writing Space: The Computer, Hypertext, and the History of Writing*. Hillsdale, NJ: L. Erlbaum Associates.

Buckingham, D. (2008). Introducing Identity. In D. Buckingham (Ed.), *Youth, Identity and Digital Media*. Cambridge, MA: The MIT Press.

Bussolini, J. (2010). What is a dispositive? *Foucault Studies, 10*, 85–107.

Carrington, V. (2015). 'It's changed my life': iPhone as technological artefact. In R. H. Jones, A. Chik, & C. A. Hafner (Eds.), *Discourses and Digital Practices: Doing Discourse Analysis in the Digital Age*. London and New York: Routledge.

Cole, J., Suman, M., Schramm, P., Zhou, L., & Salvador, A. (2013). *The 2013 Digital Future Report*. Annenberg, CA: The University of Southern California, Centre for the Digital Future.

Cote, M. (2011). What is a media dispositif? Compositions with Bifo. *Journal of Communicative Inquiry, 35*(4), 378–386.

Cote, M. (2014). Data motility: The materiality of big social data. *Cultural Studies Review, 20* (1), 121–149.

Ellison, N., Steinfeld, C., & Lampe, C. (2007). The benefits of Facebook 'friends': Exploring the relationship between college students' use of online social networks and social capital. *Journal of Computer-Mediated Communication, 12*(1), 1143–1168.

Foucault, M. (1980). *Power/Knowledge: Selected Interviews & Other Writings*. New York: Pantheon Books.

Foucault, M. (2001). *Fearless Speech*. Cambridge, MA: The MIT Press.

Galloway, A. (2011). Are some things unrepresentable? *Theory, Culture and Society*, 28(7–8), 85–102.

Goggin, G., Vromen, A., Weatherall, K., Martin, F., Webb, A., Sunman, L., & Bailo, F. (2017). *Digital Rights in Australia*. Sydney, Australia: The University of Sydney.

Gregg, M., & Seigworth, G. (2010). *The Affect Theory Reader*. Durham & London: Duke University Press.

Herring, S. (2008). Questioning the generational divide: Technological exoticism and adult constructions of online youth identity. In D. Buckingham (Ed.), *Youth, Identity and Digital Media*. Cambridge, MA: The MIT Press.

Hillis, K., Paasonen, S., & Petit, M. (2015). *Networked Affect*. Cambridge, MA: The MIT Press.

Kofoed, J., & Ringrose, J. (2012). Travelling and sticky affects: Exploring teens and sexualised cyberbullying through a Butlerian-Deleuzian-Guattarian lens. *Discourse: Studies in the Cultural Politics of Education*, 33(1), 5–20.

Lambert, G. (2016). What is a dispositif? - Part 1. *Journal for Cultural and Religious Theory*. Retrieved from http://jcrt.org/religioustheory/2016/07/11/what-is-a-dispositif-part-1/

Landow, G. P. (1992). *Hypertext; The Convergence of Contemporary Critical Theory and Technology*. Baltimore, MD: Johns Hopkins University Press

Ledbetter, S. (2015). America's Top Fears 2015. *The Chapman University Survey on American Fears*. Retrieved from https://blogs.chapman.edu/wilkinson/2015/10/13/americas-top-fears-2015/

Lovink, G. (2011). *Networks Without a Cause: A Critique of Social Media*. Cambridge, UK: Polity.

Lupton, D., & Michael, M. (2017). 'Depends on who's got the data': Public understandings of personal digital dataveillance. *Surveillance & Society*, 15(2), 254–268.

Marwick, A., & boyd, d. (2014). Networked privacy: How teenagers negotiate context in social media. *New Media & Society*, 16(7), 1051–1067.

Massumi, B. (2002). *Parables for the Virtual: Movement, Affect, Sensation*. Durham, UK: Duke University Press.

Massumi, B. (2015). *Politics of Affect*. Cambridge, UK: Polity Press.

Owen, S. (2014). Framing narratives of social media, risk and youth transitions: Government of 'not yet' citizens of technologically advanced nations. *Global Studies of Childhood*, 4(3), 235–246.

Pangrazio, L., & Bishop, C. (2017). Art as digital counterpractice. *CTheory*, 21C054. Retrieved from http://ctheory.net/ctheory_wp/art-as-digital-counterpractice/

Pearson, E. (2009). All the World Wide Web's a stage: The performance of identity in online social networks. *First Monday*, 14(3).

Peltonen, M. (2004). From discourse to 'dispositif': Michel Foucault's two histories. *Historical Reflections*, 30(2), 205–219.

Pitcan, M., Marwick, A., & boyd, d. (2018). Performing a vanilla self: Respectability politics, social class, and the digital world. *Journal of Computer-Mediated Communication*. doi:10.1093/jcmc/zmy008

Prensky, M. (2001a). Digital natives, digital immigrants, part 1. On the Horizon, 9(5), 1–6.

Prensky, M. (2001b). Digital natives, digital immigrants, part 2: Do they really think differently? *On the Horizon*, 9(6), 1–6.

Puschmann, C., & Burgess, J. (2014). Metaphors of big data. *International Journal of Communication*, 8, 1690–1709.

Rohle, T. (2005). Power, reason, closure: Critical perspectives on new media theory. *New Media & Society*, 7(3), 403–422.

Salaway, G., & Caruso, J. (2008). *The ECAR Study of Undergraduate Students and Information Technology*. Boulder, CO: Educause Center for Applied Research.

Seigworth, G., & Gregg, M. (2010). An inventory of shimmers. In M. Gregg & G. Seigworth (Eds.), *The Affect Theory Reader*. Durham and London: Duke University Press.

Snyder, I. (1996). *Hypertext: The Electronic Labyrinth*. Melbourne, Australia: Melbourne University Press.

Think Artificial (2007). The fear of intelligent machines, survey results. Retrieved from www.thinkartificial.org/web/the-fear-of-intelligent-machines-survey-results/

Thompson, R. (2016). Teen girls' online practices with peers and close friends: Implications for cybersafety policy. *Australian Educational Computing*, 31(2), 1–16.

Valenzuela, S., Park, N., & Kee, K. (2009). Is there social capital in a social network site?: Facebook use and college students' life satisfaction, trust and participation. *Journal of Computer-Mediated Communication*, 14(4), 875–901.

Wakefield, A., & Fleming, J. (2009). Responsibilization. In *The Sage Dictionary of Policing* (pp.277–278). London: Sage Publications.

Wyatt, S. (2004). Danger! Metaphors at work in economics, geophysiology and the internet. *Science, Technology, & /Human Values*, 29(2), 242–261.

4

(RE)PRESENTING IDENTITIES

The notion of identity is both ubiquitous and elusive in academic discussions of contemporary society. Back (2012, p.26) argues that as 'everything has become an issue of "identity" the notion is increasingly loosely defined and diffuse. Identity has become a zombie concept that is "little more than portentous incoherence"' (Gleason, 1983, p.931). This might appear a counterintuitive way of framing a discussion of how young people are using digital media to form and represent their identity. Yet Back's dismissal does in fact provide a useful framework through which many of the emerging issues might be understood. Most social networking sites are constructed first and foremost around an individual profile, i.e. an online representation of identity through which all social interactions on the network are mediated. On social media, 'identity' becomes attributed not only to visual representations, but also to posts, social interactions and associations. Through social media, identity has become not only more 'visible' and prevalent in daily life, but also more diffusely embedded and difficult to define and discern.

Notwithstanding this incoherence, Judith Donath (2014) explains that 'identity' refers to two different, but related phenomena. One is 'individual identity', or 'who you are as opposed to any other person'. The other is 'social identity', or 'the type of person you are and your role in society' (p.228). As she explains, a social identity is 'how people make sense of you—how they understand what sort of person you are, what type of relationship they might have with you, what behaviours they can expect from you, and how they should act toward you' (p.228). In some respects, these definitions reflect the etymology of the word 'identity', which originally meant 'sameness', 'oneness' or 'identicalness', but later came to mean the difference or character that marks an individual. In this way, identity is represented and interpreted through notions of both the individual *and* the collective.

This chapter focuses on how the young people used digital media to enact practices that were associated with their identities. While these processes are intertwined with individual identity, it is social identity that young people are representing when they use digital media. In particular, social media, manifest in distinct platforms across the digital dispositif (see Chapter 3), act to explicitly increase the focus on identity, serving as a kind of 'lens' through which users are impelled to interpret and experience this context. Not only did social media help to support visual representations of peers, friendship groups and wider social networks, but they were also used to share an accomplishment, reveal a different side of identity or reify becoming-other. Despite these findings, identity was found to be less fluid across digital contexts and over time than first thought.

Theories of identity

One prominent theory used to analyse identity is Erving Goffman's dramaturgical method outlined in his book *The Presentation of Self in Everyday Life* (1959). Goffman argued that self-presentation varies with audience. For example, an individual will present themselves differently to their employer as opposed to their partner. In this theory, Goffman delineates the ritualised and expected versions of identity presented to the world on the 'front stage' from the more honest and often contradictory version of self 'back stage'. An important part of Goffman's theory is that identity involves 'impression management', which is a conscious or subconscious process where people try to influence the perceptions of others so that particular goals and ideals can be achieved. Given the public presentation of self on social media platforms, it is not surprising that Goffman's theory of identity has been well used in research around young people and digital media (see Jones & Hafner, 2012; boyd, 2007; Mendelson & Papacharissi, 2011; Vitak, 2012).

While Goffman's theory is useful, in reality the (re)presentation of identity on digital media involves a more complex set of propositions. Rather than being distinct, 'front stage' and 'back stage' identities are contingent upon each other, meaning identity (re)presentation involves an ongoing process of reflection and recalibration. Buckingham (2008) points out that Goffman's theory implies that the 'back stage' version of self is somehow more truthful to 'real' identity than that which is presented on the 'front stage'. However, this is not always the case. The phenomenon of 'Finstagram' outlined in the opening chapter is a good example of how such clear-cut distinctions can be complicated. Further, the proliferation of identities on digital media mean there is a variety of 'front stage' identities, each cultivated in response to different social and technical conditions. While differences between 'front stage' and 'back stage' might exist, digital media also demonstrate the reciprocal relationship between the different selves, be they online or offline, 'front stage' or 'back stage'. Seen in this way, identities are fluid, reflexive and changeable, without clear-cut distinctions between front and back stage personas.

To conceive of identity as 'fluid' means that 'it is no longer conceptualised as a stable entity that one develops throughout adolescence and achieves at some point in (healthy) adulthood' (Moje & Luke, 2009, p.418). Janks (2010) argues there are benefits to imagining identity as fluid and hybrid as it can 'resist essentialising people on the basis of any one of the communities to which they belong or to which we assign them' (p.99). Nevertheless, an important aspect of identity is that it is 'recognised' by others. As Gee (2000) explains:

> Being recognised as a certain 'kind of person,' in a given context, is what I mean here by 'identity.' In this sense of the term, all people have multiple identities connected not to their 'internal states' but to their performances in society.
>
> *(p.99)*

Gee goes on to acknowledge the presence of a 'core' identity 'that holds more uniformly, for ourselves and others, across contexts' (Gee, 2000, p.100). This aligns with the narrative analysis adopted in Chapter 2 in regard to Rachel's digital past. Despite shifts and changes in Rachel's practices and sense of self, it became clear there were core aspects of her identity that could be traced across time, such as her interest in fashion and writing.

A distinct advantage of large social media platforms like Facebook is that they allow users to communicate with a wide audience quickly and efficiently. Indeed, research has shown social media sites can help users to accrue social capital (Ellison et al., 2007; Valenzuela et al., 2009). However, having a large number of 'friends' on social media can make impression management difficult due to the collapsing of contexts. Context collapse (Marwick & boyd, 2014; Vitak, 2012) is when multiple distinct audiences in an individual's social network are encountered together in the one context. The Facebook News Feed is a primary site for context collapse, as people from different aspects of an individual's life (i.e. work, home, school) become a single group of message recipients.

Context collapse makes it more difficult for individuals to adapt their language, tone and beliefs to suit different audiences. In many respects, on social media identity is 'fixed' through the profile, which brings with it audience expectations around identity representation and performance. For example, in the past it might have been easy for individuals to separate their professional and social identities, but context collapse blurs this distinction. Employers have exploited this situation with reports that it is now common to check the suitability of potential employees via Facebook (Skates, 2014). Not surprisingly, Brandtzaeg et al. (2010) found a large number of friends on Facebook led to a decrease in intimate disclosures due to fear of 'social surveillance and social control' (p.1006). In addition, if users have concerns about privacy and public disclosures on the platform then the frequency of their posts tends to decrease (Stutzman et al., 2011; Vitak & Ellison, 2013).

Navigating the advantages and disadvantages of social media use provides ongoing challenges underpinned by an ever-changing set of social and technical conditions. The 'social supernets' (Donath, 2007) provided by platforms like Facebook enable young people to share and connect with distant and intimate friends, with the possibility for increases in social capital. However, there are tacit thresholds and rules that temper the possibilities for digital identities. A further complication is the increasing pressure from platform operators to present one 'authentic' identity online. Facebook founder Mark Zuckerberg claims that 'the days of having a different image for your work friends or co-workers and for the other people you know are probably coming to an end pretty quickly' (Kirkpatrick, 2011, p.199). Questions of authenticity, context collapse, invisible audiences and the size of friend lists are all factors young people negotiate as they engage in online identity work.

Becoming

The idea that identity is socially constructed, fluid and multiple underpins the theorising of identity in this chapter, and in the book more broadly. To be specific, I use Deleuze and Guattari's (1980/2013) theory of 'becoming' to make sense of the young people's (re)presentations of identity. 'Becoming' is the process of change, flight or movement within a context and marks an important shift in language (i.e. becoming rather than being) and way of thinking about identity. Becoming challenges the idea that there are such things as stable identities and instead situates identity as symbiotic with various aspects of culture and society. As Stagoll (2010, p.26) explains, becoming is the 'very dynamism of change' and signifies the perpetual state of transformation that the individual is in. Seen through the lens of becoming, digital media shape identity (re)presentation in ways that can be difficult to identify. Technological innovation and the unique combinations and networks that result, provide a series of threshold moments for the individual— 'frontiers' for new conceptions of self. Adopting a poststructural lens, users' identities are continually shifting and transforming due to their interaction with various digital media.

Extending upon Chapter 3, in this chapter I explore how the digital dispositif becomes an architecture for becoming. Indeed, Deleuze's theory of becoming draws upon Foucault's dispositif to discern the processes involved in identity (re) presentation. As Deleuze (1992, p.164) elaborates, 'We belong to dispositifs and act within them … In each dispositif it is necessary to distinguish what we are (what we are already no longer), and what we are in the process of becoming: the historical part and the current part'. Deleuze (1992) describes the dispositif as 'composed of lines, each having a different nature' (p.159). These lines not only have the potential for 'sedimentation but also of lines of "breakage" and of "fracture"' (p.159). The aim in this chapter is to map out these lines and the ways in which they shape the processes of identity (re)presentation through the digital.

An important part of the study was to find ways to encourage a critical reflexivity in young people with regard to the fluidity of their identities as they are (re) presented and (re)formed through digital media. I explore strategies and techniques that encourage the participants to identify and reflect upon the different ways in which digital media facilitate their becoming. Specifically, I investigate how their ways of making meaning are influenced by the materialities of the media, as explained in Chapter 1. As Zielinski (2006) argues, it is important we try to understand the effect of technological systems on the individual, to 'assist the forces of imagination to penetrate the world of algorithms as far as is possible' (p.10). He argues that this is 'potentially invaluable for shedding light on a culture that is strongly influenced by media and for opening up new spaces for maneuvering' (p.10). Put simply, enabling young people to reflect upon how digital media shape their becoming is key to their criticality and agency in this context.

Young people's identity practices

Analysis of the research data revealed numerous factors involved in shaping the young people's identity practices. Photos and images were particularly important in representing identity. So too were friends and other social networks. Given the prominence of images and friend lists on the interface of many mainstream social media platforms this is not surprising. Yet digital media provided the young people with many opportunities to explore and experiment with different aspects of their behaviour, which I analyse through the theoretical lens of becoming. Despite this, interpretations of digital identities were far more prosaic, and limited what the young people felt they could 'become' online.

The role of photos

As the young people in this study explained, photos were a principal way of understanding or comprehending another's identity. Mark explained: 'I guess you can judge a lot from their profile picture … depending on what it is.' When asked to identify the most important aspect of a Facebook page, Sean replied: 'I think definitely the profile picture or their photos … you can gauge what kind of person they are.' The visual cues that these young people used to understand identity might have been related to an inherent ability to predict behaviour from expressive gestures (see Ambady & Rosenthal, 1992). This helps explain the young people's reliance on photos in the context of the fieldwork. Given the absence of other expressive cues on social media, photos take on particular significance as they become a kind of short cut to understanding another's identity. While this is a rather simplistic way to understand and represent identity, the structure of many social media platforms strengthens the reliance on this mode.

The young people used photos in a range of ways to present their identity on social media. In some instances this offered telling insights into their socioeconomic status. Two of the young women from a private school used photos of themselves at the Melbourne Races. In Australia, the Melbourne Cup Carnival is a popular event, dubbed the 'Playground of Racing Royalty'. While the races are open to the general public, many of the spaces are only available to a privileged few, with the infamous 'Birdcage' described as a 'Premium Marquee Enclosure'. Others used more playful photos for their profile pictures. For strangers, this might have provided less insight into their personalities, but for those they knew it might have signalled something quite typical about their character. Mitch used a photo in which his face was difficult to see (Figure 4.1).

As he explained, the choice of profile photo was something that happened by default:

> In performing arts last year … we were messing around backstage and we were lined up in a group and we just jumped in the air. And one of my friends sent me a message saying, 'Oh could you use this as your profile pic?' So I thought oh yeah it looks hilarious, so I did it.

In interview Mitch appeared indifferent to how his identity was represented on social media, even though he did refer to this image numerous times throughout the fieldwork.

For several young people in the study, photos were not only seen as the key to attracting attention, but also for expanding a network of friends and

FIGURE 4.1 Mitch's profile photo, January 2014

increasing social interactions. Telling someone they 'looked good' was a typical comment Penny made on friends' photos. It not only made someone more socially visible, but it encouraged Penny to initiate conversation if she hadn't seen them in a while: 'Like some of my friends that I have on there [Facebook] I haven't seen in ages, but when I scroll through and I'm like "They're looking good lately, I should go see them, I haven't seen them in ages".' It is not surprising that this made choosing a photo as a profile picture quite a complex process, as Grace explains:

> There's a lot of stuff with having a new profile picture, like how many likes you get on it and stuff like that. So it's kind of like it would have to be a *really* good photo if I was to change it, because now it's a lot more important. So it's probably a reason why I haven't changed it because there hasn't been a photo that I thought that this is a good picture.

Despite the pressures that surround the use of photos, uploading and commenting on them was described as the most common activity for the majority of girls in the study. The like button was integral, as it was the most common form of feedback and, for many of the young people, the key to popularity and social success. As Rachel said: 'You can tell someone who's popular if they have heaps of likes on their photos and stuff because then they'll have heaps of friends on Facebook.' For Rachel and several others, photos and likes became a web of signifiers central to understanding someone's social standing and identity.

But whether clicking the like button actually meant someone *liked* the content was another matter. In research Provocation 4—*Re-articulating the icons of the internet*, where the young people redesigned the icons of the internet, Grace drew a pair of eyes as one of her sketches for the like button. As she explained: 'I think the like button is mainly just to say you've seen it sort of, other people's photos and stuff.' In the end she designed a two-thumbed hand (Figure 4.2), because liking is more an acknowledgement that you have seen the content and not that you *actually* like it.

Maddy described opening up her Instagram account and scrolling down clicking indiscriminately on her friends' content—'like, like, like'. In this way liking something had become almost an unconscious process that was both integral to social media use, but also somewhat meaningless. As Maddy explained, with close friends you are obliged to like their photos: 'If it is one of your close friends, if they put something in their profile photo and it's really ugly and you don't like it, it's like I'm kind of obligated to like it. So I just like it anyway.' For the young women, there was an unspoken obligation for 'friends' to like and comment on each other's content.

While these activities might appear to be fairly inconsequential to the young people, they are clearly an integral part of the broader networks and economies in which social media platforms are embedded. What the young people describe is essentially a series of habits based around social media use. Chun (2016) explains

FIGURE 4.2 Grace's redesigned 'like' icon

that habits help us to organise our actions in the world and enable networks to be scaled, so that 'individual tics become indications of collective inclinations' (p.3). As she cautions, habits matter most when they appear not to matter at all. Indeed, likes, links and comments on social media are digital traces that can be mobilised into data economies, providing information on the individual that can be used to track, trace and profile them. While the individual can act upon this information (most often presented to them in the form of recommendations, suggestions or ratings), what might appear 'meaningless' digital practices are not without consequence.

For most of these young people the motivation to change profile or cover photos was justified in terms of coming across another, often better photo of themselves. The girls in particular were very careful about what photos to upload, as Heidi explained: 'I'm really selective of the photos that go on there.' Indeed, changing profile photos was an important event and described as a way of attracting attention, or as Stacey said '[giving] people something to look at'. Of the six girls in the study, five changed their profile on Facebook at least once over a six-month period, with three of them more than three times each. This appeared to be a more common technique used by the girls in the group, as of the five boys in the study on Facebook, only one changed his profile photo more than once. However, as Rachel explained, uploading a new profile picture could bring about a certain anxiety:

> I usually take a few photos of myself and then I wonder how many likes will this get. I feel kind of guilty for wanting likes and stuff, but I feel like it's kind of normal to crave a little bit of attention over social media.

Rachel's confessional tone resonated with the group with Stacey adding: 'Who doesn't want attention?' Amongst the girls, there seemed to be greater uncertainty about their social identity, which encouraged them to seek affirmation from their friends. Rachel was able to explore this idea when creating her map of digital and non-digital experiences. While her painting appeared vibrant, with the digital side a chaotic array of exchanges and interactions, she chose to represent herself as a tiny, faint, black rectangle just visible in the centre of the painting. She explained: 'I don't know, I feel like I'm a black rectangle [laughs] … because black always reminds me of like emptiness, I don't feel empty, but I just don't know who I am.'

When the question of social belonging and identity on social media was raised, Mitch asserted that he did not have that 'need for social belonging' and Mark claimed to feel 'the same way' because he 'made it through 2014 without all that stuff [so] I can go without it all'. The internet had only recently been connected at Mark's house, so he saw himself as 'behind' his peers and was attempting to make up for lost time: 'so now it's just trying to like get as much experience as I can and try and catch up while I can.' Several young men in the group projected an indifferent position toward social media, as if they could take it or leave it. However, whether this was due to a genuine critical distance from the platform or they were complying with social expectations around boys' use of social media is difficult to determine. Evident, however, was the marked difference in the way the boys and girls in the group engaged with social media and the manner in which these processes and practices were described and expressed in front of others.

The importance of 'friends'

For many of the young people, social media 'friends'—whether they were platonic, romantic or familial—were an important means of representing identity. As such, who they were photographed and 'friends' with were important indicators not only of who they were (i.e. family situation, where you go to school), but also what sort of person they might be (i.e. personality, social grouping). As explained in Chapter 3, mutual friends were also used as a kind of gauge to determine the character of a potential friend and whether it was worthwhile 'friending' them. For others, developing a 'list' of friends with whom you could socialise without relying on family and outside school time signalled a newfound independence.

Most commonly 'friends' were used on social media profiles to reveal various aspects of identity. All of those in a romantic relationship displayed profile photos that included their partner. For two of the boys the same photo was used throughout the duration of the study. However, as explained in Chapter 2, Rachel changed her profile photo regularly to reflect the evolving nature of her relationship (see Figure 2.1).

Friendships were also strengthened through photos, perhaps most conspicuously in a profile or cover photo. However, for two girls in the study, friends also helped to choose the best profile picture to upload, so that they were essentially 'co-constructing' their identity with close friends, as Penny explains:

I'm like 'I don't know which photo to use' and then I send them through because there would have been three or four photos from that night or another photo I had that I liked and I wanted to change my profile picture. So I'll send it through and go 'Maddy, which photo should I use?' And she'll go 'I like that one'.

This process of co-construction ameliorated the anxiety associated with posting a profile picture, as the young women were testing the representation (and those of friends) prior to uploading.

Public displays of friendships or communication were a common way of signalling belonging to a particular social group. This was commonly achieved through cover photos (Figure 4.3).

As Grace explained, who to include in the photos was important because it signalled how important different friends were to you: 'So like the people in the photos are probably like my closest friends, so Mia is in both of them, she's probably like my closest friend.'

Another way of signalling group membership was to only post information to a particular group of people. For Dylan, using Snapchat made him realise that he could continuously share what he was doing with a particular group of people, which he reflected in his timeline:

Snapchat has the X on 2013 because that's when I kind of first started using it and documenting my days with all my friends. And I kind of came up to the idea that I have like at least 100 friends I can talk to on Snapchat or just show them what I'm doing.

Membership to this group expanded Dylan's social networks and brought greater confidence to his social identities. Sean belonged to the Facebook group 'The Marauders', which was composed of fellow art students. His participation in this group heightened his sense of being an artist and provided him with a space to 'put his artwork and that sort of stuff up'. To add to the exclusivity and significance of being in this group, Sean explained that it was 'a secret page that just my friends are in'.

Friends played a pivotal role on social media, helping the young people to explore and represent various aspects of their identity. In relation to identity, a friend's list might be used to gauge personality or social standing, meaning that for many of them, friend lists were carefully curated. Profile and cover photos were a common way of signifying belonging to a particular social group or to indicate that they were in a relationship. As such, friends and followers became a type of resource in the digital context.

This was explored as part of research Provocation 4—*Re-articulating the icons of the internet*, when the young people redesigned the 'friend' icon. When prompted to critically consider the icon, Sean multiplied the figures in it and placed question marks on their faces. This design aimed to demonstrate the pressure to have a lot of

FIGURE 4.3 The importance of 'friends': participant cover photos, 2014

FIGURE 4.4 Sean's redesigned Facebook 'friend' icon

friends, even though many people did not know who their Facebook friends were (Figure 4.4).

In his icon he had tried to capture the competitive nature of 'friending' on social media:

> I think it's definitely strategic [to have lots of friends] because people can brag about how many friends they have and it's sort of a competition to

FIGURE 4.5 Trent's redesigned Facebook 'friend' icon

some people. I think people feel better about themselves if they have a thousand friends.

Trent redesigned the icon into a series of stars, because as he explained: 'I've got the stars, lots of stars, symbolising populars trying to become popular' (Figure 4.5).

Evident in Sean's and Trent's redesigned icons is an awareness of how Facebook has changed conceptions of sociality and friendship. Rather than collective groups, through social media individuals exist in loosely bound networks that are continuously expanding and changing. As Lovink (2016, p.20) explains: 'The social is the collective ability to imagine the connected subjects as a temporary unity. The power and significance of what it potentially could mean to connect to many is felt by many.' Through their re-articulation of the icons, Sean and Trent were able to explore and critique the 'friending' process on Facebook. Their use of the visual enabled them to represent processes and principles that were difficult to articulate through language, highlighting the potential for the visual as a mode of digital critique.

Identity (re)presentation—a series of becomings

A significant part of the young people's digital practices was associated with exploring and experimenting with various identities and aspects of identity. I analyse these through the concept of 'becoming' (Deleuze & Guattari, 1980/2013): an ongoing process where the social, material, discursive and affective dimensions of the dispositif connect to bring about new subjective possibilities. Over the course of the fieldwork, the young people articulated the range of ways that digital media had shaped and influenced them. Using becoming as a theoretical lens we can explore the shifts in the young people's identities as they are both agents and subjects within the digital dispositif.

For some young people in the study digital media worked in an aspirational way encouraging the development of certain qualities and beliefs, such as working hard and setting goals in life. For others, it facilitated changes in social and professional identities by helping them to develop particular skills or facilitating specific practices. Digital media, particularly social media, enabled the young people to exhibit these new identities to various 'audiences' helping to validate or formalise these becomings through public acknowledgement. In some instances the changes involved unconscious processes that occurred simply because of new unities and associations brought about through their digital networks. But, at other times, practices were carefully planned to signal conscious and deliberate changes in identity.

Professional becomings

For several young people aiming for a particular profession in life, digital media could be used in an aspirational way. They provided a 'window' to a wider world; one that was bigger than school and home and within which they could experiment with and become myriad identities. For some of the young people, coming across a new idea or source of inspiration 'planted a seed' for what they might become; this 'aspirational' self might also be woven into representations of identity to reinforce the changes that were taking place.

A large part of Simon's digital practices involved gaming. On Steam he went by the name 'Agent North', and as he explained, this character exhibited traits that Simon aspired to as a gamer:

> He's one of my favourite characters because he's a very, very smart person. You can try to hide something from him, but he'll be like 'What are you trying to keep secret?' He's also not very strict either, he's smart and laid back, but when the time comes, he'll get the job done.

Simon was not on any social media but spent a lot of time on Steam and marked finding the 'EB Games' store online as a significant moment for him on his timeline of digital practices. As he explained, 'seeing the games that were out there and then going in depth on those games', as well as seeing the 'community' built around them, was the 'start of his ambition to become a professional gamer'. Not only did this provide Simon with a sense of belonging but, as he described, he began to feel less constrained and more empowered by these experiences: 'I feel I can do something on these things because it's not restricting me to what I can do *now.*'

Digital media also provided opportunities for the young people to develop skills, enabling them to cultivate an identity associated with a particular vocation or interest. Mark and Mitch were hoping to work in the film industry when they left school and both believed YouTube was key to this process. Mitch's goal was to become a director: 'I've been planning out some different videos that I want to make in the future … I guess I want to put it out there so people can see it and get inspired themselves, because I want to be a director when I grow up.' Mark and Simon had created a YouTube channel where they made and uploaded films based around gaming called 'Screencheats'. In talking about Screencheats Mark said: 'It's just a good feeling that people want to watch your content and like what you're doing. It kind of gives you a sense of purpose.'

Mark was able to draw together the diverse aspects of the digital dispositif to create both a process and space in which he and his collaborators could become filmmakers. Not only were the materialities of the dispositif important, such as the YouTube platform and mobile devices and equipment, but so too were the affective dimensions, in the form of feedback and affirmation from friends, family and the YouTube community. The discursive construction of YouTube as a place to 'Broadcast Yourself' also appears to have played a role as they perceived few barriers to achieving their creative ideas. As Mitch explains: 'I saw these people making all these different short clips and I thought I want to do that just for fun.'

In both instances important identity work was taking place through the development of skills and the public recognition of this.

As well as skill development, social media were perceived as a way of developing and promoting a professional identity. Artist Sean explained that digital media were 'pretty important' in generating his artistic identity, as he found 'some kind of media' necessary to 'projecting your stuff outside your social bubble'. He had a Tumblr account that he could link his Facebook friends to. Feedback from friends on these social media sites was important to both him and photographer Dylan, helping them to refine their techniques and strategies. Dylan started using Flickr in 2012 to display his photographs, but his use increased exponentially when he received a new camera: 'I got my camera and I got really into photography. It's kind of accelerated more and more as I got into photography.' Not only was the feedback on Flickr important, but so too was the ease with which he could link people to the site. He explains:

> I used to post stuff, like just photos of flowers and things like that … it was just really bad shots, like amateur shots. I deleted those … and now I have some experience of working on it and putting out photos and a nice portfolio-type thing for my photography. And so if someone wants to see I can just link them, instead of sending them my photos.

Through digital media and social media, both Sean and Dylan were developing their skills and identities as artists. Here, the digital dispositif is used positively, as the boys are able to develop, package and promote their artistic attributes through digital media.

Social becomings

Digital media were also important in facilitating social changes for the young people. In some instances these becomings were brought about by conscious practices designed to show a different aspect of an individual's personality or to signal to others a sense of independence from the family unit. In other instances the young people referred to changes that had occurred unconsciously and of which they had only recently become aware, sometimes as a result of the study. In some cases, social media became a testing ground in which they could work out how to deal with particular types of people and negative exchanges. Given the temporal and physical distance afforded by digital media, several young people felt better placed to work through these complicated situations. This gave them more confidence when handling these situations offline.

Stacey began watching episodes of the anime *Uta no Prince-sama* online in 2009. As well as introducing her to 'many new words and cultures' it also modelled the idea that you 'need to work hard to get where you want to go'. This message, and the aesthetics associated with it, had resonated strongly with her, as anime has become a significant part of how Stacey represented herself online. For example, she was part of the *Uta no Prince-sama* Group on Facebook, and also clearly 'liked' Japanese popular culture. Inspired by *Uta no Prince-sama* Stacey acquired new digital practices that enabled her to create an anime version of herself, as seen in the September 2014 profile picture (Figure 4.6).

She was also able to share these skills with her class: 'There's a little app called Anime Girl and you can download it onto iPads and like iPods. And so I used it, last year, I used it to create a whole bunch and try to make it look like all the students in my class.' Despite the effort that Stacey had put into the pictures of herself and her classmates, she said in reference to her posts on social media: 'I don't usually get feedback, but it's fun to try and show.'

These experimentations with identity were primarily enabled through digital media opening up new possibilities for the young people to explore. What emerged was used as inspiration or motivation thereby changing how these young people viewed themselves and their futures. For example, Stacey's Facebook cover shot was a photo of a New York street, which she had taken when she visited with her family early in 2014. She wanted people to see the photo because it's her 'dream to go back there and do a bit of study'. With her profile photo embedded in the New York street Stacey was strengthening the dream in both her own and her audience's mind (Figure 4.7).

For three young women in the group, digital media were key to developing their social identities. It meant they were more visible to their peers and therefore more likely to receive invitations to parties and outings. All three girls were on four social media platforms: Facebook, Instagram, Snapchat and Tumblr. The fear of missing out on an invitation was an important reason for being on social media. As Penny explained: 'I also find that people that don't have Facebook, not that this is a life ruiner, but you wouldn't get invited to as many things and you don't see friends as much because the conversations you have with your friends they start and then you're like "I'm bored, let's do something".'

Opening a Facebook account was a key moment for each of these young people and was indicated as such on their timelines of digital practices. Grace said that using Facebook helped her 'catch up with people a lot more regularly'. Penny explained that Facebook gave her more independence to organise her social life:

> I think that kind of changed how I did everything … Yeah so 2010 I started talking to my friends more and I organised 'playdates' as we'd call them for myself and I was more talking to my friends rather than my parents calling their parents and saying this date, this date.

This was common across the group, as opening a Facebook account coincided with greater freedom to communicate, socialise and organise events with friends independent of parents. It was viewed as a kind of contemporary debutante for several, signalling their social emergence or becoming.

FIGURE 4.6 Stacey's Facebook profiles, 2014

FIGURE 4.7 Stacey's Facebook cover photo, December 2014

Some noted that using digital platforms meant they had to 'toughen up' in order to handle the negative people and interactions they encountered. Stacey noticed that her brother became more 'gangster' and 'hostile' when playing Grand Theft Auto: 'I've noticed with my brother when he started playing video games he started changing as well ... They're watching something and they're trying to manipulate it and they start reflecting it.'

However, the answer was not as simple as leaving the platform, as Simon explained: 'Sometimes with this one game on Steam ... you play with lots of people, sometimes it's just like they're really mean people [and] do you become bad back? It's like if I leave the group it's ruining my own fun.'

In some instances working through these negative exchanges was good practice for how they might handle these experiences offline. Sean explained that World of Warcraft helped him learn how to handle 'difficult' people: 'People are kind of nasty online because of that mask of anonymity and it sort of helps me with tougher people, which I would say was a catalysing point.' In a similar way, using Facebook enabled Sean to hide or exit from interactions that made him uncomfortable: 'I was a fairly shy person and it helped me talk to people better ... It was sort of a safe way to talk to people with not actually having to be there, and you could sort of say I have to go.' For others such interactions and experiences were not positive. It can be difficult to identify and resist the overtly negative influences being shared. In Rachel's case she had to quit her Tumblr blog, but not before she felt herself becoming upset and depressed by the content (see Chapter 2).

The digital dispositif provided a range of opportunities for the young people to explore and experiment with their identities. This could involve the emergence of a more social and public persona or the cultivation of a professional identity; either way these were all significant moments of becoming for the young people. It also enabled them to orient themselves toward the future, providing spaces into which positive attributes and skills could be organised and recognised by others. The digital context might therefore appear to have presented them with a fairly open 'canvas' from which myriad becomings emerged. However, on several occasions the young people intimated there were contextual factors that also shaped their practices

Tethering the process of becoming

Despite the post-structural framing of identity set out in the early chapters of the book, the young people's identity practices were structured and restrained by a range of forces. Specifically, their digital identities were *tethered* technically *and* socially. Technically, they were tethered by the architecture of social media platforms, which promoted particular 'types' of identity practices. A contributing factor was the young people's use of social buttons external to the platform, meaning that a wide range of internet practices become tethered to particular digital identities. Socially, their digital identities were tethered to an idealised notion of a 'real' self.

As a consequence, the young people interpreted digital identities by comparing or calibrating them to their supposedly 'real' or 'authentic' identities.

Turkle's (2006) application of the 'tethered self' is quite different to the way in which I use the concept of tethering here. Turkle is concerned with the way 'tethering technologies' shift understandings of the physical self, arguing they move individuals into a liminal space that 'reinvents intimacy and solitude' (Turkle, 2011, p.28). As a point of departure, I use the idea of 'tethered identities' to conceptualise the *limitations* to identity play and becoming in the digital context, arguing that identity is not as fluid and free as what was originally conceived. The utopian argument that online spaces offer freedom from the corporeal body and 'limitless space for constructing new identities' (Ringrose, 2011a, p.601) is questioned through these findings. Unlike Turkle, who centralises the physical identity (which she argues is becoming diluted and diminished by technology), the position I have taken throughout this book is to see digital and embodied identities as part of an interconnected network that has multiple axial points and prisms for various identities to emerge, circulate, intensify and dissolve.

Technical tethering

Facebook was the most popular social media platform used by this group of young people. Analysis of the platform at the time of the study shows how its architecture facilitated the technical tethering. To use social media individuals entered information about their identity into a structure that was predetermined by the platform. The user completed a profile (with information like date of birth, hometown, relationship status, also including profile and cover photos, etc.), and was then encouraged to enter 'Statuses' with the prompt question, 'What's on your mind?' Feedback was given via the Like/Share/Comment buttons that appeared at the bottom of posts.

Facebook then 'curated' these posts into a 'Timeline' based on the popularity of each post; a post with few comments or likes could be deprioritised on the timeline. Down the left-hand side of the 'Home' page was information about popular stories that were 'Trending', 'Suggested Groups' (based on what groups friends are in) and photos of 'People you may know' (based on your friend list). There are also buttons to 'Find Friends' and 'Find Groups', which prompt individuals to keep expanding their social networks. The structure of the site promotes a particular type of identity—one with lots of friends, 'interesting' experiences and a liking for popular culture and 'interest' groups. Notifications sent directly to the user's device provide continual feedback and information that 'binds' people to this social media identity.

As with other social media, the design of the Facebook platform encourages users to present themselves in particular ways. Rachel was candid about the influence of her Facebook practices on her sense of self:

RACHEL: Yeah I start to get notifications on Facebook, I'm like people *actually like* me and then when I get nothing, I'm like *ok*.

LUCI: *So it's good when you're popular but then when you're not?*

RACHEL: Yeah it's kind of silly but that what's it's like … I feel like because you know I'm a teenager and just sometimes I want attention and I think it's bad to say that, but I'm being really honest now.

The 'need' to receive notifications and validation is no doubt a fairly common experience for social media users, particularly for those in their teenage years. Combined with Facebook's constant suggestions and tips on *increasing* the number of friends, particular practices were promoted. For Rachel this meant becoming 'friends' with people indiscriminately. However, she was not comfortable with these practices and eventually changed them: 'Like in 2013 and [20]12, I just added [friends] you know, I knew them but I didn't know them, I just added them because I knew that I needed to have them. I started getting a lot of friends and then I'm like "Wait! I don't need this".' At this point she realised she did not need 'all those friends' on Facebook to feel 'loved'.

Yet her solution was not to review her list of Facebook friends and practices, but instead to start a new Facebook account under a different name. Compared to Rachel's first Facebook account, which had over 1,000 friends, her new one had just 327 friends. She still maintained the old account and occasionally interacted with different people and pages on there. Indeed, it may have been socially 'costly' to get rid of it altogether. However, opening the new account made her realise just how tethered her identity was to the first one—distancing herself from that was liberating: 'When I realised about Facebook and stuff I became a little bit more happier than I was. I found a little bit of myself, it sounds a little bit lame.'

Rachel's experience showed just how influential the platform was to her identity, tethering her to versions of herself that she was no longer comfortable with. Stacey summed it up in the following way: 'Most people hide who they actually are to be popular or to fit in, instead of being who they really are.' Given the way social media platforms like Facebook structure identity representation and the accompanying social pressures this brings, it is not surprising that this was a difficult space to negotiate. As Sean explained: 'You feel the need to be online at all times doing like texting, messaging, like all that sort of stuff constantly.'

Social tethering

According to Gee (2000), recognition is an important analytical tool in understanding identity; without the recognition of others these changes might be seen as ineffectual. Stacey's motivation to present an anime version of herself was to counter the perception that she was 'really shy' and 'hard studying'—she wanted her friends to see her 'fun side'. However, Stacey had received quite a bit of negative feedback on Facebook in response to these (re)presentations: 'I see some people put positive [comments up], but then others have put quite negative ones up and I just tend to ignore those or block them due to the fact that I don't want to be knowing that stuff.' She found it hard to tell if her friends were being 'sarcastic or something', suggesting some uncertainty as to how her actions and posts were perceived by others.

This was a source of consternation for Stacey. One reason Stacey might have attracted more negative attention on social media was because she portrayed a version of herself that was quite different to the one encountered face to face. Not only was the identity visually very different, but it was also more empowered and assertive. When compared with her physical identity a dissonance emerged between Stacey and her digital identities, which may account for the negative reactions she experienced. Despite the opportunities offered by digital media to experiment and explore different aspects of self, digital identities were often interpreted against embodied identities. In this way, the young people's digital identities were tethered to their corporeal identity.

Trent explained that he had been bullied a lot throughout his life: 'I've been bullied like my whole life really. It just recently stopped near the end of last year.' The bullying continued in the digital context and was 'a reason to *not* go online … big time'. In response he deactivated his Facebook account in 2012. Trent intimated there was a sense of control when this occurred as deactivation meant his digital identity was 'untouchable': 'Then you can never message me … and when I started it up I had nothing bad on there so you couldn't do anything on my Facebook.'

Another strategy Trent used to deal with this problem was limiting the circle of people that he interacted with online and using a more covert identity: 'The only thing I went on was Steam and that's where like people didn't know me and the few friends I had on Steam were really just friends that weren't bullying.' While digital media might have offered an array of opportunities and experiences for Trent to explore, his digital practices and play were limited. For Trent, digital media were not neutral spaces to explore and exhibit *any* desired identity, but were instead shaped by the external social context, which influenced how he experienced himself and others in the online space. Others perceived Trent's digital identities through the 'prism' of his embodied identity, thereby tethering him to his social experiences offline.

One significant moment for Trent was when he 'jumped back onto Facebook' and realised he was 'no longer being cyberbullied'. On reflection, he acknowledged that his use of a rather 'serious' cover photo might have helped (Figure 4.8).

The character featured in the cover photo was from Borderlines, a game based on the legend of Pandora's Box. According to Trent, the character 'is a psycho' who just 'runs at people'. As he explained, the cover photo indicated to his network of friends that he wanted to be taken more seriously:

> People don't see me as a serious person in most friend groups, so they see me as a bit of a joke. Even when I'm trying to be serious they tend to laugh at it … They see that profile and they're just like he must be serious or something.

FIGURE 4.8 Trent's Facebook cover photo, June 2014

Using this cover photo Trent signalled a decisive change to his network of friends. This was an active decision to distance himself from previous social experiences and the bullied and victimised identity he was tethered to. Trent acknowledged that it helped him to become a stronger, more serious person in real life.

Finally, there was evidence of replications of identity across different digital contexts. Mark used the same profile photo across a variety of digital contexts, as he explained: 'It's a picture I use universally for most of my stuff. I'm kind of fond of it, so I just use that.' For Mark this might have been a matter of convenience and perhaps safety; however, for others in the group the same photos frequently appeared across different social media platforms. While these photos appeared in slightly different sequences and sometimes with different comments, essentially the 'same' identity was being portrayed. Further, for many young people their friend list was composed of the same people, meaning the audience for both social media platforms was often very similar.

In light of this discussion, forming and representing digital identities becomes a negotiation between a variety of factors. These include: an identity that the individual desires or aspires to; the type of identity enabled and promoted by the structure of the digital platform; and how digital representations align with embodied identities and the practices of your social group. While the digital space enables some opportunities for exploring and becoming a variety of different identities, these possibilities are tethered by various contextual factors. Cultivating digital identities that appeared authentic, socially acceptable and interesting to others required sophisticated social media literacies.

Architectures of becoming—promises and pitfalls

Digital media expanded the range of opportunities these young people had to explore and represent their identities. While some of the young people were using an array of digital media, social media platforms were the primary sites for identity work to take place. boyd (2010) points out that a social media profile becomes the 'locus of interaction' (p.42), meaning conversations happen on and through these visual representations of identity. In many respects the young people's Facebook identities worked to condense and authenticate the other identities (re)presented in their digital networks. This was a complicated process for the young people to negotiate with several issues emerging for consideration.

First, is the complex array of pressures associated with visual representations of identity on social media. While simplistic, photos were key to representing and interpreting identity in the digital context. They were also subject to the most scrutiny with the amount of likes a photo or post received being seen as an indication of its worth. Arvidsson's (2011) General Sentiment theory explains how metrics take on value for the individual so that 'other people's evaluation of one's identity (or "brand") becomes central not only to one's sense of self-worth, but also, and increasingly, to one's objective value' (Arvidsson, 2011, p.49). All of the young people were aware of the importance of metrics on social media. The girls appeared to feel these pressures more acutely. They brought up popularity, attention and judgement as topics for discussion more often than the boys and also explored these themes more explicitly in their responses to the research provocations.

In her analysis of gender and social media, Marwick (2013) asserts that in some environments 'certain behaviour in women is encouraged while the same behaviour in men is discouraged' (p.63). Uploading attractive photos was a normalised, if not expected, visual representation of identity on Facebook for the girls in this group. However, it appeared that the boys were unlikely to engage in similar digital practices. Marwick (2013) explains that in her study the 'normative judgment on technology practices was determined by the social context of the creators' (p.70), meaning that the intentions, processes and behaviours of the creators become inscribed in the way the platform is structured. While it has certainly evolved over time, the fact that 'Facemash', Facebook's predecessor, was built as a type of game in which creator Mark Zuckerberg and friends rated photos (often of females) as to whether they were 'hot or not', sets a precedent for how the site is used (Carlson, 2010). It is therefore not surprising that users, young women in particular, feel pressure to display or exhibit their attractiveness on Facebook.

While the young people's digital networks allowed opportunities for professional and social becomings, recognising and understanding others' identities followed a far more prosaic set of processes. Digital identities were most often understood or calibrated against embodied identities, so that 'friends' judged digital representations for truthfulness or authenticity. Reinforcing this idea was the fact that Facebook, the most common social media platform for the group, encouraged users to have one 'authentic' identity. The young people explained any dissonances between identities with the idea that people are 'different' online. Identity was not fluid in the digital context, but tethered to embodied or offline identities. This fits with the disposition discussed in the previous chapter in which many young people did not see the online as confluent or embedded with the offline. Approached as a distinct space, the digital was thought to bring forth a *different identity* rather than *different aspects* of the same identity. This social tethering limited the possibilities of what people might become in the digital context.

For both Trent and Stacey digital identities were a negotiation between the possibilities enabled by their use of digital media, the identity desired by the individual and the social milieu in which they were embedded. Ringrose (2011b) argues that because social media networks are composed of students from a 'real' school community the embodied identity 'intrudes upon the possibilities of … virtual self-representation' (p.107). While this might mean the identities are more 'honest' when compared to a 'real' or embodied self, they can also limit becoming and change as the individual is tethered to an embodied identity that is, at times, just as arbitrarily attributed as any other 'experimental' identity enabled through digital media. To avoid negative feedback individuals are encouraged to align digital representations of identity with a 'real' or 'authentic' identity, meaning there are replications of self across online and offline contexts.

As a 'networked public' (boyd, 2007, p.42), Facebook encourages individuals to acquire 'friends' across different aspects of life. Rachel talked candidly about the pressure to acquire Facebook 'friends'. While she achieved this goal, she soon felt uncomfortable about having so many 'friends' and being on a constant quest for likes. Not only did it feel contradictory to her embodied self, but it also became difficult to manage the context collapse that took place through the News Feed. Rather than close this account, Rachel continued with the first Facebook page as a 'lite version of her life on Facebook' (Marwick & boyd, 2014, p.10), but posted more regularly to the second one.

The more careful and conventional digital identity Rachel presented on Facebook was less inclined to intimate disclosure, yet was able to reach a wider audience. Maintaining this profile avoided any repercussions of closing the account altogether and ensured she maintained any social capital she had accrued. Yet negotiating the context collapse she encountered on Facebook, Rachel presented what Pitcan et al. (2018) call the 'vanilla self—a 'conservative, staid' (p.2) version of the self. While Rachel's two Facebook accounts help her to work around the tensions that surface when (re)presenting identities on social media, they involved significant time to maintain and manage. Rachel's experience highlights how quickly and easily identities can be proliferated and changed through social media. While this enables Rachel to work around the tension between different identities, this has the potential to be destabilising.

The Facebook 'identity' was not only integral to maintaining social relationships, but was increasingly 'mediating' how the young people experienced sites external to the platform. The rise of Facebook Connect and the placement of like buttons on external websites prompted continual sharing with Facebook networks, meaning some participants, like Rachel, became tethered to this identity whenever they were on the internet. As van Dijck (2013) argues, this aligns with Facebook's commercial goal to tie its data to many sites across the internet through these social buttons. The upshot of this is that individuals link a 'diverse set of online practices back to the singular identity crafted on their Facebook page' (van der Nagel & Frith, 2015, n.p.). It is not surprising that several young people in the study felt pressure to present and maintain their Facebook identity.

However, the practices encouraged by the platform did not always map smoothly onto young people's experience. Presenting the self in a way that suits the architecture of the platform requires the adoption of particular digital practices, and for some participants this prompted anxiety, particularly as the representations and relationships facilitated on Facebook felt, to some degree, inauthentic. Intensifying this situation is the fact that these representations and expressions are publicly scrutinised and judged through likes, shares and comments. From a personal perspective, (re)presenting and measuring the self through the platform led participants to practices they felt were self-contradicting. Despite this, sociologist Eva Ilouz (2007) argues contradiction is simply part of the digital dispositif:

> The technology of the internet thus positions the self in a contradictory way: it makes one take a deep turn inward, that is, it requires that one focus on one's self in order to capture and communicate its unique essence, in the form of tastes, opinions, fantasies and emotional capabilities.
>
> *(p.79)*

In this way, the platform becomes the site for the self to be 'assembled', rather than just presented. However, this also requires a 'deep inward turn', which for many in the study was a confronting experience.

Negotiating identities within the dispositif involved construction and concealment of different aspects of self according to context and audience (Marwick & boyd, 2014). It also involved complex processes of comparison and contrast between the young people's personal identity and the subjective positions produced through the dispositif. These are not necessarily new processes, but as Agamben (2009, p.15) explains, the dissemination of subjectivities produced through the dispositif 'pushes to the extreme the masquerade that has always accompanied every personal identity'. The digital dispositif operates in between the discrete spaces of the platform to capture and orient the fluid identity of the individual. Indeed, dominant discourses and the young people's friends and family were often a countering force when it came to the possibilities for identity play and experimentation.

Analysis of the young people's digital identities revealed moments of 'sedimentation' and 'breakage' (Deleuze, 1992, p.159). For example, through digital media Sean and Dylan were able to develop their artistic skills and present these burgeoning identities to their social networks. The recognition and feedback 'sedimented' this aspect of their identity and provided the impetus for their becoming artist. By contrast, Trent did not want to use social media because he was worried about being bullied. However, after using an aggressive and provocative image from the Borderlands game for his Facebook cover, Trent noticed a critical 'break' in the way his friends perceived him. He believed this more assertive and 'serious' identity was the reason the bullying stopped.

Multiple lines of force were brought to bear through Trent's processes of identity (re)presentation including: past experiences of being bullied; cybersafety programmes and common understandings of appropriate online behaviour; the language, imagery and iconography of the game; the social pressures of peers; and the materialities of social media platforms. Trent's experience highlights the role of the past in the present and how it can surface to reshape the construction of self online. This digital identity was not just an attempt to redress the flow of power, but also to confront and perhaps bring closure to his past experiences of being bullied. Becoming in the digital dispositif is a process that draws together the past and the present to (re)present 'that which we are no longer, or that which we are becoming, a perpetual inventiveness' (Bussolini, 2010, p.88).

Conclusions

This chapter has presented a detailed picture of how identities emerged, condensed and dissolved in relation to various aspects of the digital dispositif. Different social media platforms enabled the young people to become different identities, yet the social and technical elements of the dispositif simultaneously tethered them to an embodied, 'authentic' version of self. Evident here is the way in which the dispositif works *between* and *across* platforms facilitated through the array of devices the young people used—mobile phones, iPods, laptop computers. In *theory* the possibilities for practices and behaviours were endless, but in *practice* what emerged was a far more convergent set of digital practices and behaviours.

In the next chapter, the perspective shifts from the individual to consider how digital media are used to make connections with others. Specifically, the chapter considers how these young people use digital media to communicate and form relationships with other people. As we shall see, communication is sometimes planned and permanent, sometimes spontaneous and ephemeral, and is shaped by a range of social, technical and cultural factors. Identity is inevitably tangled up with communicative practices; however, the chapter is particularly concerned with how social practices are shaped by the materialities of the digital context.

References

Agamben, G. (2009). *What is an apparatus? And other essays.* Stanford, CA: Stanford University Press.

Ambady, N., & Rosenthal, R. (1992). Thin slices of expressive behaviour as predictors of inter-personal consequences: A meta-analysis. *Psychological Bulletin,* 111(2), 256–274.

Arvidsson, A. (2011). General sentiment: How value and affect converge in the information economy. *The Sociological Review, 52*(2), 39–59. doi:10.1111/j.1467-954X.2012.02052.x

Back, L. (2012). Live sociology: Social research and its futures. In L. Back & N. Puwar (Eds.), *Live methods.* Malden, USA: Wiley-Blackwell.

boyd, d. (2007). Why youth heart social networking sites: The role of networked publics in teenage social life. In D. Buckingham (Ed.), *Macarthur Foundation Series on Digital Learning—Youth, Identity and Digital Media Volume.* Cambridge, MA: MIT Press.

boyd, d. (2010). Social network sites as networked publics: Affordances, dynamics and implications. In Papacharissi, Z. (Ed.), *Networked Self: Identity, Community and Culture on Social Network Sites.* New York: Routledge.

Brandtzaeg, P., Luders, M., & Sketjne, J. (2010). Too many Facebook 'friends'? Content sharing and sociability versus the need for privacy in social network sites. *International Journal of Human-Computer Interaction,* 26(11–12), 1006–1030.

Buckingham, D. (2008). Introducing identity. In D. Buckingham (Ed.), *Youth, Identity and Digital Media*. Cambridge, MA: MIT Press.

Bussolini, J. (2010). What is a dispositive? *Foucault Studies*, 10, 85–107.

Carlson, N. (2010). At last—the full story of how Facebook was founded. *Business Insider*, 5 March.

Chun, W. (2016). *Updating to Remain the Same: Habitual New Media*. Cambridge, MA: The MIT Press.

Deleuze, G. (1992). What is a dispositif? In T. J. Armstrong (Ed.), *Michel Foucault Philosopher* (pp.159–168). Hemel Hempstead: Harvester Wheatsheaf.

Deleuze, G., & Guattari, F. (1980/2013). *A Thousand Plateaus*. London and New York: Bloomsbury Academic.

Donath, J. (2007). Signals in social supernets. *Journal of Computer-Mediated Communication*, 13 (1), 72–83.

Donath, J. (2014). *The Social Machine: Designs for Living Online*. Cambridge, MA: The MIT Press.

Ellison, N., Steinfeld, C., & Lampe, C. (2007). The benefits of Facebook 'friends': Exploring the relationship between college students' use of online social networks and social capital. *Journal of Computer-Mediated Communication*, 12(1), 1143–1168.

Gee, J. (2000). The New Literacy Studies: From 'socially situated' to the work of the social. In D. Barton (Ed.), *Situated Literacies: Reading and Writing in Context*. London: Routledge.

Gleason, P. (1983). Identifying identity: A semantic history. *Journal of American History*, 69(4), 931–950.

Goffman, E. (1959). *The Presentation of Self in Everyday Life*. New York: Doubleday Publishing Group.

Ilouz, E. (2007). *Cold Intimacies: The Making of Emotional Capitalism*. Cambridge, UK: Polity Press.

Janks, H. (2010). *Literacy and Power*. New York: Routledge.

Jones, R. H., & Hafner, C. A. (2012). *Understanding Digital Literacies: A Practical Introduction*. London and New York: Routledge.

Kirkpatrick, D. (2011). *The Facebook Effect: The Inside Story of the Company that is Connecting the World*. New York: Simon & Schuster Paperbacks.

Lovink, G. (2016). *Social Media Abyss: Critical Internet Cultures and the Force of Negation*. Malden, MA: Polity Press.

Marwick, A. (2013). Gender, sexuality and social media. In J. Hunsinger & T. M. Senft (Eds.), *The Social Media Handbook*. Hoboken, NJ: Taylor & Francis.

Marwick, A., & boyd, d. (2014). Networked privacy: How teenagers negotiate context in social media. *New Media & Society*, 16(7), 1051–1067.

Mendelson, A. L., & Papacharissi, Z. (2011). Look at us: collective narcissism in college student Facebook photo galleries. In Z. Papacharissi (Ed.), *A Networked Self: Identity, Community, and Culture on Social Network Sites*. New York: Routledge.

Moje, E., & Luke, A. (2009). Literacy and identity: Examining the metaphors in history and contemporary research. *Reading Research Quarterly*, 44(4), 415–437.

Pitcan, M., Marwick, A., & boyd, d. (2018). Performing a vanilla self: Respectability politics, social class, and the digital world. *Journal of Computer-Mediated Communication*. doi:10.1093/jcmc/zmy008

Ringrose, J. (2011a). Beyond discourse? Using Deleuze and Guattari's schizoanalysis to explore affective assemblages, heterosexually striated space, online and at school. *The Power In/Of Language*, special issue, 43(6), August.

Ringrose, J. (2011b). Are you sexy, flirty or a slut? Exploring 'sexualization' and how teen girls perform/negotiate digital sexual identity on social networking sites. In R. Gill & C. Scharff (Eds.), *New Femininities: Postfeminism, Neoliberalism and Subjectivity*. Hampshire, UK: Palgrave Macmillan.

Skates, L. (2014). Job applicants' social media profiles now checked by companies as 'common practice'. *ABC News online*. Retrieved from www.abc.net.au/news/2014-11-15/social-media-profiles-of-job-applicants-checked/5888908

Stagoll, C. (2010). Becoming. In A. Parr (Ed.), *The Deleuze Dictionary*. Edinburgh, UK: Edinburgh University Press.

Stutzman, F., Capra, R., & Thompson, J. (2011). Factors mediating disclosure in social network sites. *Computers in Human Behaviour*, 27, 590–598.

Turkle, S. (2006). Always-on/Always-on-you: The tethered self. In J. Katz (Ed.), *Handbook of Mobile Communications and Social Change*. Cambridge, MA: The MIT Press.

Turkle, S. (2011). The tethered self: Technology reinvents intimacy and solitude. *Continuing Higher Education Review*, 75.

Valenzuela, S., Park, N., & Kee, K. (2009). Is there social capital in a social network site?: Facebook use and college students' life satisfaction, trust and participation. *Journal of Computer-Mediated Communication*, 14(4), 875–901.

van der Nagel, E., & Frith, J. (2015). Anonymity, pseudonymity, and the agency of online identity: Examining the social practices of r/Gonewild. *First Monday* [online], 20(3).

van Dijck, J. (2013). 'You have one identity': Performing the self on Facebook and LinkedIn. *Media, Culture and Society*, 35(2).

Vitak, J. (2012). The impact of context collapse and privacy on social network site disclosures. *Journal of Broadcasting & Electronic Media*, 56(4), 451–470.

Vitak, J., & Ellison, N. (2013). 'There's a network out there you might as well tap': Exploring the benefits and barriers to exchanging informational and support based resources on Facebook. *New Media & Society*, 15(2), 243–259.

Zielinski, S. (2006). *Deep Time of the Media. Toward an Archaeology of Hearing and Seeing by Technical Means*. Amsterdam: Amsterdam University Press.

5

CONNECTING WITH OTHERS

With ongoing technological development and innovation, digital communication and sociality are constantly in flux. Van Dijck (2013) argues that 'sociality is not simply "rendered technological" by moving to an online space; rather coded structures are profoundly altering the nature of our connections, creations and interactions' (p.20). As such, digital media platforms no longer exist in a separate sphere and, as I have suggested in earlier chapters, have become intertwined with the fabric of everyday life. Social media now mediate the ways in which young people write themselves into being (Sunden, 2003). Analysing the way these young people establish a paradigm for their participation on social media platforms brings insight into the socially constructed nature of platform participation.

Having analysed the ways in which the young people used digital media to (re) present their identities in Chapter 4, I now focus on their experiences of using digital platforms to *connect* with others. Participation on digital platforms is an area receiving interest from various fields in the social sciences, such as media and communication (Plantin et al., 2016; Bucher, 2012; van Dijck, 2013), youth studies and sociology of youth (Bennett & Robards, 2013; Hodkinson, 2015), and digital sociology (Beneito-Montagut, 2015; Dyer, 2015). I build on a growing body of research that traces the influence of digital platforms on the communication practices and socialities of young people, who are both shaping—and shaped by—the media they use. Using the digital dispositif outlined in Chapter 3 and elaborated in Chapter 4, I detail the ways in which the materialities of the digital were manifest through the architecture of the platform, shaping the young people's communication practices.

The young people used a range of digital media to facilitate their connections with others, including social media, text messaging and email. Given the prominence of digital platforms in their connections with others, I begin this chapter with an overview of the current scholarship on social media and the politics of platforms, before analysing the young people's communication practices and the tacit rules of their participation. The chapter is divided into five sections with each exploring the specific communication strategy encouraged by the digital media or digital platform. All but one young person displayed different types of digital connections, so there was much movement and 'bleeding' between the five sections outlined. I include the non-platform-based forms of communication in order to examine the full range of the young people's digital connections, as well as provide a point of comparison with platform-based participation.

The politics of platforms

Digital media platforms generate multiple ways to participate and communicate in contemporary society. Platforms such as Facebook, YouTube, Skype and Steam have become essential tools for communication and entertainment for people of all ages. These platforms are particularly powerful for many young people, who have grown up connected to the internet through ubiquitous mobile technologies (boyd, 2014; Ito et al., 2010). The possibilities for communication, interaction and entertainment are therefore continually shifting, with the associated increase in availability and affordability of mobile digital technologies having a significant influence over how young people interact with one another, both online and offline (Marlowe et al., 2016). Similarly, identity practices are now also mediated through digital platforms, with every piece of digital information a person provides—from photos, nicknames, email addresses and comments—used to make inferences about an individual's identity (Marwick, 2013). Digital platforms not only open up the possibilities for self-representation and social interactions, but also steer these in particular ways through the architecture of the platform.

Recent research into the politics of digital platforms helps to unpack the competing tensions that these young people must negotiate as part of their participation. The experience of network culture has changed in recent years and this is largely due to the proliferation of digital platforms, which funnel operations on the internet. In Chapter 3 the young people described the architecture of the platform as an overriding organisational feature of the digital dispositif, leading to a more homogenous set of digital experiences. In a similar way, Hands (2013) explains, the internet is 'vanishing'. No longer do we have a single internet, but instead a 'multiplicity of distinct platforms' (p.1), which are often accessed more directly through apps. The 'platform' has become the 'dominant infrastructural and economic model of the social web' (Helmond, 2015, p.5), enabling social media companies to position themselves both in the market, as an extension of the capitalist sphere, and to users.

With the proliferation of social buttons across the internet, such as Facebook's like button and Facebook Connect, these platforms also work to 'colonise' the wider internet. As discussed in the previous chapter, this has implications for identity practices. From a different perspective, Gerlitz and Helmond (2013) describe the presence of social buttons and plugins as 'an alternative fabric of the web … that is based on data flows enabled by and to third party devices' (p.1361). For this reason the interface privileges particular forms of information and communication, which enable it to be channelled in specific ways. Seeing these platforms as simply a neutral tool to facilitate participatory culture (Jenkins, 2006) is therefore problematic. Due to their commodification connective media platforms work in normative ways, reshaping communication practices. As such, the 'politics' of digital platforms not only refers to the technical architecture of platforms, but also to how the platform is discursively constructed in the 'cultural imaginary' to ensure their services 'make sense' to their users (Wyatt, 2004).

To tease out its sociocultural effects, Gillespie (2010) identifies four different definitions of the word 'platform'—architectural, functional, figurative and political—which are each drawn upon to develop its discursive resonance in the digital context. As Gillespie explains, through their use of the word 'platform' technology companies have moved the definition well beyond the computational:

> This more conceptual use of the 'platform' leans on all of the term's connotations: computational, something to build upon and innovate from; political, a place from which to speak and be heard; figurative, in that the opportunity is an abstract promise as much as a practical one; and architectural, in that [it] is designed as an open-armed, egalitarian facilitation of expression, not an elitist gatekeeper with normative and technical restrictions.
>
> *(Gillespie, 2010, p.352)*

The adoption of the term 'platform' is therefore strategic as it has connotations with openness, functionality, empowerment and neutrality. This elides the work of the platform interface and algorithms, which in many instances work to prioritise (and deprioritise) particular posts, photos and information, as well as the connections between users (see Bucher, 2012; Rieder, 2012). Digital platforms serve a number of different audiences, users, shareholders, third parties and advertisers, to name but a few. Part of the challenge is that they must manage the expectations of each and smooth out any contradictions between them in order to serve the financial interests of the company (Gillespie, 2010). For example, the computational definition of the word 'platform' appeals to developers, while the connotations of empowerment, neutrality and openness appeal to users, advertisers and other third parties. Ultimately these connotations imply many things about what the platform will offer, but in reality, platforms like Facebook and YouTube rely on user-generated content.

Viewed in these terms the operation and effectiveness of many digital platforms depend on users adopting a particular faith or belief in the role that it will play in their everyday life. The popular discourse associated with these platforms has successfully established the notion that digital platforms, particularly Facebook, are the place to connect with others (Couldry, 2015). Many digital platforms reinforce this idea by marketing themselves as fundamental to facilitating social interaction and self-representation. For example, Facebook's tagline is: 'Facebook helps you to connect and share with the people in your life.' Similarly, the prompts to write 'What's on your mind?', 'Share', 'Like' and '+Add Friend' normalise new social practices through the interface.

The discourse that helps to construct these platforms reaches beyond the boundaries of the technology to establish a kind 'social media logic' in users (van Dijck & Poell, 2013), which is actually the 'norms, strategies, mechanisms, and economies underpinning' (p.2) the dynamics of the platform. This logic is often tacit, shaping the practices associated with the site in unconscious ways. As such, the politics of platforms are constituted through the beliefs and assumptions that are bound up with the sites, as well as the architecture that presents and channels information. These issues present new challenges to communication practices.

Connecting with others

Using digital platforms, then, raises critical questions about how to exploit the possibilities of the interface while balancing the dynamics and demands of social relations. While the principles and processes of platforms have been identified and theorised, how these complexities map onto users' social experiences is more difficult to gauge. What follows is an analysis of the different forms of digital communication the young people engaged in, with a particular focus on how they negotiate the social and technical elements of the digital dispositif. I pay particular attention to the literacies they draw on to make sense of their experiences connecting with others.

Projecting the self—Facebook News Feed and Instagram

Eleven of the 13 young people in the study were on Facebook. For many this was the first social media site they signed up to. While this is only a small group, it is interesting to note the popularity of Facebook, given that in recent years use of the platform has been reported as decreasing among teenagers across the world (Olson, 2013). Simon and Chantelle were the only two *not* on Facebook or any other social media. However, Chantelle admitted that if she were to use social media, Facebook would be the platform she would start on. This suggests that Facebook was an initial, formative step in the social media 'ladder' for these young people with other platforms 'added on' later.

The majority of young people reported that they were users of Facebook before email. Sean explains that by the time he started communicating online Facebook had superseded email—it was easy to access and more immediate: 'I feel like it [email] was slightly earlier than most of the internet use that I did, so I never kind of caught on because we had Facebook as an alternative, because it's instant.' This sentiment was echoed by a number of young people who identified email as a significant moment in their school-related learning rather than their social interactions, as Facebook already facilitated this type of engagement.

Family played a distinct role for the participants on Facebook, but these engagements only formed a relatively small proportion of those that took place. For Penny and Grace, Facebook was a way of staying in contact with cousins who lived interstate or in the country. As Penny explained: 'I often talk to my aunties or I see things and I comment on the photos of my little cousins and then I'll show it to my mum because she doesn't have Facebook but I'll be like, "Mum look what our cousins are doing".' For Mitch, Facebook was the 'only way' he could contact his father, who lived in the Philippines. Stacey, on the other hand, described her parents acting like supervisors, ensuring she did the 'right' thing online: 'My parents have all access to my internet accounts, so they can see what I'm doing. And that also helps because that means I know I can't do anything wrong, even though I wouldn't actually.' Most of the other young people did not communicate with family on Facebook and if they did it was quite cursory. As Mark said, his sister will 'put something on Facebook and I'm like, *like!*'

One purpose for using Facebook was to help smooth transitions as life changed for the young people. Three in the study had started using Facebook when they began secondary school at age 12. This enabled them to stay in contact with primary school friends and cope with the transition to a new school. As Dylan explained: 'Getting it in grade 6 was a good idea after you drifted off to different schools, and you still remain in contact basically on Facebook.' Keeping in touch was like a kind of 'safety blanket' for the young people as they transitioned through different stages in life. However, as they eased into this change and gained new friends they relied less on Facebook for this purpose. Mitch explored this theme as part of his map of digital and non-digital experiences when he included his primary school friends, or 'ex-friends' as he called them. He drew a pair of scissors cutting the line connecting him to this group because as he explained he was 'slowly losing connection with them'.

Like Dylan, Heidi found Facebook smoothed the transition to new and different places and situations. Having attended seven different schools throughout her life, she used the platform to maintain communication with 'old' friends. In particular, Facebook was useful when she arrived in Australia, where she knew few people:

> When I moved countries I felt very alone and I felt it was all different and it was the only thing that stayed normal, because it [Facebook] hadn't changed. So I was like if I go on here it's like you look for stuff that's very familiar, that hasn't changed. So that's the one thing, for the first year I was very like … I relied on it a lot, and then afterwards, after you get your own friends, it came back normally.

In Heidi's description the constancy of the platform across countries is a distinct advantage. While everything else around her was changing, Facebook stayed the same. However, this also highlights a global 'way of being' facilitated by the Facebook platform.

The convenience of Facebook also increased the young people's use of the platform. As Sean explained, email has a more convoluted login process: 'I need to go on the internet I need to Google "Gmail" and then I have to log in … whereas I click a tab and I've got Facebook straightaway and it'll tell me if I've got notifications or messages.' The simplicity of 'checking' Facebook made it easy to form habitual digital practices, which could become hard to break. When Heidi started her senior years of high school she thought about taking a break from Facebook to concentrate on her studies, but as she explained, 'it's not worth it' because she felt the 'need to know stuff'.

Fear of missing out on posts, invitations and general gossip was a strong motivator for using Facebook. This was not surprising given that a major part of the business model of technology companies such as Facebook is to create habits that encourage the user to keep returning to the site as often as possible (Greenwald, 2015). This compulsion to check and be aware of others' affairs is established not only through the notifications users receive on Facebook, but through the type of information that is shared, so that you start, in Mark's words, 'tracking real-life friends'. As Heidi explained, the information shared gives a sense of omniscience that can become addictive:

> Well you become more sociable and you know more about lots of people because you're constantly seeing it—it's being fed to you all the time. You're in everybody's little business, which isn't always great, but you always know what's happening over there, happening over there, happening over there. Like in a school you'll have certain groups and you know what's happening in that group even though you've probably never spoken to them.

For some of the young people Facebook was key to maintaining awareness of what was happening with celebrities and the entertainment industry. As Penny explained: 'You kind of feel in the loop as well because even when stuff happens like with celebrities and stuff, I've liked Fox FM and they're often posting and you can read articles and things about what's going on in the world.' Chantelle, who was not on Facebook, felt like she missed out on things with her peers because, as she explained, 'a lot of the conversation is you know what was funny with You-Tube, what was the conversation on Facebook'. In a similar way, before getting the internet connected at home Mark felt 'out of the loop', but now he can 'actually start a conversation about something on the internet and be able to be involved in that process'. Being a Facebook user was important to both online *and* offline conversations and interactions.

All those on Facebook stated the main reason for their being on the platform was to stay informed about what was happening in other people's lives—particularly, friends, family and celebrities. As a consequence, the young people shaped their posts to suit the expectations of their audience. Heidi's posts on Facebook were designed to 'let people know what you're *actually* up to'. Whereas Dylan used Facebook to 'communicate events and stuff … it's much easier to show stuff I guess'. Digital connections facilitated through the Facebook News Feed were composed of photos and posts of events and news so that the young people were *projecting* the self into the digital space. Typically this was the participants' 'best' self—doing something exciting, such as participating in a debutante ball, performing in a dance concert or attending a relative's wedding.

Projecting the self was also about seeking the affirmation of others. While this could be a positive process, it also involved peer judgement, which could induce anxiety. Several girls posted very little on social media and reported that they did not do much apart from looking and liking others' posts. As Grace explained: 'I don't post that much. I don't know, I just like looking through what other people post, that sounds kind of weird … there's just not a lot to write about.' Similarly, Penny put up very few posts, so that her use of Facebook often involved projecting herself via photos and commenting and liking other people's photos; as she said, 'I don't write that many posts or statuses'.

Four young people in the study described their use of Facebook as 'passive', meaning they rarely engaged in creating and uploading content or communicating with others. For research Provocation 4—*Re-articulating the icons of the internet*, Heidi chose to represent a Facebook 'friend' as a link in a chain because, as she explains, 'they're more like a communication link or a link to someone else' (Figure 5.1).

She went on to explain that often when you add a friend on Facebook, 'you never communicate, you never chat with them'. To Heidi friends were not necessarily people to share a discourse with, but instead 'links' through which information passed. To confirm this the young people only regularly communicated with a small number of 'friends'. For example, Penny had 1,200 friends on

FIGURE 5.1 Heidi's redesigned Facebook 'friend' icon

Facebook, but only communicated with about 20 of them; Dylan also had 1,200 friends but only communicated with about 14 of them. It might be that the architecture of Facebook helped reify the varying levels of friendships in the young people's lives, from close to distant.

While most of the young people only communicated with a small percentage of their Facebook friends, *all* friends could see a post on the News Feed. This increased the pressures associated with uploading content, which made some young people reluctant to post at all. Sean explained, 'I have so many people on Facebook I don't really want to send them stuff that I don't want them to see'. Sean was a member of a Facebook group started by one of his friends called 'United Against Abbott', which shared political and satirical critiques of the then Australian Prime Minister Tony Abbott. Sean's posts or comments on the group's page were visible to his family and family friends, who were occasionally offended by the more controversial content. This had become difficult for Sean to manage, so he had stopped posting onto the News Feed and instead communicated with friends by text.

In doing so Sean was able to manage the context collapse (Marwick & boyd, 2014; Vitak, 2012) that takes place on Facebook due to having such a diverse audience. He described social media platforms, like Facebook and Tumblr, as 'less private' because 'anything you say can be seen by another … any person can see your profile or whatever'. He likened these social media platforms to a room: 'So instead of talking to one person you're shouting to one person in a room full of thousands of people'—an offline practice that he would never normally engage in. As a result, posts on Facebook tended to be controlled, conservative, one-way projections of self, rarely becoming interactive and spontaneous. In fact, Sean had decreased his use of social media and cited the difficulties in negotiating context collapse as a reason for this.

Both Facebook and Instagram are designed for connecting and 'sharing' with friends and family, and several of the young people did say they felt a sense of belonging when using social media. However, three others expressed a more complex array of feelings. As Stacey explained, using Facebook was just like 'browsing', not conversing or interacting with others: 'I don't join in with many of the conversations people have so it's like you don't really feel like you belong on it.' Trent and Mitch described Facebook in more negative terms, explaining that they felt more connected to the gaming platform Steam. In a group discussion, Trent, Mitch, Simon and Stacey described Facebook as a 'food chain', with the 'popular' people taking the place of the tertiary predators at the top of the chain:

LUCI: … *So you're saying that by putting people down they become popular?*
TRENT: They go up the food chain.
STACEY: Yeah, very much.
MITCH: Yeah.
SIMON: If someone's ahead of you, you make them stand down and you move up.
LUCI: *Right you …*
STACEY: It's like basically a food chain.

MITCH: So if you're down here and someone's up here [gesturing vertically], you
    have to get through all these people to be this popular.
LUCI: *And how do you do that?*
TRENT: Well you know you bully them, put them down.
STACEY: You lower the people behind, under you …
TRENT: Make them self-conscious.
STACEY: You make the ones under you feel uncomfortable and you befriend the
    ones, slowly befriend the ones that are going higher.

This discussion was revealing not only because of the hostile behaviour descri-bed, but because all those present in the workshop concurred with the depiction of Facebook as a 'food chain'. Implicit to this hierarchical description of social rela-tionships is the idea that those at the top of the chain have more power and con-trol. The 'social Darwinism' they described playing out on Facebook was an extension of the dispositions toward knowledge and power discussed in Chapter 3.

Unlike a study by Merten (1997), which found that hierarchised social networks are more common in girls, in this study both boys and girls had experienced cyberbullying. Nilan et al. (2015) describe these patterns of behaviour as 'linked fields of struggle' (p.6), where social and cultural capital are often expressed through forms of harassment. In this way, online 'peer teasing' is a 'means of building social capital with friends and classmates' (p.7). As explained in Chapter 4, popularity is also linked to likes and therefore the number of friends people have. Underpinning this system, however, is the currency itself—the 'image' or the projected identity of the individual, which becomes a kind of commodity to be cultivated and condensed through the platform. It is perhaps not surprising, then, that some young people described little sense of belonging or connection to Facebook as their digital practices often involved appraisal and judge-ment by peers. Some experienced this sense of depersonalisation more acutely and more often than others. While there were obviously other factors that contributed to the way Trent felt about himself, Facebook appeared to surface his anxieties and con-cerns as he became quite impassioned when asked about it, stating 'I hate Facebook'.

Interacting with others—Facebook Chat, text message and Skype messenger

Distinct from the digital connections facilitated via the News Feed, Facebook also facilitated messaging through its chat service. Clicking on a Facebook friend opens a chat box in the bottom right of the screen so a private message can be sent. More than one Facebook friend can be included in the message. For these young people Facebook Chat fulfilled a similar role to that of text messaging and Skype mes-senger in that the audience, purpose and context for the message were often very similar. Skype messenger is a free instant messaging service, which is promoted as an alternative to talking with friends. While text messages take place via mobile phones, Skype messenger can be used on mobile phones, laptop or desktop computers.

For many of the young people, Facebook Chat was reported to be a useful way to interact with friends and family on Facebook, and facilitated a more private and sustained dialogue. In some instances, the young people reported using Facebook Chat to organise events and complete group assignments for school via the creation of a 'Group Chat'. Text messaging and Skype messenger were also common ways to interact with others, and similarly there was often quite a functional purpose behind these interactions.

Digital interactions via these forms of media appeared to involve a more intimate group of people, typically friends and family. Text message was often used to communicate with parents, in particular to organise being picked up. As Grace explained: 'I would use like text messages and stuff quite a lot like to get picked up and let mum and dad know where I am and stuff and what I'm doing. But no social media.' Ling and Yttri (2002) call this type of communication 'micro-coordination' in which the mobile phone is used to impart 'functional and instrumental' information. Despite her parents having access to all her internet accounts, Stacey used her mobile phone only to interact with her parents. Three of the young people in the study shared a mobile phone with their siblings. The main purpose they cited for using the phone was to communicate with parents about the time and location of being picked up.

Text messaging was another important way to interact with friends. Sometimes this had a functional purpose, such as finding out about homework or, as Grace explained, to find out 'what you answered for certain questions'. But typically interactions with friends via text message were social in nature. Sean used text message to communicate directly with friends rather than social media because he 'always' had his phone on him. For Heidi, the iMessage service on her iPhone actually encouraged more frequent interactions with her peers. It was always available and free, as she explains: 'it was available all the time, so as soon as I bought an iPhone we got iMessage and I was using it all the time. And well a heap of people have iPhones and are sending free messages to you so it's an easy way, cheap way. I think it was purely money based.' For Heidi iMessage helped expand her social networks. However, for others text messaging was saved for close friends. As Rachel explained, she 'doesn't really talk to a lot of them [her friends] on social media'; she would prefer to 'call them or text them'.

The young people often described Facebook Chat as 'talking' to people on social media so that it was seen as similar to face-to-face discussion. Rachel described 'normal friends' as people she would 'talk' to online *and* offline. If friends were only offline or only online Rachel described them as 'not always there', so they were not able to share the full range of experiences. Important to Rachel in establishing intimate relationships was what Archer (2007) calls 'contextual continuity', where 'communality of landmarks together with experiential overlap facilitates the sharing of internal conversations' (p.84). As well as knowing peers face to face, an essential step in developing intimacy is being on the same social media platforms or present with them across contexts. Unlike text messaging, however, Facebook Chat can be used to interact with more than one person.

Maddy explained that once her friends reached 13 and were able to sign up to Facebook, they 'migrated' from MSN Messenger to Facebook and Facebook Chat: 'And then before you know it everyone's on Facebook and everyone who was using Messenger used Facebook so you could talk to them.'

For the girls in the study, Facebook Chat was used for a variety of purposes: to organise events; complete group projects or to simply hang out online. For example, Penny would often organise school projects over Facebook: 'If I'm in a group presentation then maybe if everyone has Facebook, I'll go "OK guys I'm doing this" and whatever. And then [organise a] group chat.' As she explained, this was easier than using email because 'you have to reply to the latest [email] rather than the other ones'. The interaction that took place as part of a group project—involving negotiation and back-and-forth discussion—appeared to be better facilitated through the chat service. Organising events and gatherings was also made easier through Facebook Chat. As Grace explained: 'We talk a lot on social media, like on Facebook we use the messenger a lot to talk, because then you can like have a big group conversation about something if you want to meet up somewhere or something like that.' But Rachel was the exception among the young women in the study, as she explained that the 'massive' group chat was a passing fad that 'just died down' after a while.

While few of the young people in the study reported using Skype to message friends and family, Penny explained that the 'younger generation' (her younger sister and her friends) used Skype messenger. Penny's observation illustrated the socially situated nature of digital media use for the young people: if friends were not using a particular platform then there was no point in being on it. As she explained, 'if you were on something like MySpace, no one is on MySpace so you are not going to be able to do what it's meant for'. Awareness of what peers were doing not only shaped which social media platforms individuals used, but also how they used them. As digital platforms exhaust themselves, new ones emerge, so that the young people's participation was migratory in nature.

Over the course of the study Stacey started using Skype more frequently, not only because it bonded her more closely to her friends, but also because it was instant and she could surreptitiously use it while at school:

> I always use Skype just to communicate with friends in other classes from school, to ask for help or if they need help they can talk to me. If they had some problem and they are not able to get out of class and they need to get it off their chest, they're able to talk to me about it.

Skype messenger enabled Stacey to let her friends know she was there for them, so, as she explained: 'If someone needs me it'll pop up and I'll quietly send them a message.' While Stacey had quite a complicated relationship with other social media like Facebook, Skype messenger allowed her to interact in a more direct way with close friends when it came to issues that were more intimate and personal. When using this particular social media platform she appeared to feel more in control of her digital connections.

Despite this somewhat more controlled and direct method of interacting with others, the young people still reported negotiating complex issues when using these chat and messaging services. Stacey still preferred 'social interactions with actual people instead of online' because, as she explained, 'I can actually tell their expressions and normally I don't misunderstand any of it'. Facial expressions and body language helped her comprehend the intentions of others. She admitted that when online, 'I misunderstand a lot of things'. This was a recurring theme in the group discussions. Dylan reported online interactions as having a specific set of challenges, as he explained that sometimes 'the tone seems off' and people can sound 'blunt and angry'. To temper this, he used emoticons to sound 'nicer' and 'less robotic'. Sean also identified the difficulty in communicating tone, and like Dylan saw the benefit in using emoticons so that people could more easily 'convey how they feel'.

A study by Fullwood and Martino (2007) found that using emoticons in online interactions conveys greater socio-emotional information, thereby alleviating 'some of the constraints associated with cue-restricted communication' (n.p.). But emoticons could also be used to disguise a spiteful message, making it more difficult for the recipient to decipher the purpose of the message. As Chantelle explained, someone can be 'brutal' and then just put 'a smiley face to make it seem lighter [so] you've no idea what they're actually doing'.

Aside from the challenges in communicating tone, digital connections of this kind afforded these young people a more private and controlled method of interacting with others. These media were often used for functional or organisational purposes to communicate with people whom they saw in person regularly (e.g. parents or school friends), but also to 'chat' with peers online. Of all the social media platforms explored in this chapter, this type of communication is perhaps closest to the spoken word in that it is usually synchronous and spontaneous. At the same time, without the gestural and expressive cues to accompany the written word, several young people explained that misunderstandings could easily take place. While the social group influenced which platform the young people engaged with, the platform architecture shaped the frequency, audience and content of the digital engagements that actually took place. Analysed in this way some platforms like Facebook Chat and Skype enabled connection with others in a more detailed and sustained way.

Cooperating with others—Steam, YouTube and Wattpad

The most popular gaming platform that these young people used was Steam. Steam is a digital distribution platform developed by Valve Corporation and was launched in 2002. It offers digital rights management, multiplayer games, video streaming and social networking services. Five boys in the study were frequent users of Steam, while one girl, Rachel, also played, but not regularly. For Mark, Simon, Trent and Mitch, Steam was the platform they spent most time on. Trent was on Steam about 15 hours a week. Sean was also a regular player on Steam. While gaming was an integral part of the boys' digital practices, it was not common among the girls in the group.

Wattpad and Quotev were writing websites that offered a similar context for cooperation and dialogue. As mentioned in Chapter 2, Rachel used Wattpad to hone her skills as a writer. Like Steam, these websites offered opportunities to collaborate with peers, creating an informal community of practice for users. Rachel's use of Wattpad and the practices she engaged in on the site scaffolded her identity as a writer.

Not only was YouTube used for entertainment and learning, but it was also seen as a positive space for discussion and collaboration with friends and strangers. As already discussed, Mark and Simon worked with others to design and create their YouTube channel 'Screencheats'. For many of the young men it appeared easier to initiate digital connections through these sorts of platforms as not only was there a common interest, purpose or goal, but social exchanges appeared to emerge 'organically' as a result of 'hanging out' together online.

The digital connections that take place through these platforms were often more cooperative in nature, as individuals worked to build skills and knowledge about particular topics. At times, they also practised conflict management and resolution. On Steam digital practices were often about cooperating with others in order to win a game. As Mark explained: 'I play a lot of games online and when I do I'm constantly with people I don't know talking to them, telling them things like "This is how we should do this!"' Part of the appeal with Steam was that players could keep their identity anonymous, only revealing their username and avatar to those they knew and trusted as friends.

Mark had organised a group on Steam so that he and his friends could 'play games at specific times'. When not playing with friends, the boys did not know or care to know who they were playing with. For someone like Trent, who spoke often about being bullied, even a small degree of anonymity was liberating. When the bullying was at its worst the only platform Trent used was Steam because, as he explained, 'that's where people didn't know me and the few friends I had on Steam were really just friends that weren't bullying'. Steam was also appealing because it was a place for fellow gamers. According to Trent, gamers are often teased by others, so sticking together was important: 'I can just get into a group of people that like playing games like me because these days people are always playing sport and things and just bagging out stuff like that [video games].'

On platforms like Steam and YouTube some of the young people found it easier to talk to others. Mark felt more comfortable initiating conversation with people online because, as he explained, in real life he felt like he needed a more explicit purpose:

> When … it's someone like you actually know online it's easier to be like 'Hi, how're you doing?' but in real life you kind of need to have something to talk to, like to talk about with them.

That said, others like Mitch felt that it was easier to initiate conversation in person as you could 'read' their 'body language' to determine whether you should approach them or not. Despite this, Mark and Simon reported that having a ready-made topic that could be shared and discussed made it easier to initiate conversation in the digital context, as Mark explained:

> If I watch a YouTube video then I'm there to watch the YouTube video and so is everyone else. So if I comment on the video then I'm not going to be like 'Hey, have you seen this?' And they're like 'No'. They're going to be like 'Yeah what did you think?' And then it's going to be a lot easier to talk to those specific people.

Mark maintained that platforms like YouTube, Wattpad and Steam 'broaden the amount of people you can talk to about a specific thing', and for some young people, like Mark and Rachel, this was clearly viewed as advantageous. While Mark and Rachel viewed these people as 'strangers', they still valued the digital connections that were forged. In Rachel's case, receiving feedback and cooperating with people on the writing website Wattpad was a way of connecting with people beyond school and home who could help her develop her writing skills.

Both Simon and Trent used Steam as a way of socialising with others. Initially Simon's parents did not allow him to have Facebook, but he no longer saw a use for it because he and his friends 'socialised' through Steam. Similarly, while Trent was on Facebook, he said 'I spend a lot of time on Steam rather than Facebook'. When a friend comes online a player receives an alert and from there they can begin a dialogue. As Simon explained:

> That's the way we connect. It'd be like we're sitting there Friday afternoon and I'd see if anyone's online and I'd start a conversation saying 'Do you want to hang over the weekend … or if you can't do anything on Saturday, do you want to do something on Sunday?'

For this group of boys Steam was their primary means of connecting online with others. As Mark said, 'all of my close friends that I have, I have on Steam … it's basically where I talk to people really online'. He explained that the content of these types of discussions might be about the game or 'anything really … like something that happened in the day or something in the game'.

However, Sean and Simon had both had negative experiences on Steam. While these experiences were not pleasant, both boys recognised that they helped them develop skills to negotiate and manage conflict in 'real life'. Working through these negative exchanges online was viewed as good practice for how to handle such experiences offline. While the main form of communication that took place on these cooperative platforms was through a chat system similar to that of Facebook Chat and Skype messenger, having a common interest or affinity shaped these digital connections so participants were essentially 'cooperating' and conversing with others.

Communicating more formally—email

Given that the iconography, language and structure of email is based on the old-fashioned postal letter (i.e. 'send', 'address', envelope symbol), it is not surprising that participants typically used this to communicate more formally with an adult audience. Mostly the email accounts were school-based; however, two young people had additional Gmail accounts. Given this context, it is not surprising that the main reason for the young people to send an email was to either find out information from a teacher or send them documents for assessment.

For three students at the same school, starting a school email account was a significant turning point in their learning. It was described as improving communication with teachers so that it was more direct and needs-based. Prior to year 7 Grace never used email to 'contact people'; however, she now found it a 'helpful' support to her 'learning'. Maddy described it as 'a new way of learning with teachers and stuff'. At another school, four students regularly used email to submit work to teachers, but not to seek clarification or missed work. Mark explained: 'Every time I need to hand something in I'll email them with the work.' Mitch suggested that emailing assignments helped teachers as well because 'if they lose it they can just re-enter their emails and get it'. Both schools had learning management systems (Compass at one and SEQTA at another); however, email was the preferred way of contacting teachers for these young people.

Simon and Chantelle were not on any social media platforms, so they occasionally used email for social purposes. Simon explained that if he could not contact someone through Steam he would email the person. Chantelle used email for 'school', 'work' and 'uni applications', and sometimes to contact friends (once in the last month). Her parents were also encouraging her to email her grandparents in Canada. For the other 11 young people, however, email was not used socially; as Grace explained, she would 'never' use it on the weekends. In Maddy's view it was the limited audience and asynchronous way of communicating that made email unappealing for social interactions:

> You can't like talk because they only have limited people there and not all your friends are there and you want to talk to them. Facebook is instant, because email is going to take a while to get through, or it just takes too long using an email, so you might want to go on Facebook and message.

While the young people viewed email as an important mode of digital communication, particularly for school-related learning, it was, in the main, used for a formal audience, with a particular purpose in mind.

Testing provisional aspects of self—Snapchat and Qooh.me

Given the ephemeral and fragmentary nature of the digital connections on Snapchat and Qooh.me, the young people tended to use these platforms for the transmission of risky content. Snapchat is a photo messaging application established in 2011 that had gained widespread popularity at the time of the study. In 2014 Snapchat enabled users to send photos or 'Snaps' to 'friends' who could then view the photos for between one and ten seconds, after which time the photos were hidden from view and deleted from Snapchat servers. Six of the young people were regular users of Snapchat. Five young people in the group also used Qooh. me, a service that allowed users to ask one another questions anonymously. However, only Rachel was still a regular user.

Both these services purposefully omit elements of communication—either the identity of the speaker in the case of Qooh.me, or the content itself after a designated time with Snapchat—encouraging a digital connection that tested more hidden and risqué aspects of self through the photos sent or the questions asked. These less traditional modes of communication encouraged exchanges that 'tested' the boundaries of identity communication between friends.

While Dylan used Snapchat for 'documenting his days with all his friends', the ephemerality of these digital connections often encouraged him to share more playful or risqué content with others. In both types of engagements, however, communication was designed to strengthen bonds with others even if it was, at times, 'testing' what was appropriate content for communication. Dylan explained that he would often reference 'a little inside joke' or 'take a picture of it' for his Snaps and send it to his friends. However, sometimes he would send more risky Snaps like a 'really ugly double chin selfie' but only to 'certain people'. As Heidi explained, the risk was not only how Snaps would be received, but also the fact that recipients 'screenshot' and 'post a lot of them' to other social media platforms, which could be 'embarrassing'.

Heidi, like Grace and Penny, followed a particular rule to protect herself against social embarrassment, as she explained: 'You've just got to be careful. I would never send anything out [that] if they did screenshot I wouldn't mind it being on the internet.' Due to the more intimate nature of the content shared, Snapchat could be used to cement or further develop social relationships as the young people disclosed more intimate details about themselves through this messaging service. In a sense the young people were testing how friends would receive these exchanges and this aspect of their identity.

At the time of the fieldwork Snapchat enabled users to make some posts visible on their timeline for up to 24 hours to create a 'story'. As Dylan explained, he put 'Snaps' that he was proud of onto his 'story':

> If it's not joking around and you're just like showing off something or you're serious about or like you're proud of something just like put it up on your story which you can for like 24 hours view it.

In this way there was a relationship between audience and content, so the more risky the content the more intimate the audience. This content was not necessarily sexual in nature, but as Dylan explained, it might be 'embarrassing' or 'something you want to keep as a joke or private'.

Despite common misconceptions, a survey of 5,475 Snapchat users aged 18–29 years by Kelly (2013) in the US found only 13.1 per cent of respondents said they used it for sexting. However, the short 'life span' of a Snap encourages users to take risks in how they communicate with others. Perhaps a more fitting explanation for the riskier content is that given by Pielot and Oliver (2014), who argue that ephemerality not only adds 'excitement', but also 'removes a need for perfection' (n.p.). In this way Snapchat offers a distinctly different experience from other forms of social media where the dominant mode of engagement is projecting pre-dominately positive and perfected versions of self for affirmation and commentary.

Another service that offered a less traditional form of communication was Qooh. me, where users could ask each other questions anonymously. Vincent Mabuza, founder of Qooh.me, says that the service 'makes it easier for people to get to know more about each other, beyond the information they post on their social media profiles' (Wilson, 2011, n.p.). In most cases the young people embedded a link to Qooh.me on their Facebook News Feed with a comment encouraging friends to ask them questions. Once they click on the link it connects to the individual's Qooh.me page, where the anonymous visitor can then ask questions. They appeared to use Qooh.me for a range of reasons, but the captions in Figure 5.2 reveal that it had much to do with alleviating boredom and loneliness. But sometimes the caption became more provocative, perhaps priming the questioner to ask more sensational or challenging questions (Figure 5.3).

Qooh.me only works if users find the individual is interesting enough to ask questions of. Revealed in these comments was a deliberate (and often awkward) ambiguity between appealing to others without trying to appear desperate or needy, hence the more belligerent or humorous approaches.

As Maddy explained, people often used Qooh.me to 'test' whether a relationship might become romantic:

> Anyone who asks something is anonymous so no one can know so you always get asked like, teenage kind of things like 'Who do you like?' And then that could be the person that likes you, hoping you would say their name.

Following the link to the Qooh.me site revealed that many discussions focused on romantic relationships (the posts at the bottom are the oldest). Maddy explained that these kinds of exchanges could lead to awkward and uncomfortable questions, particularly if a parent happened to see it:

> Someone asked me a question and my dad had clicked on it and it was so awkward, because it was not a good question that they should have asked. And I didn't answer it … I handled it well, but it was just like, really?

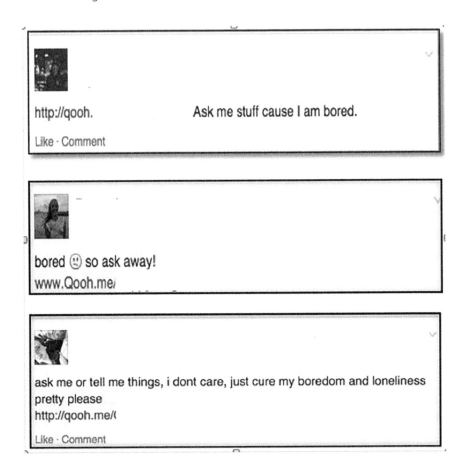

FIGURE 5.2 Screenshots of the participant's invitations to Qooh.me

Maddy, Penny and Grace had all stopped using Qooh.me; Penny decided it was just 'not interesting' and stopped doing it because 'people just ask stupid questions and some of them are really rude'.

While most of the young people treated Qooh.me in a cautiously playful manner, Rachel and Mark engaged more enthusiastically and earnestly with the service and as a result were asked more controversial, risky or challenging topics. In some instances they played the role of counsellor or confidant to the questioner, but at other times roles were reversed and they were expected to give honest, truthful answers to questions posed. Typical questions were: 'Who are your favourite people at work?' or 'Why aren't we friends anymore?' Others became more serious, with one poster asking Mark, 'Why shouldn't I kill myself?'

In these exchanges Qooh.me had become like a confessional in which the anonymous user or the respondent 'offloaded' their troubles while at the same time testing how another might respond to their innermost thoughts and feelings. If the young people gave some consideration to the questions posed, these digital

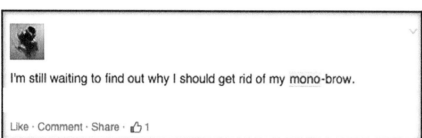

FIGURE 5.3 Screenshots of Dylan's and Mark's invitations to Qooh.me

engagements quickly became more intimate, personal and detailed. Other topics mentioned involved taking medication, issues of self-esteem and thoughts on people at school. Answers were often carefully delivered, just in case the person asking was the actual subject they were referring to. Interestingly, at times people would ask questions with their identity visible, yet these questions were still of a sensitive or personal nature, suggesting that the structure of the medium also promoted particular forms of engagement, and temporary intimacy.

While the use of these less popular forms of social media was short-lived for some young people, the enthusiasm for services like Snapchat and Qooh.me suggest they afforded something that mainstream social media like Facebook and Instagram did not. Rather than projecting their 'best' identity, these services enabled a protected way to test covert, controversial or risqué behaviour. In more sustained instances, dialogue on Qooh.me could be described as confessional in tone and style. In an era when all types of digital engagements can be logged, saved and traced, exchanges that were in some way obscure or ephemeral appeared liberating, and in some instances on Qooh.me, even redemptive.

Platform participation—technologically and socially situated

Driving the culture of online communication was a need to connect—with people, concepts and content. While the young people initiated a range of communicative strategies, this chapter has demonstrated that there were five typical patterns to their use: *projecting* the self via Facebook and Instagram; *interacting* with others through synchronous text messaging and chat services; *cooperating* with others through Steam and other affinity websites; *communicating* more formally through email; and *testing* provisional aspects of self via other social media platforms, like Snapchat and Qooh.me. This is not to deny the existence of other digital connections, but to show that despite differences in the age, education and socio-economic background, there were still obvious trends to the way the young people used digital media to connect with others.

While the structure and parameters of the platform shaped the type of communicative strategies that were established, these findings also point to the socially embedded nature of these interactions. The young people in this study were accomplished at initiating digital connections to reflect and reinforce varying levels of friendship; however, the platform played an important role in steering how these relationships were experienced. Digital media opened up new methods of communicating with others but these were directed in quite particular and sometimes constrained ways. This was a source of reticence and anxiety for some. Digital connections that involved projecting the self made several young people feel vulnerable, mainly because of the fear of being judged negatively or simply rebuffed. Complicating this was the need to be on certain core social media platforms, like Facebook and Instagram, regardless of how the young people felt about or experienced them. Digital connections that were somehow more 'protected' from the social milieu, either through the anonymity or ephemerality of the medium or through a shared goal or interest, reduced the effect of these social pressures.

Each digital platform encouraged particular types of digital connection, which often led the young people to reveal different aspects of their identity. Communicating through Facebook, for example, often encouraged the projection of their 'best' self in what might be thought of as a kind of grown up 'show and tell'. By contrast, Qooh.me facilitated more transitory or experimental versions of self. Beneito-Montagut (2015) arrived at similar findings in her online ethnography. While the participants in her study were older, she describes a 'ritual set' based around language, topics, gestures and, crucially, the 'applications' affordances' that establish 'rules of performance in an implicit way' (p.24). As she goes on to explain, 'once these rules are fixed by the use of a particular social web application or system, there is a set of ritualised procedures for pointing out deviance and correcting deviant acts' (pp.24–25).

Returning to Gillespie's (2010) definition of the platform as both 'computational' and 'conceptual' helps make sense of the young people's experiences. Connectedness is not just *within and between individuals*, but also *with the platform*, so that communication is also shaped along the lines set by platform operators (van Dijck, 2013). One example of this was the young people's ongoing commitment to Facebook, despite their negative experiences on the platform. For five young people in this study using Facebook invoked a sense of consternation. On the one hand they felt compelled to be on it, but on the other they recognised that it rarely brought them any enjoyment. While Mark did not 'hate' Facebook in the same way that Trent did, he demonstrated little affection for it, describing it as 'boring', logging in once a month at the most. Despite this, he had no intention of deactivating his account. It appeared as though it was a social expectation to use Facebook, meaning very few in the study had seriously entertained the idea of leaving this 'core' social media platform.

Evident here are the implicit forces circulating through the digital dispositif that 'summon subjects to be and remain almost always connected in already given sociotechnical arrangements' (Isin & Ruppert, 2015, p.86). Examining the young people's experiences indicates that these arrangements can be hard to shift or change. For example, email was unlikely to be used for social purposes, as Instagram, Facebook and Snapchat were *the* platforms for connecting with friends. The monopolisation of the digital context by only a few digital platforms makes it difficult for other types of digital communication to emerge. The findings in this chapter extend upon those of Chapter 3, where the architecture of the platform was found to be an overriding feature of the digital dispositif (Foucault, 1980). Analysis of the socially and technically situated nature of the young people's platform participation reveals how the digital dispositif compels them toward particular gestures, behaviours and practices. We can think about this happening at a couple of different levels across the digital dispositif.

Network effects or network externalities play a role in the creation of what the young people described as 'core' social media platforms. The theory of network effects comes from economics, and claims that the value of a platform depends on the number of users it has (Katz & Shapiro, 1986; Rohn, 2013). In the context of social media platforms, the more users a platform has the more valuable it becomes as a communication service to its members. Facebook, for example, has become the default social networking service in many parts of the world because the sheer number of users means that it is the most logical place for individuals to connect with friends online. However, institutions, companies and other community groups are also drawn to using the platform because it connects them to the public in useful ways. As participation increases, so too does the amount of data generated, which improves the reliability of the platform algorithms to suggest, recommend and match information between all parties. As Belleflamme and Peitz (2016, p.5) explain, this 'enhances the quality of the platform service and, thereby, the utility of all users'. Network effects help explain why the young people had accounts on the platform even when they felt ambivalent about its role in their lives. Through its popularity Facebook has a particular social value that many young people felt they could not afford to miss.

The platform interface was particularly important in structuring experiences. For several young people the dominance of the visual image in the Facebook News Feed was interpreted as prioritising appearance. Similarly, the use of metrics such as the likes or the number of friends one has became a source of anxiety for several participants. While digital media could provide opportunities for becoming more playful or subversives identities, often the young people were more concerned with engaging in practices that were acceptable to the specific context. As a result, each user adopted a tacit set of rules and strategies to manage these pressures. To several young people the strategy was to be present, but not actively post, while others, like Rachel, set up an alternative profile that could be more controlled and intimate (see Chapter 4). While these strategies were associated with feelings of consternation and confusion, they were largely 'interiorized by individuals' (Langlois et al., 2009, p.6) as the overriding discourse positioned them to participate.

The platform acts as a kind of framing device for the information and interactions that unfold. While platforms might appear decentralised, in reality it is only content creation that is decentralised. The platform position is one of an intermediary, managing or governing the terms of the relationships between parties through the manner and volume of interactions. Platforms are also able to increase their reach and social value by diversifying and expanding their features. For example, through their instant messaging services Facebook and Skype provide users with another reason for using the platform, claiming the space previously occupied by text message. In this way the platform becomes a kind of 'drawing and framing machine' (Bratton, 2015, p.85), accentuating particular aspects and modes of communication and downplaying others. At the end of 2016, for example, Facebook deprioritised links to the outside web in the News Feed, as operators worked to keep users on the platform for as long as possible (Tufekci, 2016). The problem is that users are not made aware of these changes, so what might appear as impartial broadcasting of posts and status updates is in fact highly organised. Most of the young people in this study were not aware of these processes, suggesting there is much work to be done in building understanding of the materialities of the digital dispositif.

Conclusions

In the last three chapters I have sought to untangle the lines within the digital dispositif. As Deleuze (1992) writes, this is akin to 'drawing up a map, doing cartography, surveying unknown landscapes' (Deleuze, 1992, p.159). The 'map' that has emerged of the young people's digital experiences is not a neat one, and there are many parts that overlap, merge and conflict with others. However, through the process of drawing up the map we have arrived at a sense of the complex and contradictory terrain young people must navigate as part of the everyday digital.

The findings of this chapter suggest that the role of digital platforms in shaping practices needs to be more carefully considered. Platforms, and the publics that emerge as a result, can become networks for participation and empowerment. However, they also raise questions of representation, social obligation and assurance, particularly with regard to the mainstream social media platforms, most notably Facebook. Of course young people have found ways to subvert the dominant ways of being and doing that platform operators encourage. Indeed, these young people provide glimpses of what critical digital literacies of the future might look like. However, these critical practices are often fleeting and sporadic.

To be enacted in a more active and conscious manner, critical digital literacies need to be discussed and practised—two factors that were decidedly absent from the young people's everyday life. At this age political and critical sensibilities are beginning to emerge, meaning educators and researchers need to consider what a critical pedagogy of social media platforms might entail. However, it is also at this time that digital platforms hobble political and critical becoming via the social and technical elements of the digital dispositif. In the final two chapters of this book I analyse the insights gathered over the course of the four empirical chapters with a particular focus on what this means for digital literacies. I consider how we might reimagine an approach to critical digital literacies that supports young people as they negotiate the challenges of the current media landscape.

References

Archer, M. S. (2007). *Making Our Way Through The World: Human Reflexivity and Social Mobility*. Cambridge, UK: Cambridge University Press.

Belleflamme, P., & Peitz, M. (2016). Platforms and network effects. In L. Corchon, M. Marini, & E. Elgar (Eds.), *Handbook of Game Theory and Industrial Organization*. Elsevier.

Bennett, A., & Robards, B. (2013). *Mediated Youth Culture: The Internet, Belonging and New Cultural Configurations*. Basingstoke: Palgrave.

Beneito-Montagut, R. (2015). Encounters on the social web: Everyday life and emotions online. *Sociological Perspectives*, 58(4), doi:10.1177/0731121415569284

boyd, d. (2011). Social network sites as networked publics: affordances, dynamics and implications. In Z. Papacharissi (Ed.), *A Networked Self: Identity, Community, and Culture*. New York: Routledge.

boyd, d. (2014). *It's Complicated: The Social Lives of Networked Teens*. New Haven and London: Yale University Press.

Bratton, B. (2015). *The Stack: On Software and Sovereignty*. Cambridge, MA: The MIT Press.

Bucher, T. (2012). Want to be on the top? Algorithmic power and the threat of invisibility of Facebook. *New Media & Society*, 14(7), 1164–1180.

Couldry, N. (2015). The myth of 'us': Digital networks, political change and the production of collectivity. *Information, Communication & Society*, 18(6), 608–626.

Deleuze, G. (1992). What is a dispositif? In T. J. Armstrong (Ed.), *Michel Foucault Philosopher* (pp.159–168). Hemel Hempstead: Harvester Wheatsheaf.

Dyer, H. (2015). All the web's a stage: The effects of design and modality on youth performances of identity. In S. L. Blair, P. N. Claster, & S. M. Claster (Eds.), *Technology and Youth: Growing Up in a Digital World*. Bingley, UK: Emerald Group Publishing Limited.

Foucault, M. (1980). *Power/Knowledge: Selected Interviews & Other Writings*. New York: Pantheon Books.

Fullwood, C., & Martino, O. (2007). Emoticons and Impression Formation. *The Visual in Popular Culture*, 19(7), 4–14.

Gerlitz, C., & Helmond, A. (2013). The like economy: Social buttons and the data-intensive web. *New Media & Society*, 15(8), 1348–1365.

Gillespie, T. (2010). The politics of 'platforms'. *New Media & Society*, 12(3), 347–364.

Gorriz, C., & Medina, C. (2000). Engaging girls with computers through software games. *Communication of the ACM*, 43(1), 42–49.

Greenwald, T. (March/April2015). Compulsive Behaviour Sells. *The MIT Technology Review*.

Hands, J. (2013). Introduction: Politics, power and 'platformativity'. *Culture Machine*, 14, 1–9.

Helmond, A. (2015). The platformatization of the web: Making web data platform ready. *Social Media + Society*, July–December, 1–11.

Hodkinson, P. (2015). Bedrooms and beyond: Youth, identity and privacy on social network sites. *New Media & Society*, 19(2), 272–288. doi:10.1177/1461444815605454

Isin, E., & Ruppert, E. (2015). *Being Digital Citizens*. London: Rowman & Littlefield.

Ito, M., Horst, H., Antin, J., Finn, M., Law, A., Manion, A., Mitnick, S., Schlossberg, D. & Yardi, S. (2010). *Hanging Out, Messing Around and Geeking Out: Kids Living and Learning with New Media*. Cambridge, MA: The MIT Press.

Jenkins, H. (2006). *Confronting the challenges of participatory culture: Media education for the 21st century*. Macarthur Foundation White Paper. Cambridge, MA: The MIT Press.

Katz, M., & Shapiro, C. (1986). Technology adoption in the presence of network externalities. *Journal of Political Economy*, 94, 822–841.

Kelly, C. (2013). Is Snapchat used for sexting? We asked 5000 people to find out. *Survata Blog: Survata*. Accessed from: www.survata.com/blog/is-snapchat-only-used-for-sexting-we-asked-5000-people-to-find-out/

Langlois, G., McKelvey, F., Elmer, G., & Werbin, K. (2009). Mapping commercial web 2.0 worlds: Towards a new critical ontogenesis. *The Fibreculture Journal*, 14, 1–12.

Ling, R., & Yttri, B. (2002). Hyper-coordination via mobile phones in Norway. In J. Katz & M. Aakhus (Eds.), *Perpetual Contact: Mobile Communication, Private Talk, Public Performance*. Cambridge, UK: Cambridge University Press.

Marlowe, J., Bartley, A., & Collins, F. (2016). Digital belongings: The intersections of social cohesion, connectivity and digital media. *Ethnicities*, advanced online version, 1–18.

Marwick, A. E. (2013). Online identity. In J. A. Hartley, J. Burgess, & A. Bruns (Eds.), *A Companion to New Media Dynamics*. Oxford, UK: Wiley-Blackwell.

Marwick, A., & boyd, d. (2014). Networked privacy: How teenagers negotiate context in social media. *New Media & Society*, 16(7), 1051–1067.

Merten, D. E. (1997). The meaning of meanness: Popularity, competition and conflict among junior high school girls. *Sociology of Education*, 70(3), 175–191.

Nilan, P., Burgess, H., Hobbs, M., Threadgold, S., & Alexander, W. (2015). Youth, social media and cyberbullying among Australian youth: 'Sick friends'. *Social Media + Society*, July–December, 1–12. doi: doi:10.1177/2056305115604848

Olson, P. (2013). Teenagers say goodbye to Facebook and hello to messenger apps. *The Guardian*. Retrieved from www.theguardian.com/technology/2013/nov/10/teenagers-messenger-apps-facebook-exodus

Pielot, M., & Oliver, N. (2014). *Snapchat: How to understand a teen phenomenon*. Paper presented at the CHI Conference on Human Factors in Computing, Toronto, Canada.

Plantin, J. C., Lagoze, C., Edwards, P. N., & Sandvig, C. (2016). Infrastructure studies meet platform studies in the age of Google and Facebook. *New Media & Society*, advanced online edition, 1–18. doi:10.1177/1461444816661553

Rieder, B. (2012). What is in PageRank? A historical and conceptual investigation of a recursive status index. *Computational Culture: A Journal of Software Studies*. Retrieved from http://computationalculture.net/2012/08/29/what_is_in_pagerank/

Rohn, U. (2013). Social network sites across cultures and countries: Proximity and network effects. *Qualitative Research Reports in Communication*, 14(1), 28–34.

Sunden, J. (2003). *Material Virtualities: Approaching Online Textual Embodiment*. New York: Peter Lang Publishing.

Tufekci, Z. (2016). As the pirates become CEOs: The closing of the open internet. *Daedalus: The Journal of the American Academy of Arts & Sciences*, 65–78. doi:10.1162/DAED_a_00366

van Dijck, J. (2013). *The Culture of Connectivity: A Critical History of Social Media*. New York: Oxford University Press.

van Dijck, J., & Poell, T. (2013). Understanding social media logic. *Media and Communication*, 1(1), 2–14.

Vitak, J. (2012). The impact of context collapse and privacy on social network site disclosures. *Journal of Broadcasting & Electronic Media*, 56(4), 451–470.

Wilson, C. (2011). SA network Qooh.me takes flight. *Tech Central*. Retrieved from https://techcentral.co.za/sa-social-network-qooh-me-takes-flight/25638

Wyatt, S. (2004). Danger! Metaphors at work in economics, geophysiology and the internet. *Science, Technology, & /Human Values*, 29(2), 242–261.

6

CRITICAL UNDERSTANDINGS OF THE DIGITAL

According to research from the University of New South Wales, 'sexy selfies' are on the rise. In a controversial article entitled 'Sexy selfies just latest step to win complex game of evolution' (Blake, 2018), researcher Khandis Blake explains that sexy selfies, in which young women pose in provocative, scantily clad ways, are more prevalent in countries where inequality is increasing. Increased inequality leads to increased competition, and beauty, according to Blake, is a 'valuable commodity' that can generate large returns. Taking a stance *against* the high moral ground Blake argues that a young woman who takes a 'sexy selfie' is not objectifying herself, but instead 'actively strategising to fulfil her own interests and to maximise social mobility'.

It is refreshing that Blake has resisted analysing these findings through a strictly moral lens. Her reading of this social phenomenon appears to be a positive one, in which she celebrates, rather than denigrates the practices of young women. Her argument is framed in 'evolutionary terms' in which these behaviours are 'completely rational, even adaptive' (Blake, 2018, n.p.). However, what is missing from this analysis is *any* mention of the role that social media played in creating this situation. According to Blake, young people are just adapting to the social and economic conditions they are faced with—social media are simply a neutral tool with which they can do that. Besides, she reasons, they can opt out if they choose. Yet following the logic of Blake's argument, opting out would relegate one to the bottom of the evolutionary chain.

The issues raised by this article go to the very heart of what this book is about. Rather than consider the role that social media platforms play in shaping the practices and behaviours of young people, they remain decidedly absent. So too do the economics and politics that govern these platforms. Instead, young people are praised for their ability to comply and adapt, with scant regard for the long-term effects such practices might have on their mental health and wellbeing. While

Blake may well be right that these women do not feel 'objectified', were they supported to make any other choice? How have we arrived at a situation in which *we* adapt to technology, rather than *it* being adapted to us?

This book set out to explore the young people's critical understandings of digital media. However, I quickly became aware of how hard it was for the participants to adopt a critical disposition. For the most part, it seemed oppositional to the practices that were encouraged by the architectures of digital platforms and the expectations of their social networks. Despite what Blake might argue, opting out is not without consequence. The participants also acted to meet the expectations that adults placed upon them, even if these did contradict those of platform operators and their peers. The problems and tensions of meeting the demands of such oppositional stakeholders were largely interiorised. This chapter brings together the findings from the previous four chapters and discusses the critical understandings young people have of the digital and how the issues, tensions and possibilities identified articulate with broader concerns.

The role that digital media played in the young people's lives

It was clear that digital media played a significant role in the life of each of the 13 young people. Penny, for example, started using the internet at age four, owned six digital devices, and was on four social media platforms. Like her friends, Maddy and Grace, Penny felt like she was missing out on something fundamental if she was made to go without digital technology. By contrast, some young people felt they had to defend their decision *not* to use digital media, highlighting the significance of digital media even when absent. Chantelle defined herself by the lack of digital media in her life, seeing herself as somehow more liberated and engaged in day-to-day living. She did not use social media and would send an email on average once a month. To Chantelle, digital technologies were a 'dark cloud' encroaching upon her family and friendships. Despite the varying levels of engagement, in both cases digital media were a defining aspect of these young people's lives.

Identity representation and formation

Digital media were clearly influential in shaping these young people's identity representation and formation. While this influence varied across the group, certain trends emerged, particularly with the 11 young people who used social media. Indeed, social media appeared to be the main sites for these young people's identity work to take place. Their first step in substantively engaging with most social media sites was the creation of a profile—i.e. a representation of the individual user's identity. Facebook was by far the most popular platform for these young people and was the first 'grown-up' social networking site they were introduced to. As such, Facebook had ongoing significance for many of these young people. Even when they explored and experimented with different aspects of their identities through other digital platforms, these were most often reported back through Facebook.

One notable finding was the way in which online identities were (re)formed and (re)presented by the preformatted structures and coded architecture of the platforms that the young people used. As described in Chapter 4, lists of friends and personal photos were a primary means of self-representation on social media—largely due to the prominence given to these signifiers on sites like Facebook. Relying on a narrow range of cues to make sense of individuals' social identity meant that certain aspects of their social media presence (i.e. photos and the number of friends) took on a heightened value.

There were often several competing pressures at play when the young people engaged with this platform. Several young people spoke of anticipating not only the value judgements of peer groups when posting content, but also the societal expectations associated with their use of social media and the technological functions and constraints of the site, such as the like button. While Dylan displayed a relatively nuanced approach to social media that enabled him to negotiate these competing pressures effectively, three of the young women in the group were more reticent about posting photos and comments, thereby restricting their digital practices to viewing others' content. Alongside self-regulation/self-censorship, another strategy that two young people used to safeguard against unfavourable peer judgement was co-curating their social media identity with friends. This involved sending a selection of photos to friends and asking them to help choose which ones should be used as a profile picture.

Becoming

Digital media enabled and encouraged the young people to explore and develop various aspects of their identity, and/or mark particular changes in their life. For most, the act of signing up to Facebook signalled a form of social emergence or marker of independence, as well as experimenting with various aspects of their identity. Several young people engaged in practices that led to professional and aspirational becomings, as they found a wider range of resources and opportunities online. Further, the relative 'anonymity' afforded by comparatively niche sites (i.e. Steam and Wattpad) meant Rachel, Mark and Trent in particular could experiment with these becomings with fewer social repercussions. These non-mainstream representations of identity often contrasted with the supposedly 'authentic' or 'real' identities that were displayed on Facebook and offered them a greater freedom to experiment with their sense of who they were and who they might become.

However, there were limitations to what the young people could become within the structure of any online site and the social milieu in which these were embedded. The young people often compared and calibrated these more transitory or experimental becomings with offline corporeal forms of identity. Stacey and Trent provided key examples of this. Stacey in particular used Facebook to experiment with more adventurous or alternative versions of herself; however, an incongruity with a corporeal identity resulted in the negative feedback of others. While it may be expected that individuals could, would or should be different online, there were also limits to how different or experimental they could be. Becomings were tethered to corporeal identities and an 'original' Facebook profile, which in tandem created an authentic version of 'self'. In this way, the experimental becomings explored through digital media were often subordinated to embodied identities. However, whether these becomings develop into more consistent and lasting aspects of self is yet to be proven.

While the study set out to understand identity through a post-structural paradigm, namely becoming, the findings highlight that a more conservative and structuring set of circumstances was at play. Despite the differences in each young person's experiences, there were dominant values and social relations implicated in their digital practice—and these most often reproduced dominant offline values and power relations. Digital media could provide opportunities for becoming experimental or transitory versions of self; however, because the majority of the young people's identity practices took place on Facebook and Instagram, it was more often experienced as a conservative, conformist environment. Steam and YouTube appeared to provide the young people with more opportunities for identity play due to the relative anonymity these platforms afforded.

Types of communication

While there was a wide range of digital media that young people could use to communicate with others, most of their online interactions took place on social media sites, particularly Facebook, Instagram and Snapchat. Which social media platforms the young people used was strongly influenced by their peers, and communication was often shaped to demonstrate their belonging to a particular group. However, the fact that each platform was essentially 'walled off' from other platforms meant that the young people often felt obliged to follow their peers to particular social media sites. Failure to do so led to an acute sense of missing out on social activities, invitations and information. In this way, having a profile on the social media platforms where your friends were became an essential element of being socially visible. Aside from social media, only a couple of other platforms and affinity spaces were found to be significant to the young people's online communication.

The gaming platform Steam was used by all the boys in the study not only as a source of interest and entertainment, but also to communicate with others. Like other similar affinity spaces (i.e. Wattpad, YouTube), the appeal of Steam was that communication was felt to occur in a more spontaneous, organic way. This appeared to lessen the social pressures associated with online communication as dialogue was based around shared goals or interests. The findings showed that the structure of these digital media platforms strongly shaped communication practices. On some social media sites the primary form of communication was the presentation of self, while on others (Snapchat) it was to test whether aspects of self warranted further development and public self-display. Distinct types of interaction were propagated by each digital platform, some of which were decidedly new and different to older forms of communication like letter writing or talking face to face, resulting in what might be best described as a series of digital connections.

Change and participation

The existing literature on young people and digital media foregrounds civic participation yet there was little evidence to suggest that the young people in this study used digital media for this purpose. The fleeting engagement with civic issues that was evident in the study group took place on social media, mainly through online petitions. Rachel and Dylan signed various petitions, but Rachel, in particular, described this in a dismissive way, indicating that she saw this type of engagement or 'clicktivism' as futile. Sean was the most politically active in the group having signed up to a 'United Against Abbott' Facebook page, and attending various protests in person organised through the site. His peer group was more politically motivated and this meant participation was tied up with a sense of social belonging and a collective group identity.

While we could presume that the young people would have studied and researched global issues through the school curriculum, however, not one mentioned *ongoing* digital practices that focused on national or international news and current affairs (i.e. membership to an online group or regular visits to a website). Sometimes 'spectacular' news events or political issues were the topic of discussion on social media. Mark had discussed recent aeroplane disasters on Facebook. Dylan said that he had talked about the controversial issue of coal seam gas on Facebook with 'friends'. However, in digital spaces the other nine participants appeared to be apolitical, as they reported that their social networks did not share information on politics, community or news. The majority of the young people's digital practices were directed at socialising or entertaining; few other forms were noted in the study group.

Critical understandings and perspectives

Despite their use of digital media, many of the young people did not demonstrate a well-developed critical disposition toward the technologies they used. This is not to suggest that they were unwilling to critique, but rather that they had few opportunities to cultivate these sorts of critical understandings. In school, the main education in regard to digital media came through cybersafety programmes. While there were some important lessons in this discourse, Trent explained that in more recent years it had used shock to convey the message.

More agentive and transformative critique built on the kind of technical, cultural and economic knowledge of digital networks outlined in Chapter 1 was not taught at any of the schools that the young people in the study attended. There was also little evidence of a metalanguage to discuss critical issues and aspects of use. If the young people *did* display these understandings they had been acquired in an informal way, through conversations with relatives or friends. Five of the young people did show some awareness of corporate ownership of content, technological convergence and media monopolies on the internet. However, having neither the technical knowledge nor an understanding of how or why these issues were significant meant most young people saw this as simply *part* of the internet, and an advantageous one at that.

Social hierarchies of digital platforms

The most common and prominent form of critique these young people engaged with related to the social currency of digital practices and the hierarchies of digital platforms. These critical understandings were primarily developed in relation to social media, and often in an *ad hoc* manner through first-hand experience or witnessing interactions online. The young people recalled feelings of social isolation if a photo or comment attracted no comments or likes, which subsequently shaped them to post content of a different nature. These critical understandings were developed through observations and trial and error so that over time most young people's understandings around these processes were finely tuned to become complex and nuanced readings of the social value of digital practices. Indeed, the semiotics of these digital texts and practices were most typically interpreted in reference to the immediate and physical social discourse and not wider educational or cultural discourses.

A case in point was the group at Bankview College who agreed collectively on the description of Facebook as a 'food chain', where the 'populars' have bullied their way to the 'top'. At the same time critiquing how their own digital practices replicated or resisted these social pressures and hierarchies appeared to be more difficult—requiring a critical self-reflexivity on the part of individuals that was neither associated with nor encouraged by social media platforms. Rachel was the only one in the group who reflected on her own practices in this way prior to the study. While the young people felt able to identify the motivations and drivers behind others' digital practices, when asked during the research activities why they did particular things themselves on social media the answer was often an awkward 'I don't know'. In fact this question yielded so few insights that it became redundant and uncomfortable to ask.

Digital connections appeared to be part of a subconscious set of practices that were shaped by the architecture of digital platforms and the social currents that underpinned the peer groups. In Chapter 3 I used Foucault's (1980) concept of the dispositif to detail how the young people arrived at these attitudes and beliefs. The findings revealed particular elements of the digital dispositif were influential in how the young people viewed themselves and their peers' behaviours and practices within and across the dispositif, as well as the circulations of knowledge and power. The structure of mainstream platforms such as Google, Facebook and YouTube, set a precedent for how the architecture of the digital dispositif was understood.

While affective relations with peers, also manifest through the platform, were also important motivators of practices. These understandings were often complicated or limited by the two prominent discursive positions promoted through the dispositif—young people as 'digital natives' and/or as vulnerable online.

Safety and security

Given the dominance of the protectionist discourse within the digital dispositif it is perhaps not surprising that the young people's critical understandings were predominately related to issues around cybersafety and security. These understandings were related to social media and involved three key messages: 'knowing' someone face to face before becoming friends with them online; remaining 'anonymous' when online; and only uploading onto social media content they felt comfortable to be spread widely and publicly. These understandings were developed at school in special cybersafety classes that were conducted by external organisations, usually charities or the police. All the young people recalled cybersafety classes from upper primary school onwards and, for many, such classes were still an annual event in the school curriculum.

In interviews and group discussion the young people drew on these cybersafety discourses to frame their digital practices. However, occasionally some in the group wilfully re-interpreted the cybersafety message to ensure their online behaviours were not restricted in any way. For example, at City College the young women interpreted 'knowing' someone as simply sharing many 'mutuals' on social media. By doing this they could continue to extend their list of friends while adhering to the cybersafety message. In this way the young people were continually negotiating issues of risk and safety associated with their digital practices.

Most considered themselves 'cybersafe', describing social media practices such as strict privacy settings, carefully chosen photos and a list of 'known' social media 'friends'. As such, they saw themselves as doing the 'right thing' online. However, two in the group acknowledged that this alone could not protect them from large corporations and/or hackers who could still access their personal information. In this way, there was a sense of powerlessness when it came to being private online. Nevertheless, strict privacy settings were seen a kind of insurance policy in helping the individual avoid blame if something went wrong online. At the root of the cybersafety message was an individualised responsibility for socially appropriate and responsible behaviours, as well as personal safety and security measures in digital spaces.

Significant others

Peers, parents and other relatives played a relatively minor role in helping young people develop their critical digital literacies. One notable exception was Mitch. Living with his tech 'expert' uncle meant that Mitch was scaffolded into more complex and critical use of digital technologies from the outset. The fact that Mitch shared his knowledge and understanding of digital media confidently and regularly in group discussions, suggests this kind of one-on-one 'mentorship' can be influential in shaping future practices and dispositions. Further, *others* acknowledged Mitch's more 'expert' reading of digital media, as when Stacey reported talking to him about some of the issues she faced. Despite this, it was surprising how little the young people spoke to peers about their experiences with digital media. While they regularly discussed the content, topics and trends that featured on digital platforms, there was little conversation around the social dynamics that contextualised and directed the flow of such content.

Aside from offering counsel and comfort on the trials and tribulations of social media, few young people spoke to their parents about their digital experiences. More typically, the young people reported that the main role played by parents was to reinforce and maintain their safety and security in digital spaces. In this way, parents were more like gatekeepers than guides when it came to cultivating critical use of digital media. Indeed, the enthusiasm and willingness of the young people to partake in the reflective and critical discussions instigated by the fieldwork might be due to the fact that there was a general lack of these conversations in young people's lives. In theoretical terms this might be thought of as drawing on *different* elements of the digital dispositif (apart from the protectionist discourse) to help young people expand the ways they might think about and understand themselves and others in this context.

Implications, insights and interpretations

Having developed a detailed picture of the relationship these young people have with digital media, it is now possible to consider how the digital dispositions, understandings and practices identified throughout the fieldwork articulate with broader theoretical concerns. Adopting a constructionist methodological approach means that the purpose of the fieldwork was to generate new theoretical ideas, and helps to modify already existing theories or uncovers, in more detail, the dimensions of a phenomenon. It also explored ways to scaffold young people's critical understandings of digital media by trialling a series of creative and visual provocations.

An unanticipated finding of the study was that the young people's engagement with digital media was more structuring and conservative in character than anticipated by the post-structural framing of the project. For this reason the discussion draws on a range of scholarship, from software studies to sociology and philosophy, as well as returning to key themes outlined in the approach, namely, a post-structuralist approach to identity, as described by becoming, and the tension between the particular and the universal. In the final chapter I return to a focus on literacies education to discuss the implications of these findings for the field of critical digital literacies.

Notwithstanding theories that help make sense of these findings, this research found young people's 'lifeworlds' to be fluid and complex. The discussion draws on *individual* experiences to challenge and extend understandings of young people and digital technology. The section is organised into five parts. The first counters the notion that digital identities are fluid and multiple, arguing that they are bound by several factors that influence the representation and formation of identity in notable ways. The second challenges the assumption of young people as unproblematically empowered by their use of digital technology, instead examining how the architecture of social media platforms strongly structured the participants' representation of identities and interactions with others. The final three sections of the discussion are interrelated—each problematising the gaps that exist between young people's experiences of digital media, academic theorisations of this relationship, and educational approaches that aim to address popular media panics.

Bounded identities

One significant finding of this study is that the young people's digital identities were not as fluid and multiple as theorised in the early chapters of the book. Digital identities were bound by several factors, including a tethering to embodied identities and an interpellation (Althusser, 1971) into the role of the 'digital native'. Binding identity at both the personal and collective levels becomes a significant constraint to how the participants represented and formed their digital identities. This also meant that there were competing discourses and complex social dynamics for them to negotiate when using digital media. While limitations to the theory of becoming are outlined below, this section focuses on the influence of the generational label of the 'digital native'.

While becoming was a helpful conceptual tool for exploring the possibilities for identity practices, it could not account for the influence of offline values and power structures, as well as the structuring nature of digital platforms (this latter point is explored in more detail in the next subsection). Like more traditional approaches to understanding identity, becoming is also socially constructed, meaning that the feedback of peers was an important consideration when engaging in identity practices. Fuller (2005) introduces this idea in his discussion of becoming, suggesting that the social, political and cultural architectures surrounding digital media are what limit possibilities. The young people's experiences confirm this as their audiences on social media were those they saw each day in school. However, it also highlights that with limited ways of interpreting and integrating the digital practices of others, the external contextual factors take on greater prominence, and sometimes in ways that were constraining.

The idea of 'generations' helps to identify the social conditions that form the backdrop to young people's lives; however, tethering their collective identity to the 'digital native' had an effect not only on how they saw themselves, but also on how adults perceived them. The idea of 'digital natives' as a 'homogenous generation' speaking and learning 'differently to preceding generations of students' (Thomas, 2011, p.4) has been critiqued throughout this book and in many other studies; however, a significant finding from this research was that many of the young people *themselves* used this idea to define their generation and explain their practices. In many respects this might be expected given how prevalent and per-vasive the discourse and labelling has been. Livingstone (2009a) argues that the notion of the 'digital native' is 'promoted by two constituencies'—the first is edu-cators, and the second is those who make and direct content and marketing at children and youth. Developing more complex understandings of young people's experiences requires an examination of the purpose and effect of these descriptors.

Generational or collective labels like 'digital native', 'net generation' and 'mil-lennials' serve a range of purposes, one of which is to control. As Selwyn (2009) explains: 'the notion of the "digital native" should be seen more as a discursive than descriptive device, employed by those seeking to exert some form of power and control over the shaping of the digital (near) future' (p.371). Within the digital dispositif, the discourse of the 'digital native' created a distinct subjective position, which both empowered and limited how young people experienced the digital. This sort of generational thinking simultaneously 'exoticises' and 'belittles' (Her-ring, 2008) young people's digital experiences, by assuming that they 'sponta-neously know everything they need to know about technology' (Buckingham, 2011, p.x). This has the further effect of reducing adult responsibility for guiding and educating critical and creative digital practices. Examining the notion of the 'digital native' through the lens of Althusser's (1971) 'interpellation' not only explains why this discourse is restrictive and reductive to both young people and adults, but also provides insight into how the effects of this generational thinking might be countered.

In his landmark essay 'Ideology and ideological state apparatuses' (1971), Althusser theorises a process whereby ideology 'hails or interpellates concrete individuals as concrete subjects'. As Althusser explains, this process relies on an imaginary misrecognition on the part of the subject in which 'ideology "acts" or "functions" in such a way that it "recruits" subjects among the individuals (it recruits them all) or "transforms" the individual into subjects (it transforms them all) by that very precise operation' (p.118). He calls this *interpellation* or *hailing* and uses the example of the 'commonplace everyday police' calling out to an individual 'Hey, you there!' To which the hailed individual will turn around. This imaginary misrecognition is what Althusser calls 'interpellation'. Elliot (2010) writes that interpellation not only creates subjects, but also assigns identity: 'It is in and through ideology that society "interpellates" the individual as a "subject", at once conferring identity and subjecting the individual to that subject position' (p.66). Through interpellation, then, individuals begin to recognise and value themselves within social and cultural frameworks. Althusser contends that it is ideological state apparatuses, including schools, institutions and mass media, which assign signification.

Despite the array of digital experiences observed in the study, all but one of the young people drew on the discourse of the 'digital native' to explain and describe their practices. In doing so the young people not only assumed a generational identity, but also sidestepped the need to explain and understand their practices in a more detailed and critical manner—they do particular things in particular ways simply *because* they are 'digital natives'. While individuals have the choice to accept their subjection, Choi (2012) writes that this is a 'forced choice' (p.29), as there are consequences for denying signification. This was evident with one young person in the group, Chantelle. She openly disavowed technology, but she recounted several occasions in which both adults and same-age friends made her feel like an oddity.

Given how pervasive the discourse of the 'digital native' is in society, young people were frequently hailed into this subject position by parents, educators and popular media more broadly. In this way, it became a 'forced choice' for the young people to accept their role as 'digital natives', which influenced the way they approached and engaged with technology. Key in this process, and in Althusser's theory of interpellation, was that this is seen as a 'free choice'. The disadvantages of this label were therefore not acknowledged. Regardless of how the young people used technology, being interpellated into the position of 'digital natives' meant they often overlooked the actual experiences and emotions evoked by their practices. This would explain the sense of consternation that several felt when using social media. There was a sense that they needed to be on particular platforms to be visible to their peers, even though their experiences might have been unpleasant and, at times, negative. The architecture of digital platforms reinforced this idea, sedimenting particular beliefs and practices in the young people.

The rhetoric of the 'digital native' restricted the ways the young people could think about and use digital technologies. Further, identifying as 'digital natives' meant they were less inclined to listen to or take on board what adults—or 'digital immigrants' (Prensky, 2001a, 2001b)—had to say about digital technologies. It is important to acknowledge that adults have played a major role in the creation of this mindset. It was adults who came up with the discourses around these generational differences, and in doing so have reinforced their own subjective position as 'protector' within the digital dispositif. The 'digital native' rhetoric inadvertently lessens the responsibility that adults have in educating young people in creative and critical digital practices. This leads educators and adults to believe they do not need to learn how to use digital technologies in innovative ways, as young people will always be more advanced. Many of these generalisations and binaries need to be deconstructed if young people are to make the most of their digital experiences and practices, particularly when it comes to developing their critical digital literacies.

The structuring nature of digital platforms

A less anticipated finding was the influential role that digital platforms had on structuring the young people's communicative practices. In Chapter 3 digital platforms were theorised as the most influential part of the digital dispositif. This idea was further developed in Chapters 4 and 5 in which the architecture of platforms and their discursive construction of these in the cultural imaginary, were influential in shaping the young people's practices. Rather than involving a wide array of practices across a number of different digital texts, the young people's online communication could be categorised into a series of digital connections or com-municative strategies—including one-way projections of self to more intimate and lasting interactions with others. These largely took place through what the young people described as a 'core' of digital platforms. This is not to deny the depth and intensity of these digital connections, but to suggest that the nature, tone and style of these exchanges were quite strongly influenced by the platform itself, rather than the content or context of the event.

Motivating and guiding the digital communication that took place on these platforms was a culture of connectivity built upon sharing and liking (van Dijck, 2013). This not only means sharing content with 'friends' and 'followers', but also with corporations. Tapscott and Williams's (2006) argument that relationships 'are the one thing you cannot commoditise' (p.44) now appears idealistic, if not naïve. The boon for technology companies like Google and Facebook came through commoditising the connections users have with others, which was made possible through the architecture of platforms. Several scholars argue that communication technologies have now commoditised feelings and affect (Dean, 2005; Karppi, 2015). It is not my intention to analyse the political economy of digital media platforms here, but rather to highlight the influence these platforms have on young people's communication practices. In doing so, the dominant ideologies of these digital platforms and the impact they have on the way young people see themselves and others might be revealed.

The digital practices explored in Chapters 4 and 5 point to what has become the prevailing culture and ideology of the digital context, but it is perhaps most clearly outlined by van Dijck (2013): 'Platform tactics such as the popularity principle and ranking mechanisms hardly involve contingent technological structures; instead they are firmly rooted in an ideology that values hierarchy, competition, and a winner-takes-all mindset' (p.21). In light of this, the prioritising and privileging of particular dispositions and understandings—including the focus on photos, increasing the number of 'friends' and attracting likes—are seen *not* as acts of nar-cissism and self-indulgence, but instead as responses to this ideology. This might also help to explain the increase in 'sexy selfies' noted at the beginning of this chapter.

Software studies (Manovich, 2001, 2013; Berry, 2011; Fuller, 2008), which focuses on the social and cultural effects of software systems, helps explain how the ideologies of technology companies take hold amongst users of their sites. One of the great advantages of software is its capacity to connect to so many aspects of social and cultural life. Yet, as Goffey (2008, p.16) argues, if we fail to understand the basic building blocks of software, 'it is unlikely that software engineering will allow us to view culture as anything other than something software plugs into'. Indeed, as technologisation is seen as inevitable and often proceeds in incremental ways, the effects of software on lived experience can be difficult to identify. Within worlds created by and augmented through software there is much room for ima-gination, play and adventure; however, the inherent formal qualities of code mean these experiences can become preordained and constraining. As Fuller (2008) explains, to interrogate these realities we need a language to talk about 'the materiality of abstraction, the interplay between formalization and the heterogenous stuff it mobilizes' (p.10). For this reason, software studies seek to build a technical language and sensibility from which to understand and critique the *lived* experiences of software.

To apply software studies to the young people's experiences of Facebook, for example, is revealing of how the imperatives of the corporation *and* the individual users' practices are mediated by the EdgeRank algorithm. On Facebook, the EdgeRank algorithm processes each digital practice (posts, comments, likes, photos) as an 'edge'. What appears in users' News Feed is determined by three things: how connected they are to the edge (affinity score); the types of stories Facebook thinks the user will find interesting (edge weight); and when the edge appeared (time decay).[1]Bucher (2012) reasons that there is a circular logic embedded in the EdgeRank algorithm in that an affinity score is determined by your interactivity with the Edge 'creator'. However, as she explains, 'for you to Like or Comment on a friend's photo or status update, they have to be visible to you in the first place' (p.1169); a low affinity score means the user and their posts will not be seen. Through the EdgeRank algorithm the functions and buttons on Facebook are hierarchised, thereby prioritising particular people and posts into users' News Feed. This creates social hierarchies and explains how some people become more visible on these platforms than others. In doing so, it is these functions and the EdgeRank algorithm that create the fear of social invisibility that the young people spoke about so regularly. To remain 'visible' these young people have little choice but to follow 'a certain platform logic embedded in the architecture of Facebook' (Bucher, 2012, p.1171). Not only does this encourage users to keep posting, but the more they share, comment and like on the platform the more personal data they generate, which Facebook can then use for commercial and other purposes.

Lev Manovich (2013) argues we are now living in a 'software society'. The impact that software had on these young people's daily experiences was evident during the fieldwork. A software studies approach draws attention to the way in which digital media shape young people's identity, communication and participation in society. Manovich argues that software is different from other technologies in three important ways: first, software is always in 'Beta stage' so that it is never 'officially completed' (p.1); second, software as a 'theoretical category' is still invisible to 'most academics, artists, and cultural professionals' (p.9); and third is that software plays a 'central role' in 'shaping both the material elements and many of the immaterial structures that together make up "culture"' (p.33).

Each of these points has significance when considering how young people use digital media to communicate with others. Not only does it point to the fact that through software culture is perpetually changing, but that from an academic perspective its effects have been under-theorised. As an example, the concept of remediation (Bolter & Grusin, 2000) has been useful in understanding how digital media remediate or incorporate old technologies; however, it also obfuscates the specific processes and qualities brought about by this new medium. Like Manovich

(2013), Berry (2013) argues that there are 'specific forms of sociality' (p.34) brought into existence by software. Even though old media may 'haunt' the new (i.e. the analogue camera icon on the smartphone), these *are* new forms of media that bring about new social and cultural processes. For example, the photo taken on a smartphone can now be instantly shared on social media. In fact, it is perhaps this continuity with old forms of media that make new media appear more banal than they actually are. Berry (2013) puts forth the notion of 'enmediation' to explain that even though the previous medium might be represented in the new, it is neither the 'same' nor is it 'contained' by it (p.33). Enmediation points to the emergent nature of digital networks, as new media resonate and shape social experiences and processes in unforeseen ways.

While much has been made of young people's reliance on digital media, what is often forgotten is that this reliance is in and of itself a product of the platforms. Young people are not inherently narcissistic and self-indulgent in the way that some scholars have suggested (see Twenge & Campbell, 2009; Twenge, 2006, 2017), but certainly they are seeking to connect with others in an increasingly fragmented and risk-conscious world. Digital platforms, like Facebook, are a way to connect with others from the safety of home; however, this involves embracing, in some way, the ideologies embedded in these platforms (i.e. promoting the self to be 'visible' to others). The lure of conviviality and friendship offered through these platforms encourages young people to share their thoughts, feelings and emotions, not only with their 'friends' and 'followers', but also with the corporations that own these platforms. While young people may not see this as a problem, the fact that technology has become indispensable to their social experiences, often in quite surreptitious and insidious ways, *is* a problem. In this way, technologies held significant power when it came to shaping discourse and ideology around social practices and behaviours.

This kind of dependence was not promoted by all platforms. It must be remembered that many young people learnt important skills of communication through their use of digital media, particularly when on more niche sites. However, it is important that academics and educators develop theories to help understand and conceptualise the new forms of sociality that are initiated through software. As Dobson and Ringrose (2015) argue, this also means more focused discussion around the new norms established by the digital context. As they explain, something that might appear normal and legitimate online can appear inappropriate in other contexts (i.e. school). Redressing the issues outlined here should not be seen as the sole responsibility of young people. Moreover, technology companies also have a responsibility to their users to be more transparent about the way these platforms work.

Young people's affective experiences of digital media

The participants were not always consciously aware of the emotions involved in and evoked by their use of digital media. This points to the difficulty in integrating and making sense of experiences *across* media. Instead, digital experiences remained a separate and distinct aspect of life. However, these young people were clearly *moved* to do particular things online, even if certain practices were difficult to rationalise in a logical way. All of the young people believed that a Facebook friendship was different, and oftentimes less meaningful, than a face-to-face friendship, yet many were still driven toward accumulating more 'friends'. A recurring finding throughout the fieldwork was the reactive and affective nature of the behaviours prompted by using digital media. In this way, affect emerged as an underlying force that shaped the young people's digital practices. I draw on social scientific applications of affect to analyse the young people's digital experiences (Massumi, 2002, 2015; Gregg & Seigworth, 2010; Hillis et al., 2015).

Affect helps to explain why the participants were subconsciously driven to particular dispositions, movements and behaviours across digital spaces in ways that were difficult to understand and identify. These subliminal *forces* were distributed and defy categorisation into typical emotions, such as happiness and sadness. McGilchrist (2009) differentiates affect from emotion by arguing that emotion is only *one* aspect of it. Affect, he argues, involves 'something much broader'. It is 'a way of attending to the world (or not attending to it), a way of relating to the world (or not relating to it), a stance, a disposition ... ultimately "a way of being" in the world' (p.184). In this sense the body and the brain work together to produce what Massumi (2015) calls 'body knowledge' (p.210). He explains that affect 'does not reduce the mind to the body in the narrow physical sense', but instead 'asserts that bodies think as they feel, on a level with their movements' (p.211).

As described in Chapter 3, the young people approached their use of digital technology in particular ways. They assumed dispositions that appeared self-evident; however, when asked to explain, they often found them inexplicable or, sometimes, even irrational. Understood through affect every behaviour, gesture or practice comes about through conscious dimensions of experience *as well as* through subconscious, embodied reactions. The findings of Chapter 3 indicated that the young people had little technical understanding of the architecture of digital platforms, and as a result they affectively 'felt' the implications of power and knowledge rather than cognitively understanding their composition and circulation. As a result, the young people's experience of the digital tended toward the affective rather than the cognitive.

The non-discursive elements of the digital dispositif are key to affect, as in its most simple form, it is the 'capacities to act and be acted upon' (Seigworth & Gregg, 2010, p.3). While the actual labels may vary, the driving force behind the young people's digital actions involved something 'vital'. Seigworth and Gregg (2010) describe it as a 'vital force' (p.3), while Munster (2013) calls it 'vitality affect' (p.104). Munster goes on to explain that 'vitality affects ... are not expressions of emotion but rather are generalised affect-sensory movements that, ontogenetically, precede the capacity to categorically express "a" feeling' (p.104). In digital networks 'vitality affects' emerge, condense and dissipate across human and non-human components in a multitude of ways. Not only are these forces kinetic and non-specific, but in digital networks they are also distributed and diffuse, which explains the young people's difficulty in identifying them. When more specifically applied to digital networks, affect explains 'how individual, collective, discursive, and networked bodies, both human and machine, affect and are modified by one another' (Paasonen et al., 2015, p.3).

The kinds of texts that young people often upload onto social networks—photos of memories, expressions of opinion, declarations of care and affection for others—highlight the importance of affect in digital networks. In this way, feelings, sensations and emotions are the very foundation of the social networking experience. Further to this, the structure of social media helps to develop what Ahmed (2010) calls the 'stickiness' of affect. Affect is sticky, Ahmed writes, because it 'sustains or preserves the connection between ideas, values and objects' (p.29). Social media platforms like Facebook are structured to promote 'stickiness'. Even inconsequential events or objects can become 'sticky' as they are uploaded onto a timeline, tagged with a caption and identified as a significant event in a person's life. Structured in this way these objects help to forge a web of affective relationships with others and increase individuals' connection to particular websites and digital tools. For marketers, stickiness is now a measure of value as it positively correlates with the amount of time one will spend on a website (Pybus, 2015). Beneito-Montagut (2015) argues that the 'emotion culture' that emerges through online relationships remains 'under-theorised' (p.4). While metrics are one obvious way to quantify affect, exactly how affect circulates on social networking sites is difficult to trace. The networked nature of affect across digital media adds another layer of complexity for individuals to negotiate.

Affect might explain why four of the young people regularly returned to the websites they used in their childhood. A technological affordance of social networks is that they can be 'archives of feeling' easily stored and accessed by large numbers of people (Pybus, 2013). These archives enable the individuals to imagine and re-imagine the communities they have participated in, hence Trent's return to Club Penguin to bring about the 'happy feelings' of the past. Sometimes, however, affective reactions emerged in unpredictable ways across digital networks. For example, Mitch assumed indifference toward his profile photo, saying that his friend had asked him to use it, as he himself did not spend much time deliberating over such things. However, in interview it was clear that bound up in this photo were happy memories of participating in the school musical and the positive relationships formed throughout rehearsals. While societal expectations might have positioned him to adopt a nonchalant attitude toward his profile picture, on another level this photo imbricated a series of significant memories and feelings for Mitch that he returned to a number of times throughout the fieldwork.

Given the role of affect in driving and shaping digital practices it is a significant finding that the young people in this study saw the behaviours on digital networks as lacking emotion. In one way or another affect underpinned much of their online behaviour. The very fact that the young people went online to spend time with people they knew and cared for suggests that these networks were significant *because* of the affective relationships they developed. Affect helps understand how young people compose and engage their digital identities and behaviours at both a conscious *and* subconscious levels, using both brain and body. It accounts for actions and behaviours that might appear irrational or inexplicable to others, but seem intuitive or right to the individual.

There is merit in prompting young people to consider how affect shapes their digital practices and their digital becoming. Identifying and naming these sub-liminal drivers is the first step in exerting some kind of control and agency over how these might be channelled through social media platforms and other digital texts. It is also important for parents, adults and educators to realise that rational or logical discourses around digital practices cannot account for affective experiences of digital media that are individualised, obscured and embodied.

The individualisation of digital responsibilities and risks

One of the well-reported virtues of the internet is the ease with which content can be accessed and uploaded. This provides opportunities for researching, communicating and learning, as demonstrated by the young people in this study; however, it also introduces new forms of risk. As Livingstone (2009b) points out, the structure and function of the internet mean that online opportunities are often inherently intertwined with risk:

> To make a new friend online, one risks meeting someone ill-intentioned. To engage even with the children's BBC website, one must provide personal information online. To search for advice about sexuality, one will encounter pornographic content also, since there is no consensual line between them.
>
> *(p.171)*

While risk and opportunity are often thought to be mutually exclusive, a large-scale study of young people's digital practices found that there was, in fact, a positive correlation between the two: the more risks one takes, the more opportunities they will encounter, and vice versa (Livingstone & Helsper, 2010). This helps to contextualise the various practices observed across the study group.

Dylan's relaxed privacy settings and willingness to communicate with strangers might be perceived as risky; however, this more open and willing disposition increased his opportunities to socialise with others. On the other hand, Chantelle, who was more risk averse, had fewer digital experiences and opportunities. Most other young people fell somewhere in between these two extreme cases; their digital practices involved negotiating the ongoing tensions between risk and opportunity. In this way, the young people used digital media with a clear sense of the 'spectacles of intimacy' (Berriman & Thomson, 2015), outlined in Chapter 1. Like the young people in Berriman and Thomson's study, these young people were also 'driven by a dual emotional imperative: seeking to navigate between the potential emotional pleasures derived through praise and recognition, whilst simultaneously attempting to avoid the anxiety and distress of being exposed to criticism and derision' (p.588). What enabled individuals to thrive in digital spaces was an ability to assess and manage these risks and opportunities effectively.

Risk, according to Beck (1992), is inextricably linked to contemporary society (a period he termed reflexive modernisation), in that it is 'a systematic way of dealing with hazards and insecurities induced and introduced by modernisation itself' (p.21). In modern society, risk is not abstract but instead fundamental to the institutions and innovations of everyday life. It is the perception and identification of risk within modern society that marks this era as different to those of the past. Through their use of digital media, the young people encountered risks and opportunities. Over the course of the fieldwork they spoke about the risk of identity theft, negative peer judgement and bullying, and the unwanted attention of strangers. However, these risks could eventuate from everyday digital practices— entering details onto a website or database, posting content and 'friending' or 'following' others online. In this way, the young people assumed the assessment and management of risk was *their* responsibility. Indeed, both the structure of the internet and the discourses that framed young people's digital practices encouraged the idea of an individualised responsibility and risk in online spaces.

Significantly, the young people in this research seemed to be voluntarily engaged with the self-monitoring that was required to manage the risks they faced online: they tried to remain anonymous in online spaces; they rigorously assessed the appropriateness of their photos or stopped posting altogether; and they used 'mutuals' to determine whether they should become friends with someone. As Sean explained, users of the internet needed to protect themselves from all the 'gross stuff' online. Insulating themselves against risk involved critically assessing the possibilities and problems of a particular situation, the credibility or trustworthiness of an individual and the fallibility of the platforms they used. Needless to say individuals *must* have proficient analytical skills if they are to prosper in digital spaces, as 'experts dump their contradictions and conflicts at the feet of the individual and leave him or her with the well intentioned invitation to judge all of this critically on the basis of his or her own notions' (Beck, 1992, p.137). Making these judgements can become an overwhelming and sometimes insurmountable task. Despite the difficulties involved individuals bear the 'full responsibility for the consequences of investing [their] trust in this rather than that example' (Bauman, 2001, p.105).

Closely associated with discourses of risk are discourses of individual empowerment and agency, such as the 'digital native' discourse, which are together, 'curiously re-embedded within official establishment discourses as a means of rationalising the increasing exposure of the individual to the consequences of their own risk-related decisions' (Livingstone, 2009b, p.178). In a risk society (Beck, 1992), not only do the state and other social institutions retract from the responsibility of managing risk, but they also play a role in shifting the responsibility onto the individual. A good example of this is Australia's *Enhancing Online Safety for Children Act 2015*, created by the Office of the Children's eSafety Commissioner.

The Act seeks to work in partnership with platform operators in tackling cyber-safety issues. Regardless of intention, as McCosker (2016) notes, the difficulty in regulating social media means it 'continues to place responsibility mainly with young people and their guardians to self-manage their social media use' (p.27).

The prominence of the cybersafety discourse in school-based digital media programmes is testament to this. It is a solution to the problem of the 'disempowered digital native', who is, according to this discursive construction, subject to a set of 'risks' and 'dangers' through their technology use (Selwyn, 2009, p.368). Sanctioned by official institutions like schools and the police, the cybersafety discourse is typically centred on zero tolerance of risk. However, in minimising risk, opportunities are also minimised. In this way, the official story young people have been told about digital media is based around risk prevention and minimisation.

The need for critical digital literacies

This book has identified and explored some of the challenges that young people experience when using digital media, underscoring the need for sophisticated critical digital literacies. These challenges might be less obvious to adults and educators, but were implicit in the many different ways the young people spoke about their digital experiences. These challenges could be summarised as negotiating the following: the complex and interrelated discourses associated with identity practices; the structuring nature of digital platforms; the often unconscious emotions evoked by using digital media; and the increasing individualisation of managing these challenges. While it is difficult to identify and explain the ways in which digital media shape lived experience, it was clear from the findings that reflecting on this held much promise in cultivating critical digital literacies.

Unlike other studies that suggest young people do not differentiate between the online and offline (Salaway & Caruso, 2008; Carrington, 2015), the young people in this study relied on more conventional and/or conservative terms to explain their experiences. Further, their explanations and discussion of digital technologies did not reflect the nuanced and complex interplay of digital media, as they were not seen as embedded in day-to-day life or as initiating emotive or embodied reactions. While it might appear idealistic to have expected otherwise, seeing the digital and non-digital as intertwined is key to developing critical digital literacies, particularly when considering the complexity of the digital context.

Malpas (2009) contends that the digital context 'does not constitute an autonomous, independent or "closed" system, but is instead always dependent in a variety of ways, on the everyday world within which it is embedded' (p.135). In many respects Malpas is identifying the digital dispositif—a layer of modern life always present to ideology and discourse. Much of what is affecting about the digital is the way it connects with and mobilises emotions and feelings. This is perhaps even more difficult for young people as a host of new emotions and experiences are emerging during these years. As Malpas argues, however, perceiving digital experiences as 'non-autonomous' to the everyday world leads to a 'more complex and nuanced conception' of the digital context, and 'its relation to the everyday, than is common in many discussions' (p.139). Developing understandings around the interplay between the online and offline should therefore be a goal of critical digital literacies.

While the young people appeared to move 'seamlessly' between the online and the offline, converging technologies and identities through the digital platforms they used, it is significant that *they* did not see it as such. This perhaps points to a shortfall in language, rather than comprehension. Without the linguistic tools and literacy strategies to make sense of these processes they remained, in many respects, beyond identification and understanding. Developing a metalanguage through which to identify and make sense of the social processes that take place across the networks of digital texts might be one step in developing the critical digital literacies of young people. As Gee (1991) explains, powerful literacy 'is control of a secondary use of language used in a secondary discourse that can serve as a meta-discourse to critique the primary discourse or other secondary discourses, including dominant discourses' (p.8).

The materialities of digital platforms appeared dominant in structuring the young people's digital experiences, so that increasing their power relative to these digital systems requires the development of a 'meta-discourse' specific to digital platforms. With few linguistic tools and even fewer material resources to help unpack and understand digital systems, the participants were left with little choice but to accept the structure and functions of these technologies without challenge. It is not surprising that three in the group expressed forms of technological determinism in their explanations and predictions for our digital futures. This suggests that they did not have either the linguistic tools or the experience to help them 'mutually shape' the digital technologies to their purposes in the way that some scholars have hoped or proposed (Lievrouw & Livingstone, 2009; Boczkowski, 1999).

The aim of sociocultural approaches to digital literacy is to build on individuals' past experiences and knowledge, and scaffold them towards increasingly complex and critical understandings of the texts they encounter. This, however, is quite a different approach to the one that the young people described experiencing at school. While there is a body of literature theorising models and approaches to teaching digital literacies (Avila & Pandya, 2013; van Dijk & van Deursen, 2014; Gillen, 2014), it seems these more innovative methods have not penetrated into the mainstream and remain niche.

The participants drew on the cybersafety message to discuss and explain their digital practices; however, the protectionist discourse was clearly limited in helping them negotiate the complex and competing pressures brought about through digital media use. These pressures include the architecture of social media platforms, the affective experiences of these digital networks and the popular media panics that shape societal expectations around use. Critically analysing the complex and interconnected nature of digital media requires information and guidance, as well as opportunities for both reflexivity and collectivity. The creative and reflective approach trialled through the fieldwork indicated promise in supporting the development of the young people's critical digital literacies. Notwithstanding this, the call for a critical digital literacy that connects meaningfully with young people's digital practices remains a priority.

Conclusions

Writing almost 20 years ago Nicholas Negroponte predicted a post-digital future, in which 'being digital' would be 'noticed only by its absence, not its presence' (1998, n.p.). Implicit in Negroponte's description of 'being digital' was an inevitability that these changes would occur. He writes: 'We have a similar blindness today, because we just cannot imagine a world in which our sense of identity and community truly cohabitates the real and virtual realms' (Negroponte, 1998, n.p.). While the young people's lives *were* digital, they still struggled to integrate, explain and make sense of the distributed and emergent digital experiences that took place across digital media. In epistemological terms, the young people were still very much 'becoming digital'. While academic understandings and theories of digital processes account for the complexity and nuance of digital experiences, they may not match the actual lived digital experiences of many young people, or adults for that matter. Providing young people with the linguistic and theoretical tools to help make sense of the new and diverse social experiences they encounter across their digital networks is an important step in developing their critical digital literacies.

This chapter has linked the findings from this study to broader theoretical concerns relating to digital media and young people. In doing so, several key challenges emerge for those concerned with the development of critical digital literacies. The first is a pressing need to increase young people's technical understanding of both the structure of digital networks *and* the coded architecture of the individual digital texts they use. Approaching social media as a digital text to be analysed would highlight not only their interpretive and flexible qualities, but also the contingent nature of their production and reception. Second, there is a need to increase technical knowledge of the way content and information flows across networks, to highlight the complex and intertextual ways a user makes meaning in digital spaces. This would not only increase technical understandings of the digital context, but also provide a basis upon which a more critical perspective might be forged. This critical perspective has a personal dimension, which relates to young people's affective experiences of digital media. A key challenge here is developing language to enable young people to unpack and examine how affect circulates, collects and dissolves across their networks.

While it is significant that young people believe that safe and secure digital practices are an individualised responsibility, it is perhaps not surprising given the rhetoric of the cybersafety message. The discourse of the 'digital native' plays into this, as young people come to see adults as 'digital immigrants' with little to offer when it comes to innovative use of technology. As a socially and culturally situated practice, digital literacies are intimately connected to young people's identities, communication practices and participation in society. It is therefore vital that they have support in developing and extending them. In the final chapter I propose an approach to critical digital literacies education that I have tentatively called 'critical digital design'. However, young people's literacies are not only the responsibility of teachers and educators alone, but in fact all those who have a stake in our digital future.

Note

1 See: http://edgerank.net/

References

Ahmed, S. (2010). Happy objects. In M. Gregg & G. Seigworth (Eds.), *The Affect Theory Reader*. Durham and London: Duke University Press.

Althusser, L. (1971). Ideology and ideological state apparatuses: Notes towards an investigation. In *'Lenin and Philosophy' and Other Essays*. London: New Left Books.

Avila, J., & Pandya, J. (2013). *Critical digital literacies as social praxis*. New York: Peter Lang Publishing Inc.

Bauman, Z. (2001). *The Individualized Society*. Cambridge, UK: Polity Press.

Beck, U. (1992). *Risk Society: Towards a New Modernity*. London: Sage Publications.

Beneito-Montagut, R. (2015). Encounters on the social web: Everyday life and emotions online. *Sociological Perspectives*, advanced online publication. doi:10.1177/0731121415569284

Berriman, L., & Thomson, R. (2015). Spectacles of intimacy? Mapping the moral landscape of teenage social media. *Journal of Youth Studies*, 18(5), 583–597.

Berry, D. (2011). *The Philosophy of Software: Code and Mediation in the Digital Age*. London: Palgrave Macmillan.

Berry, D. (2013). Against remediation. In G. Lovink & M. Rasch (Eds.), *Unlike Us: Social Media Monopolies and their Alternatives*. Amsterdam: Institute of Network Cultures.

Blake, K. (2018). Sexy selfies just latest step to win complex game of evolution. *The Age*. Retrieved from www.theage.com.au/national/sexy-selfies-just-latest-step-to-win-complex-game-of-evolution-20180410-p4z8op.html

Boczkowski, P. J. (1999). Mutual shaping of users and technologies in a national virtual community. *Journal of Communication*, 49(2), 86–108.

Bolter, J. D., & Grusin, R. (2000). *Remediation: Understanding New Media*. Cambridge, MA: The MIT Press.

Bucher, T. (2012). Want to be on the top? Algorithmic power and the threat of invisibility of Facebook. *New Media & Society*, 14(7), 1164–1180.

Buckingham, D. (2011). Foreword. In M. Thomas (Ed.), *Deconstructing Digital Natives: Young People, Technology and New Literacies*. Hoboken, NJ: Taylor & Francis.

Carrington, V. (2015). 'It's changed my life': iPhone as technological artefact. In R. H. Jones, A. Chik, & C. A. Hafner (Eds.), *Discourses and Digital Practices: Doing Discourse Analysis in the Digital Age*. London and New York: Routledge.

Choi, W. (2012). Inception or interpellation? The Slovenian School, Butler and Althusser. *Rethinking Marxism: A Journal of Economics, Culture & Society*, 25(1), 23–37.

Dean, J. (2005). Communicative capitalism: Circulation and the foreclosure of politics. *Cultural Politics*, 1(1), 51–74.

Dienst, R. (1994). *Still Life in Real Time: Theory After Television*. Durham & London: Duke University Press.

Dobson, A. S., & Ringrose, J. (2015). Sext education: Pedagogies of sex, gender and shame in the schoolyards of Tagged and Exposed. *Sex Education: Sexuality, Society and Learning*, advanced online publication. doi:10.1080/14681811.2015.1050486

Elliot, A. (2010). Social theory and psychoanalysis. In A. Elliot (Ed.), *The Routledge Companion to Social Theory*. London: Routledge.

Foucault, M. (1980). *Power/Knowledge: Selected Interviews & Other Writings*. New York: Pantheon Books.

Fuchs, C. (2014). *Social Media: A Critical Introduction*. London: Sage

Fuller, M. (2005). *Media Ecologies: Materialist Energies in Art and Technoculture*. Cambridge, MA: The MIT Press.

Fuller, M. (2008). *Software Studies: A Lexicon*. Cambridge, MA: MIT Press.

Gee, J. P. (1991). What is literacy? In C. Mitchell & K. Weiler (Eds.), *Re-writing Literacy: Culture and the Discourse of the Other*. New York: Bergin and Garvey.

Gillen, J. (2014). *Digital Literacies*. New York: Routledge.

Goffey, A. (2008). Algorithm. In M. Fuller (Ed.), *Software Studies: A Lexicon* (pp.11–29). Cambridge, MA: MIT Press.

Gregg, M., & Seigworth, G. (2010). *The Affect Theory Reader*. Durham & London: Duke University Press.

Herring, S. (2008). Questioning the generational divide: Technological exoticism and adult constructions of online youth identity. In D. Buckingham (Ed.), *Youth, Identity and Digital Media*. Cambridge, MA: The MIT Press.

Hillis, K., Paasonen, S., & Petit, M. (2015). *Networked Affect*. Cambridge, MA: The MIT Press.

Karppi, T. (2015). Happy accidents: Facebook and the value of affect. In K. Hillis, S. Paasonen, & M. Petit (Eds.), *Networked Affect*. Cambridge, MA: The MIT Press.

Lievrouw, L., & Livingstone, S. (2009). Introduction. In L. Lievrouw & S. Livingstone (Eds.), *New Media: Sage Benchmarks in Communication*. London: Sage Publications.

Livingstone, S. (2009a). 'Digital Natives': A Myth? In R. Das & C. Beckett (Eds.), *A POLIS paper*. London: London School of Economics. Retrieved from www.lse.ac.uk/media@lse/Polis/Files/digitalnatives.pdf.

Livingstone, S. (2009b). *Children and the Internet: Great Expectations, Challenging Realities*. Cambridge, UK: Polity Press.

Livingstone, S., & Helsper, E. (2010). Balancing opportunities and risks in teenagers' use of the internet: The role of online skills and self-efficacy. *New Media & Society*, 12(2), 309–329.

Malpas, J. (2009). On the non-autonomy of the virtual. *Convergence*, 15(2), 135–139.

Manovich, L. (2001). *Language of New Media*. Cambridge, MA: The MIT Press.

Manovich, L. (2013). *Software Takes Command*. New York and London: Bloomsbury Academic.

Massumi, B. (2002). *Parables for the Virtual: Movement, Affect, Sensation*. Durham, UK: Duke University Press.

Massumi, B. (2015). *Politics of Affect*. Cambridge, UK: Polity Press.

McCosker, A. (2016). Managing cyberbullying: The three layers of control in digital citizenship. In A. Mc Cosker, S. Vivienne, & A. Johns (Eds.), *Negotiating Digital Citizenship* (pp.21–39). London & New York: Rowman & Littlefield.

McGilchrist, I. (2009). *The Master and his Emissary: The Divided Brain and the Making of the Western World*. New Haven and London: Yale University Press.

Munster, A. (2013). *An Aesthesia of Networks*. Cambridge, MA: The MIT Press.

Negroponte, N. (1998). Beyond digital. *Wired*, 6(12).

Paasonen, S., Hillis, K., & Petit, M. (2015). Networks of transmission: Intensity, sensation, value. In *Networked Affect*. Cambridge, MA: The MIT Press.

Prensky, M. (2001a). Digital natives, digital immigrants, part 1. *On the Horizon*, 9(5), 1–6.

Prensky, M. (2001b). Digital natives, digital immigrants, part 2: Do they really think differently? *On the Horizon*, 9(6), 1–6.

Pybus, J. (2013). Social networks and cultural workers: Towards and archive for the prosumer. *Journal of Cultural Economics*, 6(2), 137–152.

Pybus, J. (2015). Accumulating affect: Social networks and their archives of feeling. In K. Hillis, S. Paasonen, & M. Petit (Eds.), *Networked Affect*. Cambridge, MA: The MIT Press.

Salaway, G., & Caruso, J. (2008). *The ECAR Study of Undergraduate Students and Information Technology*. Boulder, CO: Educause Center for Applied Research.

Seigworth, G., & Gregg, M. (2010). An inventory of shimmers. In M. Gregg & G. Seigworth (Eds.), *The Affect Theory Reader*. Durham and London: Duke University Press.

Selwyn, N. (2009). The digital native—myth and reality. *Aslib Proceedings*, 61(4), 364–379.

Tapscott, D., & Williams, A. D. (2006). *Wikinomics: How Mass Collaboration Changes Everything*. New York: Penguin.

Thomas, M. (2011). Technology, education, and the discourse of the digital native. In M. Thomas (Ed.), *Deconstructing Digital Natives: Young People, Technology, and the New Literacies*. Hoboken, NJ: Taylor & Francis.

Twenge, J. M. (2006). *Generation Me: Why Today's Young Americans are More Confident, Assertive, Entitled—and More Miserable—Than Ever Before*. New York: Free Press.

Twenge, J. M. (2017). Have smartphones destroyed a generation? *The Atlantic*, September. Retrieved from www.theatlantic.com/magazine/archive/2017/09/has-the-smartphone-destroyed-a-generation/534198/

Twenge, J. M., & Campbell, W. K. (2009). *The Narcissism Epidemic: Living in the Age of Entitlement*. New York: Simon & Schuster Inc.

van Dijck, J. (2013). *The Culture of Connectivity: A Critical History of Social Media*. New York: Oxford University Press.

van Dijk, J., & van Deursen, A. (2014). *Digital Skills: Unlocking the Information Society*. New York: Palgrave Macmillan.

7

TOWARD A *CRITICAL* DIGITAL DISPOSITION

Throughout this book I have sought to represent as faithfully as possible the young people's digital practices and understandings based on what they have reported, shared and made during the course of the fieldwork. I am extremely grateful for the generosity of the young people involved, and was constantly impressed by the thoughtfulness with which they constructed their responses to the research provocations. Over the course of the fieldwork we considered a wide range of issues that influence and shape their use of digital media. We have explored the contextual and historical factors and discourses that inform their digital practices, thereby identifying the connections and disconnections that exist across the digital platforms they engage with. Key insights have emerged that shed light not only on their digital literacies, but also on how research might be conducted with young people in ways that are mutually beneficial to both researcher and participant.

The methodological approach brought together social theory and creative practices to expand the ways of researching digital literacies beyond the typical frameworks of learning sciences and new literacies. I sought to develop approaches to researching young people's digital literacies in ways that were responsive to the features of the digital context, including: the interconnected network of digital texts; the coded architecture of digital platforms; and the intertwining of affective and personal responses in meaning-making processes. In Chapter 1 I argued that current models of critical digital literacy have struggled to incorporate these features, leading to a series of unresolved and unproductive tensions.

One aim of the fieldwork was to find techniques that bridged the tensions identified in Chapter 1 in approaches to critical literacies education. To do this I trialled a series of research provocations that encouraged both personal and ideological responses to the issues emerging from using digital media; marrying collective concerns with individual practices; and improving technical understandings without displacing criticality. The fieldwork explored critical self-reflection, visualisation and redesign and re-articulation as techniques for developing critical digital literacies. While these techniques do not represent an all-encompassing approach to digital literacies, they might resolve the tensions outlined and work to complement existing models of digital literacy. Throughout the fieldwork, creative processes were used as both a physical prompt and cognitive 'tool' to represent understandings and facilitate more critical perspectives from the participants.

In this chapter, I return to the literacies focus set out in Chapter 1 to identify and discuss some ways to cultivate a critical digital disposition in young people. I outline a pedagogical approach to developing digital literacies, tentatively called 'critical digital design'. Following a sociocultural approach to literacies, I maintain that learning in and around the digital should not only take place in formal educational institutions, but also, and perhaps more effectively, in the various 'non-school' settings young people encounter. With this in mind, I focus on how the various groups who have a stake in young people's digital practices might also work to improve the current situation. These groups include: schools and education officials; parents and families; technology companies; and of course young people themselves. The notion of critical digital literacies holds different meanings for each of these groups. However, an overarching conclusion that might be drawn from this book is that cultivating critical and agentive digital practices involves a more consistent approach that draws on a wider range of people and resources.

What does it mean to be critical of the digital?

While the young people in this study demonstrated an awareness of issues to do with privacy, targeted advertising and technological convergence, and some innovative critical practices, it was telling that they had little or no support for developing these understandings, at school or elsewhere. Several had acquired these practices through observation of peers or others online and often through a process of trial and error. However, young people are often just beginning to develop a critical sensibility and need help and education on how to do this (Isin & Ruppert, 2015).

Critical understandings require specific knowledge and practices, as well as opportunities to develop a *personal* sense of what it means to be critical and creative in the digital context. If young people do not understand these sociotechnical arrangements, then their potential to challenge, resist and reimagine these is limited. Digital literacies must encompass more than a set of technical skills. Learning within a sociotechnical system involves technical mastery and inquiry, analysis and critique. In Chapter 1, I described these skills as necessary for the development of a 'critical disposition', which can be enacted within *and* across digital contexts. A critical disposition, however, is not often equated with productive and successful behaviour in the digital context. As Lovink and Rossiter (2005) explain, 'It takes effort to reflect on distrust as a productive principle' (n.p.).

In this final chapter I argue that critical digital literacies need to be reconceptualised in order to provide opportunities to consider and critique the broader social, political and economic issues, alongside programmes that seek to develop technical mastery. Drawing together the insights of the last seven chapters, it is now possible to sketch out how these findings might be applied to literacies research and education. I do this to address the challenges described by the young people throughout the book.

Implications for literacies education and research

Clearly there is a need for literacies education to help young people analyse the architecture of digital platforms, as well as the materialities of digital systems. A reconceptualised approach to digital literacies might focus on how the architecture of platforms manifests and maintains systems of power and privilege. For example, there is a pressing need to develop understandings of platform metrics and how they mobilise affect and contribute to cultural and economic forms of production. However, unlike more traditional models of critique, these understandings need to be 'launched' from a personal perspective, so that an individual's beliefs and emotions might be used to guide the analysis.

While critique begins with the individual, the focus group discussions involved in the fieldwork demonstrated just how productive it was for the young people to collectively reflect and consider concerns around digital socialities. That this collective approach was so enthusiastically embraced by the young people throughout the fieldwork, suggests that there is much merit in providing an opportunity to 'speak back' to the more individualised practices that typically characterise digital media use.

Critical digital design

While any approach is likely to involve a range of practices and approaches, the aim is to distinguish the techniques that are new in this context. Reflecting on the fieldwork we can now consider which aspects of the research provocations were most effective in scaffolding a critical digital disposition. Rather than focusing on specific technologies, the goal of the research provocations was to explore and expand on the human, interpretative process associated with digital media use. Drawing out the key features of the provocations, I identify four strategies that might constitute a critical digital design approach to literacies. These are: creativity and visualisation; transcendental critique; critical self-reflection; and interpretation and re-articulation of digital concepts.

Creativity and visualisation

Pursuing a creative approach to researching critical digital literacies clearly had benefits in helping the participants understand the more complex practices and issues that emerge from their relationship with digital media. By translating digital practices across contexts and materials, participants were required to slow down and reflect upon everyday digital processes. This opened up new perspectives and encouraged them to identify how features like context and convergence can make translation (and therefore digital practices) all the more complex. The physical movement of folding, painting and modelling also prompted a physical response from participants. This called forth affective responses as 'bodies think as they feel, on a level with their movements' (Massumi, 2015, p.211). Brought together through the creative process, cognitive and physical responses were found to open up new ways of thinking about digital media.

To extend upon this further, one might draw on digital aesthetics (Cubitt, 1998; Berry & Dieter, 2014) and data visualisation (Manovich, 2013) to decontextualise or defamiliarise digital texts, tools and practices. This might be used to suspend or interrupt commonly held assumptions and views of the digital and enable the identification of the ideologies that underpin some of the dominant digital platforms. However, visualisation also expands the realm of possibilities available for daily digital practices and redesign. As a practice, visualisation can help to unpack and understand the metaphors that organise our interaction with digital media and networks. As van den Boomen (2014) argues:

> If metaphors structurally encapsulate digital practices we may wonder what they … do to our understanding of digital code, and what this means for digital code's far reaching implications for culture and society.
>
> *(p.13)*

As part of critical digital design, the main purpose of visualisation is to develop a more practical and in-depth understanding of digital networks, while at the same time questioning the conceptual tools that shape our engagement. However, visualisation could also be used to chart the elements of the digital dispositif, or even reimagine and restructure digital networks.

Transcendental critique

Implicit to creativity and visualisation is the reinstatement of a transcendental critique or critical distance from digital networks (Taylor, 2006), in which social and political issues related to digital media can be examined. The speed and ephemerality of information in the digital era have caused many scholars to argue that the 'separate space' from which to launch critical analysis has been lost; critique must be immanent and take place from inside the 'information order' (Lash, 2002, p.176). Like others (e.g. Kress, 2010), Lash equates critique with the ability to exert control from within by refashioning and re-appropriating digital media to suit our needs and desires, marking what some call a decidedly affirmative version of critique (Taylor & Ruiz, 2007).

There are intrinsic difficulties associated with developing a critical view on digital media. Not only are digital technologies evolving rapidly, but they often become embedded in everyday life before we have had a chance to evaluate their purpose and function. A transcendental perspective enables a different kind of engagement. While technical skills need to be developed in conjunction with the technology in question, when distanced from it a more critical and reflective pattern of thought is able to emerge. The creative workshops and research provocations established a critical distance on digital practices, which made it easier for the young people to identify and analyse complex issues associated with usage. There was no underlying sense of right and wrong, as these were personal interpretations and responses to a provocation, rather than 'textbook' answers.

However, there is a tendency for critique to become an exercise in mistrust, rather than a deeper, more detailed analysis. Bruno Latour (2004) argues that critique should not be preoccupied with matters of fact, but matters of concern, so that it is a constructive process, as well as deconstructive. This changes what we think of as the 'critic':

> The critic is not the one who debunks, but the one who assembles. The critic is not the one who lifts the rugs from under the feet of the naïve believers, but the one who offers the participants arenas in which to gather.
>
> *(Latour, 2004, p.246)*

This approach has particular resonance in the digital era, as the parts of the system that *should be* critiqued have become 'blackboxed' or hidden from view. As a starting point, critique needs to involve a process of revealing the structure of the internet and the architecture of platforms, so that individuals have the opportunity to make an informed choice about their actions and practices. In this spirit the research provocations opened up opportunities to reveal, analyse, reflect and (re)create. A transcendental position away from digital media facilitates this process, as the social and political issues related to digital media become easier to identify. A sense of 'distance' from digital media might be encouraged through a series of activities and provocations that decontextualise everyday use. The goal is not to mistrust the digital media in question, but rather to reassess, reflect and renew engagement with it. Subsequent to this, technical skills might then be used to realise positive changes, not only to individual digital practices but to society as well.

Critical self-reflection

Critical self-reflection was also found to be an important way to explore the relationship between personal, affective responses to digital texts and broader ideological concerns. Rather than seeing these two aspects of digital media as oppositional, through critical self-reflection the personal becomes a 'conduit' to the ideological (Misson & Morgan, 2006). This practice might begin with analysis of personal digital practices, but through analysis, discovery and provocation these practices become, in a sense, 'objectified' and are therefore seen as symptomatic of the wider digital context.

For example, through their visualisation Rachel and Stacey explored how power is circulated on social media. As part of this they unpacked the role of metrics and reflected on their own social media practices. This brought together the ideological and the personal in transformative ways, particularly for Rachel. Exploring personal digital histories with particular focus on how these are shaped by digital discourses was another way in which dominant ideologies might be questioned. Such a process might also encourage the individual to see their identity as fluid, thereby resisting the inclination to essentialise identity to any one community (Janks, 2010) or digital platform. At the same time the act of 'tracing' implies there is a core to their identity that remains consistent across time.

Critical self-reflection becomes a way in which the individual can move between the personal and the ideological while exploring and analysing concepts that are embedded in digital technologies and networks. Such a process is not simply the cataloguing of digital practices, but involves some degree of discomfort, as broader social and political issues are drawn into the exploration and ultimately linked to individual practices. As Megan Boler (1999) writes, without the critical dimension self-reflection can be 'reduced to a form of solipsism' (p.178). While critical self-reflection involves 'discomfort', it has the potential to be genuinely transformative to the individual and society. If successfully implemented, critical self-reflection encourages the individual to see personal digital practices as a form of political engagement.

Interpretation and re-articulation of digital concepts

Reconciling collective concerns with individual practices also involves questioning the rhetoric that has come to shape the way we think about digital media. For example, to describe web 2.0 as a 'participatory culture' (Jenkins, 2006) and social media as a 'networked public' (boyd, 2014), automatically links these platforms to concepts of freedom, democracy and civic engagement. Such descriptions develop positive associations that ultimately conceal some of the more complex and inequitable issues of digital media use (Fuchs, 2014). Peeling back this rhetoric to understand the reality of digital systems in provocation four was a useful way of developing a critical disposition towards digital media. While there were limited opportunities to develop technical mastery in this study, the young people's enthusiasm for the redesign and re-articulation activity demonstrated that applying newfound knowledge to transform current symbols and icons was a useful way of scaffolding critique.

Considering what concepts such as 'free', 'friend', 'link', 'like', 'online community', 'share', 'news' and 'open' actually represent in the digital context can lead to a more conscious and knowing mode of engagement. Not only are assumed definitions questioned, but it encourages examination of how and why these phrases have been redefined in the digital context. As Hodge and Kress (1988) write, texts reproduce and reconstitute 'systems' of thought and discourse. Questioning and challenging the system of signs that give digital texts their meaning also challenges the broader discourse. Coupled with redesign and re-articulation, critique becomes an opportunity for change, rather than a lesson in right and wrong. A second step in this involves the *re-articulation* (Apple, 2013) of these concepts, where they might be applied in alternative ways that seek to counter hegemonic discourse.

Listening to the young people's digital experiences over the course of a year revealed the gaps that exist between their experiences of digital media, academic theorisations of this relationship and common educational approaches to digital literacies. The four strategies outlined above for developing critical understandings of the digital were generative to both the young people and myself as the researcher, indicating that this method of critical digital literacies holds promise. However, a sociocultural approach means literacy learning takes place *across* young people's lives, not just in workshops or educational institutions. Different stakeholder groups should be involved to help build understandings, and augment and extend upon what has been learnt more formally. I conclude this book by identifying the role that stakeholders played in supporting young people's critical digital literacies, outlining how this support might be improved in the future.

Implications for schools and education officials

While the fieldwork set out to explore the significance of schools in young people's digital lives, it was notably peripheral in many instances. Part of the problem appears to be that schools assume young people already have the digital skills they need. Despite this, recent Australian research (Donaghue, 2015; Crawford, 2017) has shown that young peoples' Information and Communication and Technology (ICT) literacies are actually decreasing. The National Assessment Program (NAP) ICT literacy report, for example, 'shows a weakening in the average performance of year 6 and year 10 students in 2014' (Donaghue, 2015, n.p.). Based on the findings of this study, there are at least two ways in which schools could better support the development of digital literacies.

First, schools need to play a greater role in developing young people's technical knowledge and skill. Assumptions should not be made about young people's digital capabilities and programmes designed to expand and extend skills should still be a priority. While coding clubs and robotics classes are clearly exciting and engaging for students, this is more *extra*-ordinary digital learning. The bulk of many young people's digital experiences involve the more *ordinary* practices of information gathering, entertainment and social networking. It is important for schools and teachers to identify what their students are *already* doing with digital media, and to develop programmes and resources tailored to their needs. In regard to developing critical digital literacies, the findings of this study suggest young people need information on the structure of the internet (i.e. what it is, where it comes from), as well as greater understanding of the architecture of platforms. This might start with building a vocabulary for digital media that consists of words like: platforms; algorithms; interface; metrics; personal data; personalisation; profile; online community; security and privacy.

One way a school-based curriculum might approach scaffolding critical digital literacies is by applying Gehl's (2014) notion of 'reverse engineering social media'.

Focusing on the platform interface, Gehl argues that reverse engineering is a useful way to critique 'the final, implemented product … seeking clues as to why it was put together in the way it was and how it fits into an overall architecture' (p.10). He outlines three reasons why reverse engineering is a valuable process to engage in, all of which have relevance to the issues raised by the young people. First, in a system of 'closed code and proprietary formats' (p.10), reverse engineering looks to the interface and the artefacts, seeing how these shape uses and, more fundamentally, users. This enables a more detailed understanding of 'why some uses are privileged while other technically and equally possible uses are denied' (p.11).

Second, reverse engineering seeks to move back through time, attempting to uncover the links that contemporary technology and its metaphors have with 'prior technologies and practices' (p.11). In doing so, a more detailed understanding of the new forms of sociality might be generated for critical analysis. Finally, it also embraces positive design aspects in that it is 'a critical dissection of existing technology with the goal of building a better system' (p.12). This approach would encourage young people to consider what works well, but also what could work *better*. Whether or not the alternative social media platform is created is beside the point. By instigating critical insights, reverse engineering social media increases young people's power and agency relative to these digital platforms.

Critical reverse engineering fits with a critical digital design approach, providing a more comprehensive activity for the 'interpretation and re-articulation' section. Critical reverse engineering could be applied to other forms of digital media, including gaming platforms and music software. Not only would this approach build technical understandings of digital media, but it would also encourage young people to think about how the architecture of the platform shapes users' practices. In doing so, an understanding of what Grint and Woolgar (1997) call the 'textual organisation' or 'the relationships made possible between entities within and beyond the text' (p.73) would be developed. This takes into account the coded architecture of the software that organises the digital text, as well as the influence of other users and the discourses that frame these digital practices.

Schools would be the most appropriate site to develop critical self-reflection in young people in regard to their digital media use. Most schools in Australia do not allow students to use social media, blocking mainstream platforms such as Facebook and YouTube. While young people can work around this through their mobile phones, the principle that class time is a social media-free zone still exists. This critical distance might be conducive to initiating a more self-reflexive approach to digital media use. As highlighted throughout the book, digital texts are complexly interconnected and shaped by underlying social and political forces. From the somewhat segregated position of the school, young people might be given a different perspective on their use of digital media. This resonates with the transcendental critique outlined in the critical digital design approach and the argument of Paul Taylor (2006), which contends that the difficulties critiquing power structures in what he calls the 'new information order' point to the need for an 'elevated' or transcendental perspective on digital media networks.

In evaluating the school as a site for digital literacy programmes, it is perhaps spaces *beyond* the classroom that hold the most promise. Research by Vickery (2012) and Hull and Pandya (2004) into out-of-school digital literacy programmes demonstrated that it was not just the content of the programme that was important to its success. The mindset of the students was different in the out-of-school space and this was, in part, due to the more supportive environment created. Given the sensitive and personal nature of digital practices, establishing an environment of trust and respect is key to the success of the programme. In light of these findings, the more self-reflexive aspect to critical digital literacies might be better facilitated in spaces attached to the school, but separate from the classroom. These are essentially a 'third space' in which young people can draw on different discourses that are in-between other domains (Pahl & Rowsell, 2012; Gutierrez, 2011). This might be in a multipurpose room or some other kind of alternative space within the school setting.

Implications for platform operators

In contrast to the marginal role played by schools, platform operators shaped these young people's digital practices considerably. Their influence was not only functional (i.e. enabling access and navigation of a platform or site), but also behavioural, establishing patterns and habits for future digital practices (i.e. returning to the site to check notifications and feeling the need to stay abreast of what others were doing). However, platform operators have an *economic* stake in how users interact with their service, meaning we cannot assume they always have young people's best interests at heart. Indeed, several recent studies and events (Kramer et al., 2014; Levin, 2017) have shown how Facebook has taken advantage of having such a captive audience.

In Chapters 4 and 5 we observed how the young people become bound to the platform through affect. Young people are drawn to the platform to expand their socialities, and for many in this study that was an obvious reason for using these platforms. However, the architecture of the platform captures and mobilises the affective implications of these interactions and representations, which can then be used for a range of *other* (economic) purposes. For this reason, encouraging young people to critique digital platforms is not as straightforward as deconstructing other texts, due to the affective responses that are intertwined with their use. This was demonstrated throughout the study when the young people expressed discontent with Facebook, yet still had no plan to act differently or close their account. While finding an alternative social media platform might appear the logical response, a few key platforms have become so firmly embedded in social practices using alternatives was not a viable option.

A more effective approach might be to lobby technology companies to change some of the more problematic aspects of the social media platforms they own and manage. Given the social, political and economic conditions these platforms contribute to and create, imagining how things might be different is not easy.

Socialities have shifted in response to technology, which can make it hard to see these processes for what they are (Simondon, 1959/2010). This requires a separation of the social and the technical in order to understand how the design and structure of these platforms actually initiates and maintains particular forms of sociality via the commodification of digital practices. There are several ways in which platform operators influence the way the user comes to see themselves and their relationships to others. Identifying these is a crucial first step in considering how social media might be better.

As previously discussed, the first step in engaging with any mainstream social media is the creation of a profile, which is essentially an online representation of user identity. Despite the fact that the primary focus of social networking sites is connecting and communicating with *others*, the construction of individual identity can become a preoccupation. As Ludovico and Cirio (2014) argue, social networks are 'based on the elusive sport (or perhaps urge) to position ourselves' and to answer the 'fundamental identity question "who am I?"' (p.255). Through user profiles, many mainstream social media platforms place the individual, rather than the network or collective, at the centre of the social networking experience. If the goal of social networks is to connect, share and communicate with others then it is worthwhile considering how the collective, rather than the individual, might be the focus of the platform. This might initiate a different set of digital practices, and perhaps greater experimentation and innovation due to less fear of personal judgement.

Other principles of social media platforms that shape young people's digital experiences are the corporate ownership of content and centralised systems of control. As observed throughout the study, these principles are so deeply ingrained in the network that it was hard for these young people to see that this is not simply 'how it is', but instead a technique to raise profits for technology companies. Technology companies have an obligation to their users to be transparent in the way these platforms operate. However, these principles, particularly those to do with collecting, archiving and selling users' information, are integral to the business model of many technology companies. It is not surprising that attempts to challenge and change the policies and processes of platforms like Facebook have rarely been successful (van Dijck, 2013). Nevertheless, there are still opportunities to lessen the influence technology companies have over young people's digital practices.

One option would be to put in place a set of governmental processes that encourage and enable smaller, alternative social media platforms to flourish. While there are some alternative social media sites and applications available (i.e. App. net,[1] Lorea,[2] GNU social,[3] Diaspora[4]) there need to be many more. Gehl (2015) argues that 'corporate social media', like Google, Facebook and Twitter, have in fact 'intensified some of the problems of mass media power and anti-democratic communication' (p.1), because of a for-profit model, which is hostile to alternative ideas and discourses. He argues that alternative social media, not corporate social media, 'offer a more fitting suite of tools for people to both make media and shape media distribution infrastructures' (p.2). This would enable young people to choose from a variety of social media platforms that represent a range of different principles and processes. Diaspora, for example, is based on three key philosophies—decentralisation, freedom and privacy. Lorea, on the other hand, gives people or networks of people the option to participate on any of the existent social networks, or create their own network.

These platforms expand the range of ways one can communicate online, providing an alternative to the increasingly homogenous structure and function of mainstream social media platforms. In 2015, Twitter, for example, dispensed with the 'Favourite' button and replaced it with the like button, thereby aligning with Facebook's social buttons and in many ways decreasing the range of expressive functions available on mainstream social media platforms. Given the dominance of platforms like Google and Facebook, the government needs to reinstate its role in regulating the media landscape. Policy frameworks that regulate and support a more diverse range of technology providers are needed to give smaller technology companies with a different business model (i.e. collective, decentralised) a greater chance of competing with the main players.

Finally, because their business model is dependent on the labour of everyday people, technology companies should also be required to give something back to citizens. Microsoft and Intel have developed digital literacy programmes geared towards young people; however, there need to be more programmes of this kind. The extensive reach and resources of companies like Google and Facebook means they are well placed to improve the overall digital skills and literacies of citizens. However, whether they do or not is dependent on regulation. Governments could put in place legislation that makes doing business in their country contingent on the development of educational programmes for citizens. This could be a series of digital tools or programmes that help to build the digital literacies of young people. Alternatively, it could be workshops or mentoring programmes that provide opportunities to develop innovative digital practices or even career pathways. There is great potential for governments, community groups and everyday citizens to work with these companies to improve their skills and digital literacies.

Implications for parents and families

Parents and guardians played a minor role in these young people's digital lives, with their main concern being protecting their child in digital spaces. Not surprisingly, most of the young people in this study identified as 'cybersafe'. They used strict privacy settings on social media and were wary of interacting with strangers online. They were also mindful of balancing time spent online with time spent offline. As far as developing their digital literacies, however, parents were decidedly absent. One reason for this situation was the life stage of these young people. Teenagers are in the process of individuating themselves from family, meaning there is a natural struggle between parental control and a growing sense of independence. A contributing factor is that many of the young people identified as 'digital natives', meaning they may not have seen their parents or older relatives as a source of information or guidance.

Increasing parental involvement would begin by countering some of the popular myths that have shaped the way adults have come to think about young people's relationship with digital media. Given the colonial undertones of the 'digital native' argument, it is not surprising that adults believe they need to play a role in 'civilising' these young people, sometimes in a rather didactic way. Overturning this thinking would encourage parents to see that many young people, like adults, self-monitor their use of digital devices and are not as uniform or innovative in their practices as might be thought.

It would be far more useful for parents to initiate an ongoing dialogue with their children about their digital experiences. Most parents have familiarity with the various aspects of their children's lives, including home life, school, hobbies and extracurricular interests. Parents are well placed to help young people make sense of how their digital practices crisscross these domains. This involves more than parents becoming Facebook friends with their child. Observing online behaviour in this way might work to allay (or perhaps stir) parental fears; however, by itself this does little to help young people work through the challenges that emerge from social media use. Furthermore, as Marwick and boyd (2014) explain, social stenography (hiding in plain sight) is a technique commonly practised by many teenagers that makes it easy to hide content and posts from parents on social media.

If parents are to play a meaningful role in scaffolding their children's digital literacies, a supportive dialogue needs to be initiated much earlier. Analysis of these young people's socialisation into the digital context shows that the patterns for parental involvement were set early. Yet it seems the adults remained in the role of protector, missing opportunities to discuss their children's increasingly sophisticated and complex digital needs. As protector, parents are more likely to be seen as a barrier than a support to their children's digital practices. This is exacerbated by the myth of the 'digital native', which reinforces the idea, to both parent and child, that adults have little to offer when it comes to developing digital practices.

Providing parents and families with more support and resources on how to talk to their children about digital media is one way forward. Much of the support available to parents today is directed at keeping children safe and tends to frame the issues through shock and fear. A more generative starting point is to see digital media as providing opportunities for young people, and supporting them to make the most of these. With this in mind there is a need for further resources and programmes that help parents support their children in the digital challenges they face. These need to be grounded in a local or national context, as young people's digital practices are given meaning through the social and cultural discourses in which they are embedded. Increasing the number of community-based digital literacy programmes might also help. While coding clubs are becoming more widespread there is room for these programmes to include a critical dimension, as well as being more inclusive of parents and families.

Implications for young people

Peers were shown to influence which digital platforms the young people were introduced to and how they came to use them. In this way, peers could be thought of as expanding and guiding, but also constraining the kinds of digital practices that were engaged in. Despite seeing many of their peers each day at school and meeting them online through the various digital platforms they used, there was only a minimal amount of discussion amongst these young people about more *critical* interpretations of digital spaces and practices. Instead, their discussions of digital media could be typically traced along the lines of the platform (i.e. what was posted, what was trending), or the social dynamics of their peer group. In this way, peers were influential on digital practices, but not in ways that challenged the status quo. The young people *did* demonstrate a latent desire to talk about the more critical and complex issues that took place on social media platforms; however, the challenge is how to make critical perspectives and practices an everyday topic of conversation.

Making digital literacies a desired form of social capital is one way this might be achieved (Pinkard, 2015). In this context, social capital refers not only to the dispositions and skills of the individual, but also the conversations and insights that they can share with other young people. Digital mastery is often associated with the 'geek' or a socially isolated 'uncool' person. While this image might be changing, making digital literacies a desired form of social capital would require breaking or reconfiguring some of these associations. Promoting inspirational role models and mentors for young people in digital technologies might be one way of doing this. While the young people demonstrated a growing criticality, these dispositions need to be more readily recognised and valued by society.

Increasing the social capital associated with digital literacies might also be prompted by a series of digital tools and resources that promote more critical understandings of the way platforms and technology companies work. For example, digital tools that help young people become aware of how personal information is made available to technology companies and other third parties through their use of digital platforms is a good place to start. Data Selfie,[5] a browser extension that is designed to show your Facebook data traces and the personal profiling that takes place through machine learning algorithms, is free and easy to use. Another approach might be to create an online critical 'tool shop', where innovative digital resources that exist freely through websites like GitHub are collected and presented as experimentations into more critical use of digital technology.

The key would be for these kinds of tools to 'catch on' in much the same way that other mainstream digital platforms have. One way might be to harness the propensity for some digital content to 'go viral'. Although Munster (2013) explains it is hard to predict why certain videos, memes or ideas go viral, initiating a series of online campaigns or promotions based around critical digital practices would be worth experimenting with. In doing so, a more general and collective criticality might be established through the building of skills. Given the 2018 Cambridge Analytica scandal and the growing distrust of mainstream social media platforms, the time is ripe to launch such an approach. While these tools already exist, it is about bringing them to the attention of young people and giving them the kind of cachet that other mainstream digital media possess.

Facilitating conversations *between* young people in regard to the challenges they face when using digital media was also helpful. One benefit of the conversational format of the fieldwork in this study was that through the group discussions participants came to realise that others were experiencing the same issues. Up until that point it appeared these issues were something that most had worked through privately. It was revelatory for many of the young people to find that others had had similar experiences. As Archer (2007) writes, 'experiential overlap' (p.84) across contexts is important to expanding familiarity with others. Increasing the frequency of these types of discussions might therefore instil a more collective response that bonds young people and speaks back to the more individualised experiences of social media reported.

It is up to all stakeholders to reinforce the idea that these private experiences are actually felt by many. This simple shift in thinking echoes the broader aspiration of turning private issues into a public concern. In many respects this has been a goal of this book. As Mills (2000) writes, the social scientist should try to make connections between the personal and 'public issues of social structure' (p.8). However, as has been discussed, it is even more transformative for young people themselves to make those connections through everyday conversations and discussions. In this way they would 'translate personal troubles into public issues, and public issues into the terms of their human meaning' (Mills, 2000, p.187). In bringing these issues to a more general discussion we might be better placed to address them. While the critical digital design approach holds promise for digital literacies education, there is not one single way of improving young people's critical digital literacies—a whole range of resources, people and programmes are required to facilitate discussions that respond to the current and emerging issues identified throughout this book.

Final comments

This book has only scratched the surface when it comes to identifying and understanding the range of complex issues that emerge from young people's use of digital media. While new and different directions in developing critical digital literacies have been explored, in many respects it has raised more questions than it has answered. It joins a growing body of research in the area, underscoring the fact that the digital practices of young people should no longer be considered a novelty. Researchers need to develop questions, methods and interpretations of young people's digital lives to help identify, understand and provide support to the challenges that emerge. These are issues that look set to have longevity in the study of young people; they demand ongoing exploration from a range of different groups and people. Regardless of technological innovation, young people should never be conceived as a homogenous group of 'digital natives'. They will always be in a state of 'becoming digital'—never having all the answers and struggling to make sense of the shifting nature of their practices. In light of this, academic research that takes a similarly exploratory and speculative approach is needed.

Notes

1 See: https://app.net/
2 See: http://p2pfoundation.net/Lorea
3 See: www.gnu.org/software/social/
4 See: https://diasporafoundation.org/
5 See: www.dataselfie.it/#/

References

Apple, M. (2013). *Can education change society?*New York: Routledge.

Archer, M. S. (2007). *Making Our Way Through the World: Human Reflexivity and Social Mobility*. Cambridge, UK: Cambridge University Press.

Berry, D., & Dieter, M. (2014). *Postdigital Aesthetics—Art, Computation and Design*. Houndmills, Basingstoke, Hampshire, UK: Palgrave Macmillan.

Boler, M. (1999). *Feeling power: Emotions and education*. New York: Routledge.

boyd, d. (2014). *It's Complicated: The Social Lives of Networked Teens*. New Haven and London: Yale University Press.

Crawford, M. (2017). *ICT in Schools for Teaching and Learning. New South Wales Auditor-General's Report—Performance Audit*.

Cubitt, S. (1998). *Digital Aesthetics*. London: Sage Publications.

Deleuze, G., & Guattari, F. (1980/2013). *A Thousand Plateaus*. London and New York: Bloomsbury Academic.

Donaghue, G. (2015). *Report highlights need for renewed focus on digital technologies* [Press release]. Retrieved from: www.acara.edu.au/verve/_resources/321S1001.pdf

Foucault, M. (1980). *Power/Knowledge: Selected Interviews & Other Writings*. New York: Pantheon Books.

Fuchs, C. (2014). *Social Media: A Critical Introduction*. London: Sage

Galloway, A. (2011). Are some things unrepresentable? *Theory, Culture and Society*, 28(7–8), 85–102.

Gehl, R. W. (2014). *Reverse Engineering Social Media: Software, Culture and Political Economy in New Media Capitalism*. Philadelphia, PA: Temple University Press.

Gehl, R. W. (2015). The case for alternative social media. *Social Media + Society*, July–December, 1–12. doi: doi:10.1177/2056305115604338.

Grint, K., & Woolgar, S. (1997). *The Machine at Work: Technology, Work and Organization*. Cambridge: Polity Press.

Gutierrez, K. (2011). Developing a sociocultural literacy in the third space. *Reading Research Quarterly*, 43(2), 148–164.

Hodge, B., & Kress, G. R. (1988). *Social Semiotics*. Cambridge, UK: Polity Press in association with Basil Blackwell, Oxford, UK.

Hull, G., & Pandya, J. (2004). What is after-school worth? Developing literacy and identity out of school. *Voices in Urban Education*, Winter/Spring/Winter/Spring.

Isin, E., & Ruppert, E. (2015). *Being Digital Citizens*. London: Rowman & Littlefield.

Janks, H. (2010). *Literacy and Power*. New York: Routledge.

Jenkins, H. (2006). *Confronting the challenges of participatory culture: Media education for the 21st century.* MacArthur Foundation White Paper. Cambridge, MA: The MIT Press.

Kramer, A. D. I., Guillory, J. E., & Hancock, J. T. (2014). Experimental evidence of massive-scale emotional contagion through social networks. *Proceedings of the National Academy of Sciences,* 111, 8788–8790.

Kress, G. (2010). *Multimodality.* New York: Routledge.

Lash, S. (2002). *Critique of Information.* London: Sage Publications.

Latour, B. (2004). Why has critique run out of steam? From matters of fact to matters of concern. *Critical Inquiry,* 30(2), 225–248.

Levin, S. (2017). Facebook told advertisers it can identify teens feeling 'insecure' and 'worthless'. *The Guardian Australian.* Retrieved from www.theguardian.com/technology/ 2017/may/01/facebook-advertising-data-insecure-teens

Lovink, G., & Rossiter, N. (2005). Dawn of the organised networks. *Fibreculture Journal,* 5. Retrieved from http://five.fibreculturejournal.org/fcj-029-dawn-of-the-orga nised-networks/

Ludovico, A., & Cirio, P. (2014). Face-to-Facebook: Smiling in the eternal party. In G. Lovink & M. Rasch (Eds.), *Unlike Us Reader: Social Media Monopolies and their Alternatives* (pp.254–258). Amsterdam: Institute of Network Cultures.

Manovich, L. (2013). *Software Takes Command.* New York and London: Bloomsbury Academic.

Marwick, A., & boyd, d. (2014). Networked privacy: How teenagers negotiate context in social media. *New Media & Society,* 16(7), 1051–1067.

Massumi, B. (2015). *Politics of Affect.* Cambridge, UK: Polity Press.

Mills, C. W. (2000). *The Sociological Imagination.* Oxford, UK: Oxford University Press.

Misson, R., & Morgan, W. (2006). *Critical Literacy and the Aesthetic: Transforming the English Classroom.* Illinois, USA: National Council of Teachers of English.

Munster, A. (2013). *An Aesthesia of Networks.* Cambridge, MA: The MIT Press.

Pahl, K., & Rowsell, J. (2012). *Literacy and Education.* London: Sage Publications.

Pinkard, N. (2015). *An ecological view of equity: Reframing our understanding of youth access to connected learning opportunities.* Paper presented at the DML: Equity by Design, Los Angeles, CA.

Simondon, G. (1959/2010). The limits of human progress: A critical study. *Cultural Studies,* 6(2), 229–236.

Taylor, P. A. (2006). Putting the critique back into a critique of information: Refusing to follow the order. *Information, Communication & Society,* 9(5), 553–571.

Taylor, P. A., & Ruiz, N. (2007). Zizek! A conversation with Paul A. Taylor. *Kritikos,* 4. Retrieved from http://intertheory.org/taylorandruiz.htm

van den Boomen, M. (2014). *Transcoding the Digital.* Amsterdam: Institute of Network Cultures.

van Dijck, J. (2013). *The Culture of Connectivity: A Critical History of Social Media.* New York: Oxford University Press.

Vickery, J. (2012). *Worth the risk: The role of regulations and norms in shaping teens' digital media practices.* PhD, The University of Texas, Austin, TX. Retrieved from http://repositories. lib.utexas.edu/bitstream/handle/2152/ETD-UT-2012-08-6246/VICKERY-DISSERTA TION.pdf?sequence=1

Woolgar, S. (1991). The Turn to Technology in Social Studies of Science. *Science, Technology, & Human Values,* 16(1), 20–50. doi: doi:10.2307/690038.

APPENDIX 1

Detailed description of the fieldwork

First phase: online questionnaire with participants

The aim of the online questionnaire administered via the 'Qualtrics' platform was to acquire background information on the participants regarding their use of digital media. It comprised a series of closed and open questions to gather a range of quantitative and qualitative points of data on participants' digital media use. By establishing a basic picture of digital practices for each participant, later discussions and responses were better contextualised.

Online observations: The participants were asked to connect with/friend a social media page set up for the research. This enabled ongoing contact as well as a more continuous picture of social media use. The most common social media site used by participants was observed which, at the time of the study, was Facebook.

Provocation 1: mapping digital and non-digital experiences

The aim of the first provocation was to encourage participants to visually represent their digital networks. This provocation was an individual activity that required participants to map the people they interacted with and the 'real life' places they visited in a typical week. They were asked to think about the role digital mediation played in facilitating these relationships and experiences. They were also asked to trace the digital devices they used onto a transparent piece of paper laid over the map. Identifying their patterns of use in this way encouraged participants to think carefully about their everyday use of digital media.

Second phase

Provocation 2: visualising the internet

This provocation aimed to uncover participants' understanding of the structure and function of the internet and, most crucially, how humans fit into it. This involved visualising the structure of the internet and modelling it through analogue materials. At the conclusion of the first visit, participants were asked to suggest the materials they thought they could use for this task. This varied from site to site but typically participants suggested things like wire, pipe cleaners, plasticine, newspaper, paddle pop sticks, cotton wool, foil and other art and craft materials. In groups of two or three the participants used the various art and craft materials to visualise the structure of the internet. Participants presented their models to the group.

Interview one with individual participants

In the first interview the basic digital practices of the participants were established. Screenshots that I had previously collected from their Facebook pages were also discussed. For example, participants were asked about their profiles, including reasoning behind posts, images and other information. They were also asked about the social relationships and communicative events evident on the pages and links to other pages or groups they associated with. The aim was to develop an understanding of how social media facilitated social relationships, communication and participation.

Participants were also asked about the skills they draw on when using digital media and where they learnt or developed these. The interviews were semi-structured and involved a series of open questions. The reason for using open questions was to allow participants to answer on their own terms, as well as allow for unforeseen or unexpected answers. Each interview was recorded and transcribed.

Third phase

Provocation 3: timelining digital practices

The aim of this provocation was to develop a temporal picture of participants' digital practices to explore how digital media had influenced their identity, communication and learning *across time*. It involved participants creating a timeline of the main websites and digital applications they had used since their first use of the internet. These were plotted on dot matrix paper with coloured conté (hard chalk). They used a coloured line to represent each website and were encouraged to manipulate the line to represent something about their use. For example, if their use of a website greatly increased for a couple of years they might thicken the line through those years. Given the popularity of certain websites, one colour was used to represent these on their timelines (i.e. Facebook—blue; Google—green;

YouTube—red). This enabled participants to compare and contrast their timelines during the group discussion more easily. They were also asked to identify three moments of significant change on their timelines to do with their identity, learning or communication, which they marked with a black cross.

Interview two with individual participants

In preparation for this interview, the 'Wayback Machine',[1] an internet archive site, was used to collect a screenshot from one of the main websites participants used in their childhood (identified through their timeline). The aim was to use this archived website to take the participants back to their childhood, so they could consider how their digital practices and identities had changed or evolved since then. This activity, in combination with the timeline, aimed to explore the history of participants' digital practices.

The screenshots used in interview one were digitally filed and brought out for re-examination in interview two. The participants were asked to reflect on how their social media profiles, posts and photos from the last interview shaped their sense of self and social relationships across the intervening months. In this way, the influence of digital media on the process of becoming and participation was explored. As with the first interview, current screenshots from social media pages were also shown and discussed.

In addition, participants were asked what role the school played in developing their digital literacies and how it connected to their out-of-school practices. These interview questions were adapted and refined to draw on particular areas of interest for participants.

Fourth phase

Provocation 4: re-articulating the icons of the internet

The aim of this provocation was to explore the semiotics of the icons of the internet. This provocation focused on how meaning is made and re-made through digital symbols and texts. By redesigning these icons it also provoked an interpretive and critical response from participants. Participants were presented with the most common icons of the internet (search, like, friend, link). In groups of two, participants were given some information on one of the icons in order to develop an alternative or critical perspective on it and the purpose it serves in digital networks. The intention was to encourage participants to think more consciously about the role played by these icons in their everyday digital practices. Bearing their new perspective in mind, participants were asked to individually redesign and redefine the icon. The redesigned icons were presented back to the group for further discussion and analysis. This final group session also involved a collective debriefing of the project and general research findings.

Interview three with individual participants

This final interview followed the basic structure of interview two, asking questions about digital media use and identity. In addition, it debriefed the participants individually on the project and asked for constructive feedback on the research process. For example, participants were asked to consider the skills they had drawn on throughout the year, and whether the provocations had encouraged them to be more critical or mindful of their digital media use.

Exhibition

In February 2015 the creative works produced by the young people were displayed to the public at an exhibition in the Monash University library, entitled *Becoming Digital: An exploration of digital media in young people's lives*.

Note

1   See: http://archive.org/web/web.php

APPENDIX 2

Participant snapshots

The participation of the 13 young people in the project was completely voluntary and I worked with the teachers, principals and directors at the schools and youth arts centre to gain informed consent of all those participating. Each of the young people, as well as the school and youth arts centre, has been given a pseudonym to protect the privacy of those involved. The fieldwork took place at three different settings, so I have presented the young people below according to the context in which I worked with them.

Bankview College

Bankview College is a government secondary school in outer Melbourne. This was the largest group of students in the study and the workshops were negotiated with the teacher as part of their media class.

Stacey, 15 years

Stacey was an avid user of digital media and owned a number of digital devices (an iPod, a tablet, a mobile phone, a computer and a laptop), which she used across home and school. She considered herself to be a hardworking student with a fun side. Her digital practices centred upon education (English and Maths games, research), anime (fan sites and creating anime figures online), and social media. Stacey had mixed feelings about social media, as she sometimes found it difficult to identify and interpret the nuances of communication and had also experienced negative feedback from her peers. She was close to her parents and was required to be 'friends' with them on Facebook, so that they could make sure she was 'doing the right thing' online.

Rachel, 15 years

See Chapter 2.

Mark, 15 years

Mark was an enthusiastic user of digital technologies. At the time of the field-work, the internet had only recently been connected at his home, meaning his digital practices had been largely school based. He relied heavily on his school-issued laptop. He felt his digital practices were 'behind' his peers and that he had a lot to catch up on. This led to newly emerging tensions in the home, as his mother believed he spent too much time online. The majority of his digital practices took place on YouTube and the gaming platform Steam. On You-Tube he and his friends had started their own channel where they uploaded screencasts with audio narration of themselves playing particular video games. Mark saw starting his YouTube channel as an important step in developing a career in the media arts.

Trent, 16 years

Trent started using the internet at age seven and described many positive experiences with digital media as a child. However, in recent years he had become quite ambivalent about his use of digital media, particularly social media. While he liked gaming and spent a considerable amount of time on Steam, his experiences with social media, particularly Facebook, had been quite negative. On Steam he felt more 'protected' as only close friends knew his avatar. However, on Facebook he felt the 'bullying' that he experienced offline was easily translated to the online context. He struggled with schoolwork and rarely used technology to help him research or complete assessment tasks. Trent regularly returned to the websites that he had used as a child, such as Club Penguin, to bring the 'good memories' back.

Mitch, 15 years

Mitch was a confident user of digital media and directed his practices toward gaming and making films. He spent a lot of time on YouTube and had uploaded a number of his own films to the platform to receive feedback on his work. He owned a number of devices including a mobile phone, desktop computer and a school-issued laptop. As he explained, much of his confidence stemmed from his early years of using the internet when his 'tech expert' uncle would help him to understand some of the more complex and technical features of digital technologies. Mitch felt he was largely unaffected by the feedback systems and ratings on social media, but recognised this was an issue for many other young people today.

Simon, 16 years

Simon enjoyed learning and study, and had aspirations of working in the gaming industry. He was introduced to the internet through his interest in gaming and spent a lot time in his early years on Miniclip and Minecraft. In more recent years the majority of his practices took place on Steam. His parents did not let him use social media, but YouTube was an exception. On YouTube he worked with Mark on developing their channel, which was a cause for them to get together regularly after school. Simon shared a mobile phone with his sister, but admitted that he was the only one in his family with a genuine interest in gaming and digital technologies.

City College

City College is a private, co-educational school in inner-city Melbourne. The workshops with these students were negotiated with the year 9 coordinator and took place at various times in the students' timetable.

Grace, 15 years

Grace came across as a quietly committed and studious young person. She had started using the internet at five years of age, when an older cousin introduced her to Club Penguin. However, for Grace, like many other participants, the school domain was where she was introduced to many news websites and digital practices, either socially through friends or academically through teachers. As such, a significant proportion of her digital practices were directed toward educational outcomes. Like the other participants from City College, Grace used a mobile phone, a school-issued laptop, an iPad and she also had access to a desktop computer at home. She was an avid user of social media and had profiles on Snapchat, Facebook, Instagram and Tumblr. While Grace could see that being 'visible' on these social networking sites was socially important she rarely felt the need to post anything herself, and admitted that peer feedback could be a source of anxiety for her.

Maddy, 15 years

Maddy was first introduced to the internet at school when she was eight years old, in order to play English and maths games. While games were in her early years of using digital media, particularly Club Penguin and Moshi Monsters, Maddy admitted that now she would much rather socialise on Facebook than play a game. As with other City College participants, Maddy was on four 'standard' social media platforms: Facebook, Instagram, Tumblr and Snapchat. Despite her commitment to social networking there was some uncertainty about her practices. She said that she used to post a lot more comments; however, when her older brother told her that she posted too much on Facebook, she limited her posts.

Penny, 15 years

Penny was a chatty and animated young person, who enjoyed sharing her opinions with others. The internet had been an important part of her life for quite some time, with her first use being traced back to when she was four years of age. Like Maddy and Grace she had enjoyed Club Penguin as a child, not so much for the games, but for the ability to connect with friends beyond the schoolyard. Also like Maddy and Grace, the majority of her digital practices now took place on social media sites, including Facebook, Instagram, Tumblr and Snapchat. She started using Facebook in grade 4 and in the early days used it to play games and organise 'playdates' with friends. As such, Facebook was integral to her gaining a sense of independence from parents and family.

Williams Road Collective

Williams Road Collective is a youth arts organisation in outer eastern Melbourne. It provides a studio space for young people to come and make art as well as sessions with local artists based around developing particular practices or skills. The workshops were organised through the director of the collective and took place during free studio sessions on a Wednesday afternoon.

Sean, 19 years

Sean was a quiet and reflective young person, with aspirations of becoming a professional artist. He had already exhibited a number of his paintings and used social media, particularly Tumblr, to promote his work beyond the gallery space. While Sean started using digital media at school when he was eight years old, he felt that school offered him little in learning how to use digital technologies effectively. In his own time he used YouTube to develop his painting techniques and learn new skills. Sean appeared to be far more critical of social media toward the end of the fieldwork period, actively resisting the pressure to be online all the time. That said, Sean was already a fairly critical user of digital media having installed Adblock, a virus protection system and other security measures on his computer.

Heidi, 16 years

Heidi started using the internet at age nine, with most of the early websites she used introduced to her at school. Indeed, Heidi acknowledged that school 'opened up' the internet for her and was significant in shaping her early practices. Her digital practices expanded steadily across time helping to facilitate the various aspects of her adolescent life—including education, entertainment and socialising with friends. This was reflected in her timeline of digital practices, which revealed that the range of websites used, along with the time spent online steadily increased. The main devices Heidi used were a laptop and mobile phone. She admitted she was so 'reliant' on the internet that if she were to go without it for a few days she would 'really suffer'—socially and educationally.

Chantelle, 16 years

Chantelle first started using the internet at age nine. Given her intermittent use of digital media across the years it would be fair to characterise these as a series of episodes, rather than a set of practices. This was perhaps due to the fact that Chantelle's use of the internet tended to be purpose driven. Unlike other participants, who described themselves as influenced by what their peers were doing, Chantelle's choice to use a particular website was determined by how it would help her to learn or present her work in a better way. Her father, who was a web designer, carefully monitored her use of the internet and did not allow her to use any social media until she was 16. While opening an account was now an option for Chantelle, she still chose not to, seeing herself as free of some of the more negative effects. She appeared confident with this choice, but acknowledged that in the future she might need to change things. She wanted to work in the performing arts and believed that having some kind of social media presence would be necessary to achieving this goal.

Dylan, 16 years

Dylan started using the internet at eight and immediately became curious about what it was and how he could use it. Club Penguin was one of the first regular websites he visited, and he spoke fondly of gaining enough points to buy his penguin a special outfit. His digital practices were largely developed outside of school. The only time his digital media practices really intersected with school learning was when he tried to use more formal language when making an 'opinionated' status on Facebook to 'dress it up' and appear more credible. During the fieldwork period, the majority of Dylan's digital practices took place on social media, namely Facebook, Instagram and Snapchat. As a budding photographer he also used Flickr to display his work. Across these different social platforms he had accrued quite a following and his teacher explained that he was viewed as a bit of a 'microcelebrity' at school. Online Dylan came across as quite extroverted and opinionated; however, this contrasted with the shy and softly spoken way Dylan presented in person.

INDEX

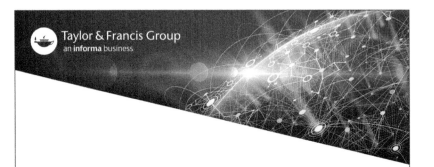